C. S. LEWIS THEN AND NOW

DATE DUE

JAN 0 3 2012	

C. S. LEWIS
THEN AND NOW

◆ ◆ ◆ ◆ ◆ ◆ ◆ ◆ ◆

WESLEY A. KORT

OXFORD
UNIVERSITY PRESS

OXFORD
UNIVERSITY PRESS

Oxford   New York

Auckland   Bangkok   Buenos Aires   Cape Town   Chennai
Dar es Salaam   Delhi   Hong Kong   Istanbul   Karachi   Kolkata
Kuala Lumpur   Madrid   Melbourne   Mexico City   Mumbai   Nairobi
São Paulo   Shanghai   Taipei   Tokyo   Toronto

Copyright © 2001 by Wesley A. Kort

First Published in 2001 by Oxford University Press, Inc.
198 Madison Avenue, New York, NY 10016

First issued as an Oxford University Press paperback, 2004

Library of Congress Cataloging-in-Publication Data

Kort, Wesley A.
C. S. Lewis then and now / Wesley A. Kort
p. cm.
Includes bibliographical references and index.
ISBN 0-19-514342-6; 0-19-517663-4 (paper)
1. Lewis, C. S. (Clive Staples), 1898–1963. I. Title.
BX5199.L53 K67 2001
283'.092—dc21   2001021324

1 3 5 7 9 8 6 4 2

Printed in the United States of America

ACKNOWLEDGMENTS

I completed this project while in residence as a senior fellow in the Erasmus Institute at the University of Notre Dame. While I spent most of my time there on a work that is still in progress, a book on belief and the language of place-relations in modern English fiction, I was able from time to time to turn to this one. I also had opportunities to share parts of it with the other fellows, and I am grateful to them, especially to Roger Lundin, for their encouragement and help. I want to thank the administration of the institute, especially Professor Jim Turner, for providing me the opportunity to work there.

I showed parts of the manuscript to several people: Dr. Mary Smith and her husband, Professor Philip Rolnick, Mr. Brett Patterson, the late Professor Tommy Langford, Dr. Anastasia Gutting, and my daughter, Eva. I am grateful to them all for their interest in my work and for their many helpful responses to it. I am also grateful to Ms. Cynthia Read at Oxford University Press, who read the manuscript with care and offered many helpful suggestions and corrections.

Finally, I want to thank my wife, Phyllis, both for her interest in this project and for her help in my attempts to write in a way that would make the book available to a wide audience.

CONTENTS

C. S. LEWIS THEN AND NOW

INTRODUCTION

A few years ago, a major in our department who had taken a couple of my courses asked me to offer her an independent reading course on C. S. Lewis. I knew of her active involvement in evangelical student groups, and I was not surprised, when I asked about her interest in Lewis, to learn that she was intrigued because he was both a "Christian"—she gave extra force to that word —and a well-positioned academic. She wanted to see how he managed that. She wanted help bringing together two important parts of her own life, her strong religious beliefs and her energetic intellectual pursuits. I suggested that she reconsider, because the course would not give easy answers but rather would raise tough questions and call for difficult choices. When she returned she said that six of her friends wanted to take the course, too. I proposed a seminar to maximize discussion. Due to demand I have been offering the course to large classes ever since.

I am intrigued both by the widespread, serious interest in Lewis among undergraduates and by their parallel desire to explore the relation of religious faith to the world opened up to them by their academic experiences and their intellectual curiosity and energy. Discontent with the prospect of a life divided into personal or internal and intellectual or public compartments seems widespread among students, as is also the willingness both to work at the question of the relation of intellectual inquiry and critique to religious faith and to incur the risks that such work entails. Lewis, I have found, becomes an occasion and guide for students to undertake in their own way and with varying degrees of success, a process of healing breaches in their lives.

I am also intrigued by the pedagogical opportunity their interest in this process and in Lewis offers. Usually an instructor must work hard to engage students in the topic of the course and to sustain that interest over the semester.

Little of that is needed in my Lewis class. Students enter with eager, inquisitive attitudes, and their engagement deepens as it becomes more informed and critical. I welcome this pedagogical opportunity because Lewis, who combines sophisticated and diverse literary and philosophical interests, a complex critique of modern culture, strong religious convictions, and a fascination with difficult theological questions, is worth the attention that the course requires. In addition, I would always rather talk about religion and modern culture in relation to particular case studies than in some general or self-warranting way. Lewis challenges students to examine the relation of cultural to religious studies, to assess the role of moral and religious belief in cultural criticism, and to evaluate the relevance of his work to their own situation as contemporary Americans. Whatever one's opinion of Lewis, there can be no doubt that he brings to attention important, even constitutive aspects of modern culture, and he does so with strong and explicit interest in both moral theology and cultural theory. Religion, moreover, is not for him something external and complete that either clashes with modern culture or stands as a substitute for it. Religion prompts Lewis to raise questions that complicate and enlarge an understanding of what culture could be, and his understanding of religion is affected by the culture he both criticizes and affirms.

The centennial celebration of Lewis's birth—he was born in 1898 and died in 1963—sparked my decision to write on themes in Lewis that seem of particular importance today, especially for Americans working in contemporary academic cultures. The topics I have chosen focus on his imaginative fiction, cultural theory and criticism, and moral and religious thought. These topics do not exhaust Lewis; nor will they answer all the questions readers may have about modern culture, religion, and their relation to one another. Rather, they are topics that mediate a relation between Lewis and the challenge faced by many, especially young people today, to understand their cultural location in ways that engage religious belief. Made conscious of transition by the century's turn, such young people are concerned about relating the traditional to the new, the academic to the moral, and the public to the personal, not despite but because of how troubled one or both parties in each set of contraries may be.

I view this project as a retrieval for several reasons. First, it causes me to go back to the enthusiasms of my own earlier years, finding much there to be treasured and reinvested, especially the belief that religion, if it is mature, should offer what was called back then "a world and life view." Second, Lewis is dated. There can be no question of simply deploying his work in relation to present challenges. He lived and worked in a world very different from, indeed as much worse as it was better than, our own. As I say to my students, I do not think it is possible to move Lewis's construction to this place and time and inhabit it. But in his work there are strategies, critical moves and insights, and large bits of construction worth imitating and using. Third, I call this effort a retrieval because in this country Lewis has largely become the property of a particular set of religious and political interests, and I find that confinement odd, at best. Among several reasons why, the most important is that Lewis above all else wanted and tried to live in a larger, more commodious world than that made available by modern culture. This does not mean that for Lewis anything goes. But his principal interest is in that larger world and one's relations to and within it. Lewis would be more engaged by a non-Christian who lived in a large world and related to its particularities variously and appreciatively than by those Christians who press the world into the shape of their own agendas. I think the company Lewis would prefer to keep, were he working in our culture today, would not be provided mainly by those who claim and treat him now as their own.

Lewis located himself within a specific cultural context, and he was fully aware of that context. I take my attempt at retrieval as consistent with his theoretical point, namely, that cultures, like characters, are always particular. What is arresting and useful in his work lies not so much in its theological content, which by his own admission is rather standard and minimal. Rather, it lies in what he does to create suitable cultural and personal conditions as a context or ground for talking about religion and morality effectively and truthfully. And that task is made ongoing and particularized by differing and changing historical and cultural locations.

To put it somewhat differently and, perhaps, more forcefully: Lewis avoids two mistakes that are pervasive in contemporary American Christianity. The first is to read modern culture as inevitable and irremediable. Lewis, by not reading modern culture as human culture that has come to fruition, does not accept modern culture's self-assessment. Modern culture must be redressed, made, that is, more complex and human. Indeed, that is for him a primary objective. The second mistake that Lewis avoids is thinking that religion can be self-enclosed, that it can separate itself from its cultural context. He agrees that Christian spokespersons and church leaders have often been too influenced by modern culture and have consequently compromised or distorted Christianity. But he believes that this is not because they have failed to separate Christianity from culture but because they have accepted modernity as an adequate form of human culture. The task is not to eschew culture, as though that were possible, but to affirm another, more adequate way of understanding human beings in their relations to one another and to the world they receive and are creating. Indeed, for Lewis one cannot begin to understand Christianity without major distortions unless that task is first undertaken.

Americans also tend to misunderstand or misappropriate Lewis because they are conditioned by modern culture's habits of abstraction. Just as they shop in malls without an interest in where and under what conditions products were produced, so they want answers, especially religious answers, without an interest in the problems to which those answers are responses. Furthermore, American Christians are, like their nonreligious neighbors, conditioned by the culture to establish their identities by difference, by standing out or standing apart. Religious identity becomes yet another culturally inspired form of taking exception to or being noticeable in the culture. Lewis cannot be conscripted into supporting either of these tendencies and habits. For him, the question, problem, or mystery is always primary; the response, especially when it takes the form of an answer or solution, remains to a degree inadequate and provisional. And Lewis, while prizing particularity, did not use religion as a way of standing out. He was in a number of ways an ordinary man. His dress and personal demeanor as well as his intellectual goals were designed not to be off-putting but to heal, not to champion the eccentric but to restore the everyday. While he was always ready to provoke, debate, and, if necessary, criticize sharply, he always acted with a sense that there were more important things to worry about than standing out. The challenges and joys of living for Lewis lie first of all not in the extraordinary but in the commonplace, not in conflict but in relationship.

I find Lewis's ordinary and practical way of proceeding to be one of the reasons he appeals to students. It allows him to articulate credible understandings of the relations between persons and between them and what they encounter in their worlds. If anything is to count for him as cultural criticism, moral philosophy, or religious belief and practice, it must do so in a way directly relevant to the everyday life of ordinary people. His principal task was to find a language that would help people to make sense of their world and their experience of it. The implied invitation to the reader is to give a religious account of things a try, to compare it with other options. This very practical approach appeals to American readers, especially students. This is because many Americans take it as a matter of course that it is up to them to develop "personally tailored religious worldviews." They tend to see religion not first of all as something final to which they conform but, rather, as "a way to make sense out of ordinary experience." They are intensely interested in religion when and because it helps "in creating and maintaining worldviews that permit them to give meaning to life."[1] Students entertain Lewis's views because what he says is offered as something suitable, not forced onto their lives. If his work arose from and required institutional or dogmatic conformity, it would provoke from students equally assertive exceptions and rebuttals. To use a market metaphor, Lewis can be read as one who has confidence in his product, and he simply puts it out there for the reader to try. He talks up its value when he compares it with secular competitors. As R. Laurence Moore points out in *Selling God*, Americans are accustomed to having religion presented to them as an option placed alongside other options.[2] American students, I am not surprised to learn, find Lewis's approach congenial. They are willing to sample options, to try things on for size.

Lewis's account of the world and of human deportment in it comes with an invitation to fill in the blanks or to engage in constructing a similar account of one's own. His work appeals because he presents his account as consistent and applicable but not as complete and rigid. He reveals his way of doing things, but the reader is set free to finish it off or to turn it toward his or her own situation and sense of things. The account is flexible, and the reader is invited to get the hang of it, to alter it, and to go beyond it. Lewis, in other words, empowers the reader. He has no interest in devotees or in carbon copies of himself. He could hardly have been more emphatic or inventive in emphasizing the particularity of a person's life, especially of a Christian's life. Christians should differ not only from other people but also from other Christians. He would have agreed with Nicholas Wolterstorff that "authentic Christian commitment as a whole, but also the belief content thereof, is relative to persons and times. One might insist that there are certain propositions which belong to the belief-content of all authentic Christian commitment whatever. Probably so. But certainly they will be few and simple."[3]

Lewis also appeals to American readers because his work is expansive and inclusive. Lewis tries to bring into focus not only the complexities of personal life and relationships but also the relation of people both to culture and to the natural context of their lives.[4] Students are intrigued by a thinker who, rather than being intimidated by a complex world and retreating from it toward private communities and internal awareness as locations and objects for religious reflection, engages and even affirms that large and complex world, especially because of its largeness and complexity.

Finally, Lewis's work appeals to students because it is deeply relational in its thrust. Indeed, his implied theory of internal relations is, I think, one of its most crucial and useful components. This emphasis speaks strongly to American students. They are presented with many analyses of the world around them, both social/political and physical, and many analyses of the self. These analyses tend not only to break things down into parts but also to define parts as distinct from and even in opposition to one another. It is left to the student to put the pieces together again. I think that they find it refreshing to encounter a critic who works with a basic belief in substantial, primary relations between aspects of the self, between the self and other selves, and between the self and the larger world. This emphasis is healing for those whose lives otherwise are sundered by great gaps or constant conflicts, especially between desires, feelings, and ideas "in here" and what exists "out there."

Young people, raised on an academic diet of difference and opposition, are easily intimidated as they contemplate our complex society. They become uncertain about their own resources and question if there is a place in society where they can fit. One of the most unnerving questions you can ask an undergraduate is what he or she plans to do after college. This question is always before them, and it carries a kind of apocalyptic thrust. This anxiety is produced by an underdeveloped sense of the relation of self to others and the world. Lewis would argue that it arises from a tacit recognition that the kinds of analyses and criticism students learn in their classes are inadequate and problematic because they make external relations, that is, difference, competition, and conflict, central. One appeal of Lewis for undergraduates, it seems to me, lies in his sustained and complex attack on the culturally orthodox doctrine of external, negative relations. He posits the primacy of relations that students have been otherwise led to think of as secondary and insecure.

I think these characteristics of Lewis are also suggestive in the larger context of American religious and cultural studies. In a situation in which religion and morality are regularly relegated to internal states or separated communities and academic interest in religion is limited largely to psychological, social-political, and historical descriptions of it, it is challenging to be reminded that religious beliefs and moral convictions have a positive, public potential. In a culture such as our own in which religion easily becomes a form of group- or self-preoccupation, it is refreshing to encounter Lewis's robust and morally muscular sense of the person's place in the world. He refuses to relegate religion and morality to private feelings and behaviors, and he refuses to define the larger culture that we conspire to make for ourselves as wholly evil or irremediable. He does not allow his strong sense of the separation between good and evil or the creative and destructive in human living to carry over into other kinds of separations, such as between religion and culture, faith and reason, or daily life and religious discipline. And that is what I find in his work most encouraging to my own: his sense that the positive and the negative, the continuous and the dissonant, and the familiar and the unexpected are always found together. The engaging uncertainty of living arises from not knowing how much of which there will be and how each will manifest itself. His over-riding affirmation is that these contraries do not only militate against one another but also are complementary or mutually revealing.

This book is intended, then, to take the reader into what I think of as the most useful aspects of Lewis's work for people attempting to articulate "world and life views" that are both relevant to our current location and informed by religious beliefs. I have placed the chapters in their present order for two reasons. First, they progress toward the middle chapter, the one on culture, and then away from it, the first three being less and the latter three more religious in emphasis. The second reason is that this arrangement is intended to move the reader from first to final considerations, from beginning to completion. The Conclusion is really an introduction, a gambit for opening a conversation about the role of belief in contemporary American culture.

The direction of this book is primarily outward. Its emphasis is construction. In these ways it stands in contrast to the book that immediately precedes it.[5] The direction of that book was primarily inward. Its emphasis was deconstructive, and its tone, suited, perhaps, to a century's ending, was negative. It moved the reader away from the world and from his or her relations to and within it. It was a study of the religious discipline of reading a text as scripture. The main point of that book was that reading a text as scripture involves world and self-rejection. The primary focus was on exit from the culture, abandoning the world, and divesting the self. In this book things are turned around. The tone here is primarily positive, suited, perhaps, to a century's beginning. The goal now is to reinstate and affirm relations.

A positive attitude toward the world and human culture carries two beliefs. The first is that a person cannot live only at the exit or only in rejection of the culture. It is fashionable among current cultural critics, both religious and secular, to think that one can live with no affirmative attitudes toward culture, no sense of the whole, and no positive relations with others. Attempts to live that way, in both their religious and secular forms, assume that human living is basically alienated and nomadic. While I believe that cultural divestment and personal abjection are indispensable to a healthy life, especially for a religious person, I also believe that they are not the whole story. Reentry, affirmation, and relations are just as important and just as difficult.

The second belief implied by the direction and tone of this book is that understanding the world and one's relations to and within it is not simply there, granted by reality, institution, or creed. It has also to be constructed, and that construction is ongoing. It is not as though a person, by exiting the culture or divesting the self, enters a more real world, whether, in its religious form, a church or body of truth or, in its secular form, the material reality that supports society or the unconscious desires that underlie the self. Living in a world and in relations to and within it are the consequence of trusting, acting, and reflecting. To paraphrase one of Lewis's comments, it is like living in a house while also engaged in its construction, inspection, and renovation.

It is not clear to me which side of this double story, the negative half of divestment or the positive half of affirmation, is the more important and with which half one ought to begin. While some people identify themselves more with one side than with the other, excluding either side results in a partial and eventually distorted understanding of both religion and life. Indeed, each side implies the other, and one without the other is incomplete. A religious life without the negative side, without cultural exit and self-abjection, becomes calcified, and a religious life without world affirmation and construction becomes self-preoccupied. Consequently, the two sides of the story should not divide the religious world, as though the one side, the negative, is conservative and the other side, the positive, is liberal. Indeed, I have tried to undercut this knee-jerk judgment by using theorists for the negative, more "conservative" project who are hardly conservative, who are not theologians or even known for their religious beliefs: Maurice Blanchot and Julia Kristeva. And now, for the positive, more "liberal" project of world and culture affirmation I have chosen to work primarily with C. S. Lewis, a person who is widely thought of as "conservative."

This book differs from the one that precedes it not only in direction, emphasis, and tone but also in style. It seemed incongruous to write a book dealing with the work of C. S. Lewis that would not be available to a rather wide range of people. Accessibility is a distinguishing feature of his work, and I have tried to emulate it. I am always distressed when intelligent and motivated readers find my work difficult to read. This happened again with my previous book. A church group composed of able people read it and invited me to talk with them about it. They all, to my surprise, found the book tough going. I tried to keep this audience in mind while writing this book. A book on Lewis should not exclude the many intelligent readers outside academic walls who find him in many ways helpful in assessing the world in which they find themselves. Lewis, by writing in an accessible way, does not simplify complex issues or attempt to gain popularity. Writing that way is a feature, I believe, of his relational view of his audience. His style affirms rather than distances the reader. In addition, he wrote clearly because he wanted to draw attention neither to the style nor to himself but to the topic at hand, primarily the intriguing and problematic world in which we find ourselves. His style, in other words, was consistent with his belief about relations, consistent, in a word, with love. I could not hope for anything more than that this book would have a share, however slight, in these characteristics.

The reader will notice at times that I have run the risk of speaking for Lewis. There are expositions of his work in my book, but there are also interpretations, reformulations, and extensions. I think that these liberties are in line with his approach to things. The greatest sign of appreciation or indebtedness is the attempt not only to see the world as another sees it but to build on that person's sense of things and to direct that person's insights toward new potentials and challenges.

I do not pretend to address or represent the whole of Lewis. There are parts of him that have a more specialized interest. There are also parts that are less useful to us here and now. And, it is important to add, there are parts that will or should put the reader off. For example, racism appears in his work. The most troubling instance is his depiction of the evil Calormenes in *The Last Battle* in terms consistent with the longstanding English disdain toward darker-skinned Mediterranean peoples. Lewis seems unaware of his racism, and it is particularly troubling that it appears in one of the Narnia Chronicles, a book intended for children. The sexism in his work seems to moderate over time. This may be due to the positive effects on Lewis of the abilities of Joy Davidman, and it is especially true of his last novel, *Till We Have Faces*. But even some of his later work carries sexist traces. Homophobia seems to increase as Lewis matures. He takes a charitable stance toward homosexual activity in his *Surprised by Joy*, which may reflect an earlier attitude, but in *That Hideous Strength* homosexuality seems tied to the culmination of evil. Homosexual people in *The Four Loves* are dealt a particularly condescending and dismissive swipe. I do not take these moments in Lewis as incidental, random blips. They indicate serious structural flaws. But I also do not think that they constitute reasons to reject the whole, as though all the construction is a concealment or justification of these personal and political beliefs. Nor do I think that we are free of equally damaging assumptions, however unconscious of them or of their implications we may be. One always must ask questions. Additional questions should be asked of Lewis: What in his work is simply English? What is upper middle class or culturally elitist? What, for all the breadth and orientation to the future, is still marked by nostalgia for a world long gone? To what degree, for all its cultural criticism, does it still carry some of modern culture's negative traces? Questionable parts of Lewis only lend force to the point that his project cannot be uncritically extended to our own place and time. His work, rather, should provoke the reader to take what is instructive and useful and to "try it for yourself."

More than that, this book is an attempt to challenge both religious tendencies to live increasingly in rejection of culture and the tendencies of cultural theory and criticism to discount or distrust religion. For this challenge to be effective, more than Lewis is required. Even more is required than a study that attempts critically to select from Lewis those parts of his work that seem most relevant to the present situation and to deploy them within it. What is called for is a rigorous refusal to allow well-entrenched distinctions to determine thought on the relation of religion and modern culture to one another, distinctions like religious and secular, private and public, internal and external, values and facts, liberal and conservative, and reality and ideology. These terms, rather than markers, have become magnets that draw people into differing camps and that allow difference to be the defining and justifying basis for identity. All of that should be relegated to a previous century. What Lewis does most of all is to allow us to recognize that resources for alternative ways of thinking are also available in that century. Lewis provides an occasion to go back in order to recover routes not taken, routes that indicate positive possibilities for the future, possibilities that do not dissolve, sever, and repress human potentials and relationships but call for their healing and release.

I

* * * * * * * * *

RETRIEVAL

The recent centennial of C. S. Lewis's birth marked a time not of decline but of increase in the potential importance of his work for American readers, especially in academic settings. Some of the earlier academic neglect is traceable to the diversity of his oeuvre, its cultural engagements, rhetorical style, and contributions to popular culture, especially science fiction and children's literature. But the academic climate, especially in literary studies, has changed. The formalism and disciplinary orthodoxy characteristic of English departments a few years ago kept them from accommodating the full range of Lewis's work. But now literary studies are interdisciplinary and take into account matters of theory and practice that also engaged Lewis. These include education and curricula, the consequences of bureaucracies for social space, value theory, the continuities between high and popular culture,[1] the relation of power and ideology to beliefs and ideas, and what are taken to be the moral consequences of intellectual and technological imperialism.

The combination of literary with historical, theoretical, cultural, critical, and moral/religious ingredients normalizes Lewis's work in current literary studies. Literary studies increasingly are marked by intersections where literary and cultural interests, questions of belief and value, and awareness of popular culture, rhetoric, and social/economic power meet and interact. C. S. Lewis sounds at times like Stanley Fish, a major mover in recent changes within academic literary studies. At one point Lewis writes, "I do not think that Rhetoric and Poetry are distinguished by manipulation of an audience in

13

the one and, in the other, a pure self-expression, regarded as its own end, and indifferent to any audience. Both these acts, in my opinion, definitely aim at doing something to an audience and both do it by using language to control what already exists in our minds."[2] One could stitch that statement into one of Fish's essays on rhetoric in literary-critical work without leaving a seam.

Half a century ago literary environments were inhospitable to such collapsing of distinctions and such diversity of interest and genre. Academic attention to Lewis was primarily established and sustained by people drawn to the specifically religious aspects of his work. Lewis encouraged conservative Protestant literary scholars to relate their intellectual interests to their own Christian identities and beliefs. During the decades immediately following the Second World War, faculty in evangelical colleges and religiously conservative literary scholars in other institutions turned to Lewis as someone who articulated traditional Christian beliefs and values to academic culture. Lewis provided a model for those who wanted to maintain the role of Christian faith in intellectual life or were unwilling to let an increasingly secular academic culture marginalize the religious aspects of English and American literature and declare religious beliefs irrelevant to literary-critical tasks.

At the same time, there were other models for increasing the role of moral and religious interests in academic work. While Lewis appealed primarily to conservative Protestant intellectuals, scholars like Jacques Maritain provided a similar model for their Catholic counterparts. Like Lewis, Maritain received his education in an increasingly non- or even anti-religious academic environment that he also finally found personally unsatisfying and philosophically vulnerable. Maritain searched for alternatives to secular and materialist assumptions, converted to Catholicism, and worked out of a general Thomist philosophical orientation. Coming to the United States at the beginning of the war to teach philosophy first at Columbia and then at Princeton University, Maritain was able, along with others, to promote Thomist philosophy in secular settings. He extended the interests of Christian faith not only into moral philosophy but also into wider areas such as political and aesthetic theory. Lewis, while not so fully Thomist as Maritain, also drew heavily on medieval texts of Christian literature and philosophy, criticized modern culture for its neglect of traditional values, and articulated religious interests in scholarship and an intellectually examined religious account of the world. Both, in their differing ways and for differing audiences, were crucial figures for the changing climate of postwar American academic culture, which increasingly allowed for the articulation of moral and religious beliefs within literary, philosophical, and cultural studies.

During the latter half of the twentieth century, academic culture underwent a gradual reversal of the tendency during the first half to marginalize or exclude religion and religious interests in or from intellectual work. The increasingly confident secularism of the prewar decades was replaced by greater uncertainty and by an appreciation for the religious life of different cultures, particularly Asian. The traumas of war, rapid social change, and the internationalization of American culture have all contributed to an increased incorporation of religion into academic life. This new academic interest in religion joins the increasingly complex character of literary and cultural studies to presage a relevance of Lewis's work to academic, particularly literary, culture today.

Academic interest in Lewis has all along been paralleled by the continuing interest in Lewis among intelligent Christian readers in America outside the academy. It is perhaps more difficult to account for this broader admiration. Lewis, a smoking, alcohol-drinking British academic without strong doctrines of biblical authority or the Holy Spirit, seems exotic in relation to American evangelical culture and theology. His appeal very likely lay in the combination of his readable style with certain characteristics of his theological views. We should note that Lewis, like evangelicals, did not position himself primarily within or in defense of the church but spoke from and to a more personally oriented and construed faith. He was also sharply at odds with the main currents of modernity, as were readers of a conservative Protestant orientation. It was very likely helpful, too, that Lewis could be read as politically and socially conservative. This was possible not only because of his focus on personal faith rather than on a social gospel or political theology but also because he desired not to subvert public institutions but instead to realign them with their traditional sources. Finally, Lewis gave encouragement to intelligent lay readers in the face of disconcerting and popular theological currents of the postwar period such as the aggressively marketed "death of God" movement.

Academics and laity who admired Lewis and used his work as a resource and model for the redeployment of Christian belief in the context of modern culture came together to create centers of Lewis study such as that located at Wheaton College in Illinois. An evangelical institution of high academic standards, Wheaton melded the scholarly interest of some of its faculty in the work of Lewis with the popularity of his books among its intelligent constituency, and that combination has characterized similar institutions throughout the country.

Americans' interest in Lewis was not confined to such circles, however. The Narnia Chronicles found their way into public and school libraries throughout the country. Some of his work also had a recognized academic standing, although not on a level equal to other major English influences on American literary and philosophical studies during the period. Several of his books were standard in bibliographies of medieval and Renaissance literature and on Milton, and some of his writings on theodicy, miracles, and religious experience found their ways into anthologies and college textbooks on philosophy of religion. This broader interest, both popular and academic, was exploited, if that is not too harsh a word, by the Hollywood filming of *Shadowlands*. More sentimental than the BBC filming of the stage play, it constructed a relation between Lewis and themes dear to Americans, such as the inadequacy of intellectual, particularly theological, formulations in relation to experience, especially suffering, and the healing resources of the natural context of human life. However, it is fair to say that although the work of Lewis has had a wider currency in the culture, its appeal remains concentrated in the homes, offices, and institutions of conservative Protestant Americans, academic and lay.

It would be unfortunate if that limited concentration continued. In my opinion Lewis is increasingly relevant to the culture of American literary studies. At century's end, literary studies resemble hardly at all what was dominant a half century ago, and the change is such that it produces a far more fertile ground for the dissemination of his work. It is possible now to retrieve Lewis's work from the quarters in which during the past decades it has been largely confined, while also fortunately guarded and admired.

The attempt to position Lewis's work more fully within the interests of current literary academia involves a two-part effort. It must first demonstrate that Lewis should not be confined to parochial religious and cultural interests. It must then challenge an academic, literary culture that, due to the loss of certainty, is governed increasingly by the dynamics of distrust and the vagaries of personal, professional, and institutional power.[3]

Mention of some negative strains in current literary culture should not send us in search of more receptive academic terrain in departments of religion or theological faculties. Those settings are presently structured by two contrary movements both inhospitable to Lewis. The first is sponsored by the ongoing attempt to subordinate religion to other ends, either to account for it in social scientific or historical terms or to harness it to political or psychological interests. The second movement is one that, rather than account for religion in other terms or subordinate it to something else, allows religion to be an account of the world and of people's relation to and in it but only in the context of specific religious traditions, communities, and institutions. Lewis can be aligned with neither of these two contrary and mutually aggravating campaigns. He does not subject religion, either in its origin or in its consequences, to other interests or terms, and he wants the account of things that religion can provide to be tested in and related to public culture.

Lewis, as I understand him, thus finds more potential appreciation and use in departments of literature than in departments of religious studies or theological schools. His diverse interests in cultural theory and criticism, rhetoric and power, in institutions, moral theory, popular culture, and even children's literature suit today's literature departments. While it would not do to call Lewis a postmodernist, it is nonetheless true that the interests that drive and shape his work (and that alienated him from mid-century academic culture) conform with those that mark current literary studies. However, Lewis also represents a potential challenge to current literary culture. That challenge asks whether the breakdown of traditional barriers, authorities, and distinctions in literary studies commits departments of literature to anti-religious and amoral ideologies. While Lewis shares much with the present ethos of literary and cultural studies, he does not share their present obsession with and deference to power, especially to power governed by nothing more than a market economy, the boundaries and directives of the profession or institution, and the self-interests of those who count themselves among the academic stars.[4] There are, however, close parallels between the interests and style of Lewis and those of current literature faculties. They share a penchant for autobiography and personal reference, an intense but critical interest in culture, including popular culture, a skepticism toward the prevailing centers of academic and social power, and a strongly polemical style. But Lewis reveals that these interests and styles are not necessarily wedded to skeptical or self-serving motives and results but can also serve positive, public moral and spiritual ends.

It is helpful to notice that Lewis did not advocate religion and morality as something extraneous to literary scholarship and imparted to it from some other source. Religious and moral interests were integral to the material he studied and the critical work in which he engaged. As he points out in his autobiography, he was led to Christianity because it allowed him to take more fully into account what was important to many philosophical and literary texts and also to those intellectual and aesthetic experiences that he found to be significant and engaging.[5] No source or authority, institutional or textual, needed to be invoked other than those already operative in and for his work: literary texts, their cultural contexts and consequences, and the tools of literary and cultural theory and criticism. A moral and religious disposition, he believed, provides a more adequate or appropriate setting or context for critical, interpretive, and constructive literary and cultural work than its modern, skeptical alternatives. Lewis could speak from religious belief and moral concern without alienating himself from or disenfranchising himself within English literary, humanistic academic culture.

The challenge to current literary studies that lies in Lewis's practice should not be missed. He did not have to pursue the moral and spiritual aspects of literary texts by bringing something to them from the outside. But literary studies unable or unwilling to take such matters into account and, *a fortiori*, those that actively discount them or reduce them to something less or other, must do so by deferring to something extrinsic to the reading of texts.

Finally, it is important to note that Lewis stressed those elements of religious faith and practice commodious and flexible enough to take the moral and religious aspects of literary and cultural studies into account and to provide critiques of them. He was unfettered by ecclesiastical authority, theological dogmatism, or religious controversy. He employed moral inquiry and religious categories within a cultural tradition largely supplied by the texts that, as a philosopher turned literary historian and critic, he studied and taught. These materials needed only to be retrieved, selected, and redeployed. Understanding and appreciating literary and philosophical texts require taking them seriously as accounts of the world and of people's relations to and within it. It is necessary to imagine oneself into the worlds they make available. In analyzing a particular textual account, it is not extraneous or gratuitous to ask what is and is not illuminating or satisfying, particularly when compared to other accounts. This inevitably raises and addresses questions of moral and religious belief.

American literary academic culture has recently seen a thawing of the secular certainties that for decades sustained a repression or occlusion of the moral and religious language of literary texts or of their relation to the moral and spiritual needs and potentials of the culture. We find ourselves today in a situation in which Lewis's project should receive fuller hearing. Indeed, his project contains potential value for efforts now either beginning or called for to explore the relation of religion and ethics to cultural studies and critiques that have changed the nature of literary scholarship in America. The centennial observance of Lewis's birth coincided with the emergence of a literary culture suited to his broadly catholic and intellectually complex religious orientations and convictions. My attempt to retrieve Lewis is largely a response to these new cultural conditions.

I

It is helpful to recall the historical context in which Lewis prepared for and entered his vocation. It was a context in which cultural retrieval had convincing voices and a ready audience. Lewis engaged English studies at just the time when they became legitimate fields of academic inquiry at Oxford and Cambridge. An academic field newly institutionalized, English rapidly gained visibility and prestige. Perhaps the British literary critic and theorist Terry Eagleton exaggerates when he writes, "In the early 1920s it was desperately unclear why English was worth studying at all. In the early 1930s it had become a question of why it was worth wasting your time on anything else." He contends that in a very short time, one during which, we should keep in mind, Lewis entered the field as a student and as a teacher, English became the central subject, "immeasurably superior to law, science, politics, philosophy or history."[6] But several factors give at least some credence to Eagleton's claims.

English, when Lewis entered it, had very much what we would now call a "cultural studies" shape. One reason for this is that literature was the chief source of England's cultural capital. In addition, the legitimacy and popularity of English studies were assured by the social concerns of young scholars who took it up. English provided the cultural content for an emerging academic population of middle-class sons among whom Lewis can be included.[7] It provided a canon that both was subversive to the cultural authority of aristocrats and countered the emerging radical force of a political and social left.[8]

In addition to such matters of cultural capital and authority and more to the point of our interests here, the rise of English studies also carried strong moral aims. English studies brought scholars in touch with the nineteenth-century affirmation of literature as a unifying and morally rectifying resource. Indeed, identification of literature and criticism with the moral and spiritual prospects of society was a constant in the nineteenth century, reaching its fullest statement in the work of Matthew Arnold. The retrieval or continuation of this agenda was undertaken both despite the consequences of the First World War and because of them. In the period immediately following the war, sharp discontinuities were felt between the post- and prewar societies. Radical changes in behavior and values, accompanied by greater mobility and rapidly increasing urbanization, created moral uncertainty and a diminished sense of shared values and norms. The rise of English as an academic discipline offered a counter-thrust to these radical changes by retrieving the moral content of the literary tradition and critical vocation, redeploying them in postwar culture. English studies created continuity with the literary tradition and warranted the role of the literary scholar as cultural critic and moral theorist.

Powerful philosophical currents also supported the emergence of English literary studies as a dominant intellectual force in Oxford. Idealism, with its stress on human reason, morality, and spirit, was very much a part of the academic climate of Oxford in the years of Lewis's development as a scholar.[9] This encouraged him to bring classical and modern idealist perspectives to his literary work. They helped to shape his understanding of the imagination, to support his interest in the comprehensive range and unifying force of myth, to sustain his attention to essences and universals, to substantiate his confidence in human rationality, and to give relevance to medieval philosophy and literature and to such particular writers as Spenser, Milton, and the Romantics. Indeed, Lewis's philosophical and literary canon can be seen as strung on an idealist line from Plato to William Morris.

Retrieval, then, was a primary scholarly, cultural, and moral project for Lewis. But retrieval was never for him simply a matter of return. It could be argued that Lewis was infected with the kind of nostalgia that marked the Romantics he so much admired. I believe, however, that Lewis was as much a forward-looking person, both as scholar and as believer, as he was a retriever of the past. He looked for yet unheard-of advances in human development, and in this way he participated very much in the spirit of modernity.[10] But he was also convinced that these advances would go awry if not steadied and directed by relations with the past. Respect and appreciation for the past does not mean control by or limitation to its achievements. It is a modern caricature of retrieval that sees it only as reactionary. The past is neither irrelevant to the present nor a repository of answers to the questions raised in and by present time.[11]

Our own retrieval of Lewis also will be neither only a return to him nor an attempt to install his views as fully adequate to the needs of our present cultural location. We will walk a path between advocates of the present literary culture who see Lewis as hopelessly bound to and by his own culture and those opponents of current academic culture who are willing to see Lewis as adequate in the present time for recovering relations between religious/moral interests and literary/cultural studies. This work is aligned with his by its opposition to both these options. Lewis had a strong sense of historical change, and he understood that religion and morality are articulated and practiced in and for specific cultural situations.[12] His own views and methods are both relevant to us now because some aspects of his culture persist today and not relevant to the extent that his situation as a mid-century Englishman differs from ours as Americans beginning a new century. Indeed, Lewis contends that appreciation of the past is necessary if a person is to recognize the present as also a distinct period and as having, therefore, its own limitations and "characteristic illusions."[13] Given both the continuities and the contrasts between our cultural location and his, our retrieval of his work must be as selective, as relevant to the present situation, and as forward-looking as was his own.[14] It is in the spirit of his retrievals, in other words, that this one is undertaken.

II

English academic culture is only one of the factors that help us to understand the development of Lewis's vocation. His own life experience, drifting away from his Christian upbringing and experimenting with a variety of belief options, also shaped his sense of vocation and academic identity. The post- or anti-Christian views he adopted as a young man were those he would later attack. Indeed, it is fair to say that he saw his own life as an epitome of a larger pattern that English culture could be seen as following.[15] As he in his own life drifted away from Christian moorings into improvised and eclectic spiritualities and popular materialism and narcissism, so English culture neglected its ties to the past and its sense of shared morality and spiritual aspiration. He could address competing ideologies and orientations as one who knew them from within and had found them wanting. As he felt compelled to retrieve a relation to his religious past, so he also believed that the culture required a comparable change of orientation. It would be greatly impoverished if it did not and foreboded a severely limited and morally distorted future for English people. His analysis of the culture of the twenties and early thirties led him to see his own conversion and identity change as needed as well for those around him, especially in academic culture. It led him to attempts to compel them also to retrieve.

Lewis, like many others in the society, had given himself gradually to a popular, uncritical materialism. His conversion or return to Christianity by way of idealism led first to a recognition of the inadequacy of materialism's account of the mind and imagination. Idealism also allowed for an orientation to the Absolute, which Lewis understood as personal and active. Lewis, with his strong interest in moral theory, then recognized the moral identity of God and finally God's intrusion into human life. As he put it, "my own progress had been from 'popular realism' to Philosophical Idealism; from Idealism to Pantheism; from Pantheism to Theism; and from Theism to Christianity."[16]

This sequence of events suggests the distance between his cultural location and our own. We live in a culture in which philosophical idealism does not provide, as it did for Lewis, a culturally available bridge to religious belief. Nor can attention to the moral and spiritual language of literary texts be defended, as it once was, by idealist philosophical beliefs. The decline and eventual disappearance of shared cultural idealism constitutes a major challenge today for any attempt to take the moral and religious significance of literary culture into account.

Can the moral and religious languages of literature and their relevance to the culture be taken adequately into account without first attempting to reinstate some form of idealism? This question will shadow this work throughout. The objections most common to the materialist and power-oriented stances of current literary studies appeal implicitly or explicitly to idealist vestiges in American literary culture. I contend, however, that it is not necessary to restructure literary culture according to idealist beliefs in order to address the moral and religious potential of literature. If we take literary discourses as primary, we need only clarify, develop, and reformulate their recognizable moral and religious language or bring to the surface the norms by which they positively or negatively depict or judge aspects of human life.

We can understand the relation in Lewis between his literary, cultural work and his religious faith more clearly if we look at some details of his conversion to Christianity. We will ask, what was his conversion, and, in particular, what was it not? First of all, it would not be appropriate to say, in a phrase one often hears, that Lewis "accepted Christ into his life." The language of acceptance, appropriation, and possession is contrary to what is basic for Lewis. For him it is essential that the Christian not think of belief as a way of bringing something into his or her life but, rather, as a way of being brought out into a larger world or sense of the world. As he puts it, "This, I say, is the first and deadly error, which appears on every level of life and is equally deadly on all, turning religion into a self-caressing luxury."[17] Lewis militates constantly against self-preoccupation and especially against narcissism. An interest in Christianity that would amount to accepting something into one's life would be only another form of self-expansion.[18] The direction of conversion for Lewis is very much the opposite, of moving outward into something larger and more important than the self. A religious person, for Lewis, lives in a very different world from that of his or her modern, secular neighbor when that neighbor has been conditioned by modern culture to be self-preoccupied, to limit interest to the boundaries of a private world. To put it another way, a non-Christian who is genuinely engaged by and concerned about the larger world is closer to Lewis than the professed Christian who is self-preoccupied.

Lewis's conversion, second, was not characterized primarily by a desire for heaven or fear of hell. Convictions about things eternal do have their place in Lewis, but by extension. To be a Christian primarily because of desires for and fears of the eternal again fashion religion from the stuff of self-preoccupation. As he says, "happiness or misery beyond death, simply in themselves, are not even religious subjects at all. A man who believes in them will of course be prudent to seek one and avoid the other. But that seems to have no more to do with religion than looking after one's health or saving for one's old age. . . . They are hopes for oneself, anxieties for oneself."[19] Or again, "Until a certain spiritual level has been reached, the promise of immortality will always operate as a bribe which vitiates the whole religion and infinitely inflames those very self-regards which religion must cut down and uproot."[20] In addition, orientation to the eternal implies disregard for and evasion of the immediate and real, the everyday world and a person's place within it. Christianity leads to things eternal, but it does so for Lewis through things temporal and of this world. When Christianity is seen as a way by which people are linked immediately with the eternal, it can easily reinforce the tendency to discount what lies outside a person in the surrounding world, a tendency to which moderns in their self-preoccupation are already deeply habituated. Christianity for Lewis leads to the eternal and teleological, but they are extensions of the everyday world and a person's orientation toward it, not a substitute for them. For Lewis, becoming a Christian cannot be a way of rejecting the everyday for the sake of the eternal.

Lewis's conversion equally does not focus on the church, its authority, sacraments, or communal life. He does not, as one might expect, offer an escape from the distortions of modern culture by exchanging it for a culture defined by a religious institution or community. As one of his closest friends at Cambridge put it, "neither in conversation nor in his works did he show much interest in organized religion. He was orthodox in belief but seemed to have little sense of the Church."[21] This does not mean that he is antichurch; rather, Lewis the convert locates himself not first of all in an institution or community but, rather, in a world differently constituted and differently understood. Conversion did not call him out of the culture and into the church but to work at the complex relation of Christian beliefs, values, and norms to the culture. This is why, in the last novel of his space trilogy, the normative community and the source of judgment on a secular and wholly self-possessed society is not the church but St. Anne's, a place that houses crucial moral and spiritual resources of English cultural history.[22]

Finally, conversion for Lewis is not based on reading the Bible or recognizing the Bible's authority. While Lewis draws heavily on St. Augustine and John Calvin for his theology, he is unlike them at this point. The Bible and its authority exert their weight or force for him more indirectly and implicitly. Lewis does not take his cues as a Christian believer and thinker from a need to accept and defend the infallibility or even the sole authority of Scripture. Let us hear him on this important matter; he says of the Bible,

> It carries the Word of God; and we (under grace, with attention to tradition and to interpreters wiser than ourselves, and with the use of such intelligence and learning as we may have) receive that word from it not by using it as an encyclopedia or an encyclical but by steeping ourselves in its tone or temper and so learning its overall message.[23]

The role and standing of the Bible are as much indirect as direct for him. For Lewis, the Bible and the tradition of English literature are mutually supportive and revealing. Alan Bede Griffiths, O.S.B., who was at Magdalen College, Oxford, when Lewis was undergoing his conversion to Christianity, said, "Both he and I came to religion by way of literature."[24] This does not mean that Lewis treats the Bible as though it were literature—indeed, he speaks against doing that.[25] It means, rather, that the meaning and authority of the Bible are to be found not only in itself but also in its recurring and formative role in English literary culture. I see this as a variation on the Catholic affirmation of the relation of Scripture to Christian tradition. While tradition does not displace or upstage the authority of the Bible, the authority of the Bible is actualized in and exerted by tradition. For Lewis, that tradition is less ecclesiastical than cultural.

Lewis's conversion cannot be described in any of these ways, therefore. It is not first of all an acceptance of Christ into his life; it does not arise primarily from a desire for heaven or a fear of hell; it is not primarily inclusion within the church or Christian community; and it is not based on acceptance of biblical authority. How, then, should it be described? What difference does Christianity make for Lewis?

To put it simply, Christianity provided Lewis first of all with what he found to be a minimal, satisfying, and flexible account of the world and of the relations of people in and to it. This does not mean that Christianity provided all the answers to recurring and important cultural and personal questions.

Nor does it mean that Christianity could be presented as a theory, that is, an account requiring no personal transformation. It provided Lewis a personally involving and fulfilling but publicly defensible account of the world and the place of humans in it. That account revealed other, competing—that is, secular—accounts to be inadequate, confining, and inflexible.[26] To say that for Lewis a Christian account of the world is adequate and satisfying does not mean that for him Christianity is true simply because it works. He is not a pragmatist, and he certainly would not turn Christianity into a means to some other end. Christianity works because it is true. But since Christianity both works and is true, his stress, for apologetic reasons, is on the first part of it, on Christianity as an account that works, that is, an account that is adequate and satisfying.

It is fair to conclude that for Lewis the crucial failure of modern culture is that it renders people unprepared to give an account of the world in which they find themselves and of their behavior in it. They are unprepared because the narcissist and materialist assumptions under which they operate are unable to provide an account that is adequate and coherent. People conceal this failure by denigrating the accounts of others that are not based on self or materiality. Cynicism and skepticism are defenses against giving an account. But if a person can be led to enter a process of reflection and analysis that leads to giving an account of the world, that person may become able to entertain Christianity as reasonable and adequate. Lewis, in other words, is neither a rationalist nor a fideist when it comes to the relation of intellect and belief.[27] He believed neither that arguments could lead to belief as a rational conclusion nor that religious beliefs were non- or anti-rational. Giving an account of one's world leads a person to recognize the role of beliefs in that account, and it raises questions about the warrants of those beliefs and their moral implications. The act of giving an account of the world implied by one's attitudes, actions, or goals holds promise for revealing the relative moral and spiritual merits of various accounts. Analysis and reflection for Lewis can serve to present a Christian account of the world and of a person's relations to and within it as viable, even as more adequate than secular accounts.

Readers of Lewis who are theologically oriented to an anti-cultural and anti-rational understanding of Christian faith may counter my description of his conversion and of his positive attitude toward human rationality and culture by quoting a statement that Lewis repeats several times. He says that Jesus in the Gospels was either "a raving lunatic of an unusually abominable type, or else He was, and is, precisely what he said. There is no middle way."[28]

This statement seems to construe the person and work of Christ—and consequently Christianity—as contrary to human reason and cultural interests as we normally understand and value them.[29]

The fact is that for someone in the cultural world of the New Testament to say such things about himself as Jesus said or to have such things said as were said about him by others was not as bizarre as it would be today. There was an active tradition of prophetic claims and royal ascriptions that posited extraordinarily close and unique relations between an individual and the presence of God's word, name, and action in the world. The question that arises in New Testament texts about such claims or ascriptions has to do not with lunacy but with legitimacy. The offense is not so much that a person would say such things or have them said of him, as that such things would be said by or about this particular person.

The cultural world of the New Testament, then, was more prepared than ours to hear and understand the claims made by and about Jesus. I take it as consistent with his work that Lewis calls our own culture into question because of its inability to take seriously—not to speak of understanding and accepting—such statements about Jesus. It is consistent, furthermore, for Lewis to point out that the desires and needs to which these statements by or about Jesus speak are true also of people today and not unique to those living in first-century Palestine. But in our own culture such desires and needs have been repressed or directed toward other sources of satisfaction.

Why does Lewis make the statements in question? In part he is attacking a nineteenth-century liberal project. That project sought to dissociate Jesus from the early church's interpretation of him and to regard, instead, the ethical teacher that was the historical man. Lewis's comments are really an attack on modern culture's desire to evade the matter of Jesus's incompatibility with modern culture not by challenging the culture but by appropriating what in the Gospels is morally and religiously compatible with it and relegating the rest to the distant past. With his statement, Lewis asks his readers to judge the poverty of modern culture by its lack of interest in language by or about Jesus that sets him apart from the ranks of religious teachers or founders. When heeded, that language can be recognized as speaking to needs and expectations not limited to first-century people but shared by readers living today.

In addition, juxtapositions of this kind—lunacy and truth—are a kind of argumentation that Lewis often employs. He often poses exclusive disjunctions that yield two clearly contrary conclusions, one of which is too repugnant to accept.[30] So, this comment should not be elevated to some normative status that defines Lewis's understanding of the relation of faith and intellect or of Christianity and culture to one another. The statement should be seen as part of a rhetorical strategy, as the last phase of an argument that tries to force a conclusion by making its alternative unacceptable.

My interpretation of this uncharacteristic, even unfortunate, statement by Lewis does not imply that he lacks a stout Christology. He holds to orthodox beliefs about the nature and work of Christ. However, it should also be pointed out that Lewis took ancient myths and literary culture as providing modern readers with multiple instances of heroes and descending gods. These recurring types not only can prepare the modern hearer for understanding Christological talk, but they also indicate the continuing human need and desire that such stories should be true.

Furthermore, Lewis, while working with a sense of continuity between culture or rationality and religious faith, does not shrink from what is harsh and confrontational in Christianity. That harshness has both a cultural and a personal side. On the one hand, he militates against the distortion or dismissal by modern culture of those human needs, desires, and potentials for which Christianity gives an account. On the personal level, Lewis is also uncompromising; at some point a person will have to recognize that a Christian account of the world and of his or her place within it calls for a sacrifice of self-centeredness. It is not only a matter of choosing one's priorities, a matter, that is, of deciding that something outside is more important than the self. Such a decision can be finally self-serving, because the other as desired—nation, lover, commodity—can enhance the self by association. No, what one must finally confront is the realization that to go further in a Christian account of things is to give the self over altogether, to be radically altered. An illustrative example of this difficult and radical change is the experience of Eustace Scrubb in *The Voyage of the "Dawn Treader."* It is not enough that Eustace feels remorse for his selfish and arrogant behavior; he must undergo a painful transformation, which takes the form of having several layers of scales and skin scraped and pulled off him. A self-denying and radically reorienting act eventually is required. But for Lewis that change occurs when a person has come to see its necessity. The change is, then, consistent with one's own sense of need and desire. This is why Eustace finds the pain inflicted on him desirable.[31] As in Aristotle's theory of dramatic plot, the most propitious time for radical change coincides with recognition. The initial, basic change effected by conversion is a new understanding of the world and of one's place and relations in it.

For Lewis the offense and the sacrifice of Christian faith make sense when they come to awareness within the context of a gradually emerging Christian account of things. This is especially true today. We lack the kind of orientation to religious language that marked not only the culture of Jesus' first audience but also Western culture (until recent times) and all other cultures as well. As we shall see, modern culture is for Lewis exceptional in this regard, namely, in neglecting or repressing its moral and spiritual content. Lewis wants to reestablish a culture which comprises the spiritual and moral factors that allow people to understand religious language. Without such a culture, religion in general and Christianity in particular will appear, if not as absolute lunacy, at least arbitrary or excessive. Even more, they will be distorted in ways that allow those who do accept religion or Christianity, especially when presented in radically anti-cultural terms, to use them in the service of modern obsessions with exceptionalism, self- or group-identity, and power.

Lewis did not think it necessary to transport his readers to the first century in order to find a general religious culture that would allow a Christian account of the world to appear adequate and coherent. He needed to go no further than the nineteenth century, a time when ancient, medieval, and renaissance Christian beliefs and values were still alive or were being reappropriated. An exemplar is Matthew Arnold, who still admired at least some of Christianity's most enigmatic and paradoxical motifs, especially its particular wisdom that only by losing one's life can one begin to find it. For Arnold, this paradox was central to Christianity and was its most characteristic, provocative, and truthful point.[32] When Lewis remarks on the offensiveness of Jesus, he is reinforcing a cultural tradition that many in the nineteenth century, including Matthew Arnold, shared and restated.

III

Lewis also addresses two objections that modern culture has accepted as adequate grounds for rejecting Christianity as a viable account of the world. One of these domesticated cultural objections is that Christianity has no answer to the problem of suffering. If there were a good and all-powerful God, as Christianity contends, such a God would not allow suffering to occur, especially in the lives of people who do not deserve it, such as children. The second objection is that Christian belief requires acceptance of miracles, and miracles are an offense to a modern sense of an ordered, reliable, and even predictable cosmos. These two objections are so powerful because they complement or reinforce one another. The first finds fault with belief in a God who does not interfere in human affairs when people suffer beyond their deserts, and the second finds fault with belief in a God who does interfere in an otherwise orderly world. Together they constitute a formidable, well-entrenched opposition to the viability of Christian belief. Lewis takes on each of them.

Lewis responds to the first objection not by trying to dispel it but rather by reducing its size. He implies that the problem cannot fully be solved because that would deny mystery and unpredictability to God. He begins *The Problem of Pain* with a discussion of Rudolf Otto's category of the "numinous," that is, the often-dreadful power of deity.[33] He goes on to question what it means that God is powerful and that God is good, arguing that God's power is not without intrinsic limits and that God's goodness is not without harshness. Finally, he points out that much suffering is inflicted on people by other people, that it is often also a result of people's own decisions and actions, and that suffering and pain often have productive results, such as improvements to moral character. In this way, while not solving or dissolving the problem of suffering, Lewis reduces its enormity and its adequacy as a reason for rejecting Christianity.

He also takes up the problem of miracles and its role in the portrayal of Christianity as unacceptable to the modern hearer.[34] He argues that miracles are possible, that they are likely and that, indeed, they have occurred, and he posits an understanding of God and of our world that allows for the possibility and even likelihood of miracles. A cosmology that from the outset is open to divine intervention is basic to his position, as is the idea that miracles are harbingers of things yet to come. He implies an analogy between God and the cosmos, on the one side, and the human mind and the body on the other. It may be said that Lewis also indirectly addresses the problem of miracles whenever he engages in imaginative work by presenting alternative or possible worlds, worlds in which unexpected, amazing, and desired events occur. He implies that one of the reasons modern people find miracles so problematic is that they live in a world that is otherwise so flat and simple. If we confine ourselves to a world that we understand and control, the idea of a miracle becomes bizarre. As we will see in the next chapter, moderns do tend to live in a world of their own making, one very much under their control. Appreciation of miracles, Lewis implies, depends on restoring our ability to perceive the world as not limited to and by what we understand and control.

In addition to these standard and entrenched modern objections to Christian belief, Lewis also seems aware of objections that also became strident in the modern period: the motives of clergy, especially their misuse of authority, and the hypocrisy of Christians in general. Lewis seems to share many such reservations. He is critical of Christians, especially clergy, who have given over their identity in pursuit of fashionable views and flattering company. But he points out that Christians who are objectionable might be even more so were it not for their religious beliefs.[35] He also exposes the elitism implicit in the refusal to be associated with less than admirable people.[36] In addition, the behaviors of clergy and other Christians do not pose for Lewis nearly so great a problem as they do for those who place the church as central or crucial to a Christian account of the world and of one's relation to and within it. Christians, including clergy, are ambiguously related to Christian faith and to accounts of the world that it sponsors.

IV

Lewis's intention is to retrieve and reconstruct a relation between religious belief and English culture. He affirms a Christianity that is directly relevant to people in their actual worlds. It is not detached from common, everyday life by being confined to the heavens, institutions, or people's interior lives. He deals with objections to Christianity that are lodged in the culture, but he does not see an easy passage from nonbelief to Christian faith. The difficulties in a Christian account of things go beyond the standard objections to Christian belief pervasive in modern culture. The more difficult questions are these: Will people allow their attention to be drawn toward things outside of themselves as of importance equal to or even surpassing their own interests? And will they also be willing to undergo the radical transformation of self that the life of faith requires?

American readers of Lewis who want to continue his work and apply it to their own situation need to undertake acts of retrieval as well. Those acts must reach not simply to Lewis but to resources available within American cultural history. One problem Americans face, when contemplating retrieval now in some way analogous to what Lewis accomplished in his own time, is that the effects may be quite contrary to those for which Lewis pressed. While retrieval for Lewis's context could have a unifying effect, giving people something that to a substantial degree they could share, retrieval in American culture threatens to divide people because of the plurality of traditions that go into the making of that culture. A major effect of retrospection and cultural retrieval is to remind Americans that they have many pasts. Retrieval in American culture not only emphasizes differences but also carries, it often seems, the desire of one kind of Americans to establish their own, particular tradition as authoritative for all. Such an attempt, even if made in the name of what may be argued is a majority tradition in American culture, is divisive and hegemonic.

While retrieval was a complex effort of interpretation and criticism for Lewis, retrieval in our own situation must be even more cautiously engaged and even more consciously selective, inclusive, and reconstructive.

Retrieval will not, in any American version, be as distinctively Christian or even as fully religious a cultural project as Lewis's. This does not condemn the project to such vague and insubstantial results as to question the value of the effort. Nor does it mean that American Christians ought to lose interest in any cultural project that does not favor what is central to their own religious and cultural locations or identities. A call for retrieval need not mean either elevating one tradition above others or having no relation whatsoever to viable moral and spiritual beliefs. There are resources that can be retrieved and reconstituted without necessarily being divisive. They provide moral and spiritual beliefs that Americans from various traditions in their various ways can recognize, albeit for different reasons, as viable, sharable, and restorative.

We have considered Lewis's relation to the past, his acts of retrieval. We have seen this in the context of his location in English academic, especially literary, culture. We have also seen him in relation to the wider cultural context in which his work came to prominence, in relation to his conversion, and his interest in making religious belief first of all a cultural project. We now can move from considerations of his relation to the past to address the question of the present: What kind of changes must occur to enable a person to view the world in a way that will be open to the spiritual and moral content of literary culture?

2

. . . .

REENCHANTMENT

Lewis was convinced that before modern people can understand what reli‐
gion is all about, they must change their relation to the world and how they
understand their place within it.[1] This change is necessary because modern
culture, particularly modern rationality, has reduced people and damaged
their relations to one another and to their world in such a way that it is no
longer possible to entertain religious belief without distortion.

Lewis believes that religion can be rightly understood only by people
who live in a world that is at least to some degree *enchanted*. An enchanted
world is one that intrigues a person and that presents itself as being, at least in
some respects, more significant than the person and his or her own interests.

To the degree that they have been affected by modern culture, people to‐
day live in a disenchanted world. They think of the world as subject to their
own interests and designs. Having drained the world of significance, modern
people conclude that nothing outside themselves is more important than they
are.[2] Religion that is presented under such conditions is bound to be distorted.
For this reason it is imperative that religious people and advocates of religion
pay attention to the culture. Prior to, or as a major component of, any apology
for religion must be an address to the culture. Rather than shape or sweeten re‐
ligion to fit it to the culture or to make it palatable, spokespersons for religion
must try to free themselves from the characteristic effects of modern culture
and address its lacks and distortions.[3] Specifically some terms must be set for
the possible reenchantment of the world. As Lewis says, "In emptying the

dryads and the gods (which, admittedly, 'would not do' just as they stood) we appear to have thrown out the whole universe, ourselves included. We must go back and begin over again: this time with a better chance for success."[4]

Lewis echoes analysts of modern culture who find the consequence of rationalism to be what Max Weber (1864–1920) called *Entzauberung*, or disenchantment.[5] Rationality has increased the power and prestige of the human capacity to analyze and control the world. A result of that increase was—and continues to be—a shift of the locus of meaning and value away from the world to the human capacity to understand and control it. This characteristic shift has produced, since the time of Lewis, a variety of refinements, but it remains largely intact today. One aspect of Lewis's work that remains relevant to our own situation is his critique of modern rationality.

However pointed his critique of modern rationality, Lewis does not reject or attack modern culture totally. In this, he differs from many other literary artists and students of modern culture of his time and from Christian theologians who took their cues from, or found support in, them. For example, T. S. Eliot and Graham Greene, two writers who were in other ways very much unlike one another, both articulated the feelings of cultural loss and emptiness felt by intelligent and sensitive people between the wars. As William Golding said, the feeling of disillusionment was so deep that it created, beneath the surface of daily life, a "deep cavern of the soul" in which people felt "stunned." Generations of people, beginning in the second decade of the century, felt that they had, Golding writes, been "conned into the mincing machine" for which they were unprepared.[6] The so-called neo-orthodox theologians developed their sense of the human condition and of the religious prospects for human life out of this feeling of shared disillusionment with modern culture.

While Lewis does not underestimate the trauma and disillusion created by war, he points to a wider cause of disillusionment. Many critics of culture are disenchanted, he thinks, because they had never lived in an enchanted world. The culture of "hollow men" is at least to some degree projected. As he says, "The world is full of imposters who claim to be disenchanted and are really unenchanted: mere 'natural' men who have never risen so high as to be in danger of generous illusions they claim to have escaped from."[7] People evince cynicism, suspicion, and cultural alienation not only because the war has forced them to but because they were predisposed by modern culture to such attitudes. Modern people prefer to live in a world drained of value and meaning because they then are free to treat that world with disdain.

The disenchantment of the world, while it takes its sharpest turn between the wars, stems from assumptions or habits of mind characteristic of modern rationality. The first, usually identified with the influential work of René Descartes (1596–1650), is a separation between the world as an object to be known and the human mind as knower of it. This subject/object distinction produced an increasingly wide gap between humans with their conscious awareness and a reality perceived as different from and even alien to human consciousness. As Paul L. Holmer, in his treatment of Lewis, put it, "One of the most familiar distinctions in the modern intellectual world is that between facts and values. It is so widely espoused that hardly anyone thinks *to* it any more; on the contrary, it has become almost axiomatic, so that most people think *from* it."[8] The subject/object split allowed nonhuman reality to be defined primarily as brute, without inherent meaning or value, and human beings to be defined primarily as conscious minds. That opposition became basic to the typical modern description of the world and the position of humans in it. Western people increasingly and characteristically understood themselves as living in a world with which, by virtue of their consciousness, they had essentially nothing in common. Lewis puts it this way: "the world of facts, without one trace of value, and the world of feelings without one trace of truth or falsehood, justice or injustice, confront one another, and no *rapprochement* is possible."[9] When matters of any kind are divided into two, one of the two is usually taken as superior to the other. In this case, Western culture is marked by the assumption that the human capacities to analyze, understand, and control the surrounding world not only sever humans from their context but also elevate them above it. The nonhuman world becomes defenseless, apart from its own complexity and intractability, against the designs of humans on it. The surrounding world becomes, then, either an obstacle to or a resource for the advancement of human knowledge and power. By the mid-nineteenth century these attitudes gain currency; they become dominant at the turn of the century. And by mid-twentieth century they are assumed as "natural." As we shall see, Lewis not only rejects this understanding of a gap between consciousness and reality but believes that, within a culture that assumes this gap, religion will be distorted. For Lewis no such gap exists.

The second assumption characteristic of modern culture and causally related to disenchantment is that meaning and value arise from human consciousness and are projected by it onto the world. This does not mean, finally, that moderns have come to associate value with themselves, although that also is true. It is more that value becomes a matter of conscious construction, choice, and assignment. Value holds a questionable position when it is detached both from the surrounding world and from human attributes, attitudes, and behavior. Human life, including consciousness, can then be thought of apart from value. As Anthony Cascardi writes, "[Max] Weber would accept the premise that value-freedom constitutes a value in its own right, but it is this very attempt to hold values in suspension that finally places the very notion of value into doubt."[10] Moderns think of themselves as constructors of value who selectively assign value and meaning not only to things and events in their world but also to other people and to themselves. Consciousness becomes the source and arbiter of meaning and value, and meaning and value become associated with the power of a person to generate and assign them. The diabolical human behaviors that Lewis depicts in his fiction characterize people who recognize no value outside of themselves, even in other people, and who think that questions of value do not precede but are secondary to the extensions of their own interests and will.

The third disenchanting assumption characteristic of modern rationality is that analyzing, understanding, and controlling entities and events in the world depends on reducing them to their simplest or most basic parts. This method becomes part of modern science through the work of Francis Bacon (1561–1626). Bacon extended the tradition of reading nature as a text, a second scripture. For Bacon reading nature was a process by which the "reader" not only would be divested of previously learned notions about nature but could discern its simplest designs. From the beginning, then, modern forms of scientific analysis worked against the stream; the inquiring mind resisted the complex appearances of things in order to work past appearances to their simple, determining characteristics.

Starting with Giambattista Vico (1668–1744), Bacon's method was transferred to the study of human events and history and eventually to humans themselves. As Bacon wanted nature "read" against the stream, against how it presents itself, so Vico read the history of nonbiblical peoples against the stream because, Vico believed, people misrepresented their histories particularly by depicting their origins as edenic when actually they were not. So, Vico read the history of people against their own self-understandings. This negative or resistive approach underlies the attitude of suspicion that characterizes typically modern forms of analysis and interpretation, particularly of human materials. The prevailing assumption is that the way humans present or understand themselves and the way they really are should by no means be taken as the same thing. In fact, it is assumed that humans present themselves in the ways they do precisely to conceal from others and even from themselves what actually is the case. This suspicion finds its most influential articulations in the work of Karl Marx and Sigmund Freud.[11] As we will see, Lewis does not object to reduction and even suspicion as particular kinds of analytic acts, but he objects to them as general attitudes or as definitive of relations with one's world and, particularly, with other people.

These three modern assumptions or habits of mind conspire to disenchant the world: 1. separation or alienation of humanity, especially consciousness, from its nonhuman context, 2. dissociation of value and meaning not only from the nonhuman world but from humans as well, making value and meaning the results of conscious construction and projection, and 3. belief that knowledge and understanding arise mainly if not exclusively from the reduction of things and events, including humans and their behavior, to their simplest components, and the tendency to view humans as presenting themselves in ways that conceal what is actually true of them. It is against a situation so constructed that Lewis carries on his work. War may have been a precipitating event or created situations in which attitudes already implicit in the culture became overt, but the disenchantment of the world is not primarily caused by war. It is more the result of the willingness of modern people to define themselves and their world in terms shaped by these modern assumptions and attitudes. And I would contend that our situation today, while complicated by the subversion of modernist assumptions in postmodern theories and criticism, cannot be understood unless these three cultural assumptions are taken into account.

I

People interested in religion and its viability within present-day culture commonly respond in one of two ways to the situation that we are summarizing with the term *disenchantment*. Lewis avoids both of these common responses.

The first response that Lewis avoids is to discount the value of rationality or view it as hostile to religious life. Since Weber had identified rationality as the cause of the disenchantment of the world, its rejection would be an obvious path to follow toward the goal of reenchantment. The overvaluation of rationality and the unbridled curiosity of the modern intellect could easily be countered by advocates of religious faith who devalue rationality and call for greater intellectual restraint and passive credulity in human life. Such advocates could, for example, counter the primacy of rationality by arguing further that feelings and actions are more important for human life than mind and thought.

Lewis does not respond to the disenchantment of the world by diminishing the importance of rationality. He resists that part of the Christian theological tradition that in the name of faith throws suspicion on reason and the acquisition of knowledge. He does not posit faith as contrary to reason, and he does not identify humility as incompatible with the advancement of learning and the development of natural and human potential.[12] Lewis does not think that humans can be too rational or know too much about their world. Furthermore, he does not assume that various aspects of human life, such as intellect, feeling, and will, are or should be separated from or opposed to one another. What one thinks, what one feels, and how one acts should be very much related to one another. One aspect of the moral life is a matter of right relations between these distinguishable but not separate human potentials.[13]

Lewis implies that limits or counterbalances should be placed not on rationality and the acquisition of knowledge but rather on specific modes of modern rational and scientific analysis. There should be restraints on the practices of separating things or events from our sense of their significance and value, of assigning value and meaning to things and events, and of reducing things and events to their simplest components. These marks of modern rationality and analysis can be and often have been productive and illuminating, but they become damaging when they operate as inclusive cultural attitudes. As accounts of reality that articulate and determine the relation of human beings to their world they create mischief.[14] Affirming the validity of modern rationality and modern forms of analysis while militating against their excesses constitutes a more difficult project than Lewis would have were he, in the name of Christianity, simply to oppose rational and scientific analysis altogether.[15]

The second path that Lewis avoids is to see the modern disenchantment of the world as a theological gain and an apologetic opportunity. Moderns and their disenchanted world, their sense of alienation and emptiness, and the depictions of the "human condition" in modern art and literature (especially during the half-century beginning with World War I) as "hollow," shadow-like, lost and lonely, a "Waste Land," were taken by some as theologically productive. They were read not only as the results of disbelief in God but also as revealing what human culture necessarily becomes in the absence of true religion. Christian theology could be taken as making common cause with these descriptions of the modern human condition by redeploying the traditional language of original sin and human wickedness. The Christian theologian could posit a dialectic by which theological intensification of the world's disenchantment could provide the negative pole to which a positive, contrary possibility, namely, revelation and redemption, could be opposed. That contrary was presented as coming from a source outside of and even antagonistic to human culture and history. That "outside" could be, for example, the internal human potential for freedom, a location transcending human history, or a community of faith cut off from transactions with its cultural surroundings.[16]

However, as Kenneth Surin points out, one cannot view rationality and its effects as the basis for a Christian *contemptus mundi* without turning rationality into a cause or consequence of evil.[17] This radical opposition of the divine and the human is, in my opinion, itself a product of modern culture, with its habit of dividing things into contraries, especially the contraries of agent and object, and its use of opposition to clarify identity. While Lewis by no means minimizes the power and consequences of human evil, he does not believe that evil has left humans and their culture bereft of anything to be affirmed and even loved. It is possible for humans to become so evil that no further relation with them is possible—Weston's condition toward the end of *Perelandra*, for example—but modern people and modern culture have not reached that point. Because the radical separation of religious belief from human culture is, for Lewis, a fundamental error, any theological construction built on it is basically flawed as well.

Lewis follows neither of these well-worn paths. He does not diminish the value of rationality, and he does not believe that the description of modern culture as a "Waste Land" and of modern people as "hollow" provides a base for theological construction. He affirms rationality, proposes its exercise within a healthier cultural context, and points to the necessary relation between the cultural reenchantment of the world and the prospects of religious faith.

Lewis, then, sees the typical marks of modern rational inquiry—distinguishing fact from value, consciously projecting value, and reducing entities or events to their simplest components—as defensible. The problem, Lewis implies, especially in *The Abolition of Man* and in the space trilogy, is that these modes of rational and scientific analysis have been so extended that they have come to characterize the relation of modern people to their world and to other people. Lewis does not see this extension as an inevitable consequence either of rationality or the pursuit of scientific inquiry. As he says, "It is not the greatest of modern scientists who feel most sure that the object, stripped of its qualitative properties and reduced to mere quantity, is wholly real. Little scientists, and little unscientific followers of science, may think so. The great minds know very well that the object, so treated, is an artificial abstraction, that something of its reality has been lost."[18] For Lewis, the negative characteristics of modern culture arise not from rationality and scientific inquiry, as Weber argues, but from pride.[19]

Pride, while not a consequence of modern rationality and scientific analysis, flourishes under the conditions they create, especially when they become all-encompassing accounts of the world and of people's relations to and in it. When such accounts become commonplace, there is nothing left to check the growth and exercise of human pride. The world is drained of value and significance except for what I decide to project onto it. I can begin to subject the world, including other people, to my own interests and designs. This grants me unbridled power over the world and freedom from accountability to anything or anyone else. Limits are set only externally, that is, by those who do not want my self-interests to impinge on theirs. When strategies of rational analysis are turned into an account of the world, they allow pride and self-preoccupation to flourish unchecked. Human beings, because of the root nature of pride, are always ready to take advantage of a situation in which pride is not held in check, and modern culture provides just such an occasion.

What is unique about modernity is that rationality and other forms of human power are not set within a culture able to check their excesses, direct them outwardly, and secure their relation to worthy goals. The question is this: What provides the critical and moral context for the exercise of human power? The answer for Lewis is that this possibility lies first of all with literary culture. Literary culture can and should counter the tendency of modern people to assume that nothing is more important than—indeed nothing is important at all except—themselves.

II

Lewis views the problem of modern culture as arising not from rational or scientific methods but from the human pride that abuses them; this emerges in his depictions of schooling in England. His attacks on the school system are directed not first of all toward what is taught in the classroom, which would include training in modern forms of rational and scientific analysis, but toward the attitudes that schools inculcate. Arrogance and disdain, characteristic of the more privileged among England's youth, foretell a population of future leaders who form "a bitter, truculent, skeptical, debunking and cynical *intelligentsia*."[20] When the tools of modern rational and scientific analysis are put into the hands of people with such attitudes, when those tools are deployed in the absence of a morally restraining or directing cultural context, they inevitably are used to expand the power and pride of detached and elevated selves. And, as he points out in *The Abolition of Man*, modern pride and self-interest find their true goal not in understanding nature or even in exercising power over it but, rather, in the imposition of power held by a few onto the lives of the many.[21] Pride and arrogance easily can flourish under conditions created by the belief that rational and scientific methods of analysis provide adequate descriptions of the world and of the relation of people to it and to one another.

In *The Abolition of Man*, Lewis challenges one of the major results of the disenchantment of the world: locating value in personal feeling and preference. This practice, an example of which he cites from a recently published literature textbook, is defended on the basis that students thus are liberated from the values of others and enabled to make value judgments of their own. The advocacy of skepticism and subjectivism as a defense against dogmatism and tyranny already reflects, according to Lewis, the situation that it attempts to avoid. The real threat of domination lies not in a situation structured by values but in one drained of them. It is only when teachers and students share values that there can be anything like freedom and anything like the conscious scrutiny of and debate about value.[22] Without shared values, those in authority stand under no limits and can exercise their power unabashedly. Nothing is already in place, nothing is shared by students and teachers that will limit and direct the imposition of authority over the minds and feelings of children. Without shared values, only power remains. Without shared values children suffer the imposition on them of adult will, a process not distinguishable from the training of animals.[23] When education is divorced from shared values and a world that has inherent value and meaning, the principal result becomes not freedom but subjugation. Students either succumb to this power or respond to it negatively, directly or covertly, by an exercise of power that they take as their own.

What grows in the open ground where shared value has been drained out is not freedom but self-interest. Self-interest compensates for or seeks to replenish the world drained of value and significance by projecting onto it the value and significance of self-interested selves. Lewis knew intimately Milton's depiction of the newly fallen Satan in the opening books of *Paradise Lost*. Detached from the shared values of heaven, Satan marshals his followers by force of rhetoric in order to project value and significance on a value-free hell by means of his own, self-serving ambition. Freed from what he construes as the constraints and repression of heaven, Satan and his followers will create what Satan projects as a fabulous, alternative world of their own in hell. Power, which alone is left when the restraints of shared value and meaning are gone, can appear arresting and convincing. In both *The Screwtape Letters* and the temptation scene in *Perelandra*, Lewis improvises on Milton's Satan. In each case he makes clear that this exchange of shared value for a value-free arena determined by power leads to conditions of absolute evil.[24]

We must notice that in Lewis's space trilogy it is the representatives of modern disenchantment and power who make Elwin Ransom's visit to other planets possible. Without the scientific knowledge of Weston and the entrepreneurial sponsorship of Devine, Ransom would not have undergone the process of correction and sanctification that results in his ultimately redemptive role. The journeys to other planets are implicitly affirmed, and Weston deserves the primary credit for them. Although the physicist is portrayed more favorably than Devine, the entrepreneur, there is also some implicit defense of the relation of business to science as productive for human explorations and learning.[25]

Ransom favors Weston, we assume, because physicists are in a position, comparable to that of few others in our culture, to appreciate the scope and complexity of the world in which we find ourselves. A physicist will be able to recognize that something beyond the human is primary to and in some respects more important than the human. Devine, the entrepreneur, lacks that awareness and is merely parasitic on Weston's advances of knowledge and technology; he subjects the entire enterprise to his own self-interests: "ocean-going yachts, expensive women and a big place on the Riviera."[26] Weston increasingly resembles Devine because he treats whatever he encounters as simply an extension of his own intellectual powers and control. He does not recognize the dependence of his scientific knowledge on the world that has opened itself to his exploration. His arrogance depends on discounting the value and significance of what lies outside himself. Weston and Devine, although they seem by the force of their work and intelligence to have expanded the world and human access to it, thus live in a smaller world than Ransom because they think only about their own interests and are actually closed to anything unexpected or new.

Lewis frequently makes the point that moderns, although they think they live in a world that is larger and more interesting than the worlds of those in previous and in other cultures, actually live in a smaller, more uniform, and less interesting world. Moderns tend to subject the world in its vastness, complexity, value, and significance to the sharply delimited boundaries of their own self-interests. For example, *Prince Caspian* indirectly but unmistakably depicts such a culture. As in the modern West, the domain of King Miraz has been falling under the sway of various kinds of disbelief. The result is a culture that has also become increasingly cut off from what lies beyond the borders of its own control. The inhabitants of the culture have grown alienated from what they do not know, and they more and more fear it.

Because he does not find the cause of the world's disenchantment in rational and scientific methods of analysis and does not think they inevitably lead to arrogance and self-interest, Lewis can grant room, within a less problematic culture, for skepticism and rigorous analysis. In *That Hideous Strength*, for example, Ransom welcomes the rational skepticism of MacPhee in the community of St. Anne's; MacPhee resembles "The Great Knock," the tutor who prepared Lewis for Oxford and whom Lewis so much admired.[27] The critical, even suspicious and negative side of rational inquiry is not itself responsible for the disenchantment of the world. Within the cultural context of St. Anne's, MacPhee's skeptical and analytic stance plays a useful role. But when it becomes identical with inquiry, when values are subjected to it, and when it serves as descriptive of the world and of our relations to and within it, fertile ground is created for unrestrained human pride and a self-absorption that results in the disenchantment of the world.

Although played out in another key, we find a similar case in Uncle Andrew in *The Magician's Nephew*. His principal fault lies neither in his curiosity nor in his interest in magic. Rather, his fault lies in the arrogance and disdain for others that allow him to isolate himself from his context and to use others for his own designs. He limits possibilities to his own self-empowerment, and, consequently, he is unable to hear intimations of new realities when they occur, as in the music of Narnia's creation. For all of his apparent desire for magical possibilities, Uncle Andrew lives in a disenchanted world and is deaf to the magical qualities of what is occurring when Aslan creates the world of Narnia.

It is important to recognize, while considering the disenchantment and reenchantment of the world, that modern people are highly susceptible to false forms of enchantment. In a world that is largely disenchanted, people are vulnerable to compensating relations and are likely to fall under the sway of enchanters. *The Silver Chair* presents a very good example of such susceptibility. In the Underworld, where Jill and Eustace find themselves, they must constantly resist the attempts of the witch to enchant them. This resistance takes forms of suspicion, questioning, and even skepticism that resemble very closely the strategies of rational and scientific analysis. The distinction in Lewis between a reenchantment of the world that is preparatory to religious belief and falling under the sway of modern enchanters and their manipulating power is similar to the distinction he makes between destructive and creative acts of the imagination, which we shall consider later on. Both distinctions are crucial, but both are difficult to make because the mistaken or evil option in both cases is a perversion or misdirection of something good.[28]

Distinguishing between good and bad enchantment or between creative and destructive uses of the imagination is not rule-governed, not a matter of applying some simple test. It depends, rather, on the ability, developed and nurtured over time, to distinguish the good from its counterfeits. Living in an enchanted world has nothing to do with coming under the sway of enchanters, such as modern advertising and the enchanting and enticing world of commodities and consumption that it offers.

Separating fact from value, projecting consciously constructed relationships, and reducing entities and events to their simplest parts—strategies of rational and scientific analysis—produce particularly sinister results for Lewis in the social sciences. It is not simply, as Paul Holmer says, that for Lewis "general laws do not and cannot explain human behavior"; it is that modern forms of analysis cannot be readily transferred to the study of human beings because human beings should not be treated as without value.[29] One should never deal with other human beings as though they lacked value.[30]

Mark, in *That Hideous Strength*, is a sociologist, and his training and intellectual methods fit him perfectly into the ideology of the National Institute of Co-ordinated Experiments, or N.I.C.E. Mark thinks of people and of human relations in the abstract. He is more interested in intellectual categories than in human beings, and he displays attitudes toward people that bracket out the question of their value. This attitude allows Mark to become increasingly separated from the interests of the people for whom he is developing policy. The shift from treating people apart from their value to treating them impersonally or abstractly and then treating them with disdain and with a will to control them are all-important stages in Mark's degeneration. They are, as well, both typical of modern intellectual culture and easily taken as natural or inevitable.

When social scientists apply modern forms of analysis to the study of human beings, they not only separate human beings from value but also reduce them as much as possible to their simplest or most basic ingredients. Reduction becomes a view of people by which everything about them is taken to be less than it appears. Joy Davidman described very well what happens when this mode of analysis becomes a worldview: "In 1929 I believed in nothing but American prosperity; in 1930 I believed in nothing. Men, I said, are only apes. Virtue is only custom. Life is only an electrochemical reaction. Mind is only a set of conditioned reflexes, and anyway most people aren't rational like ME. Love, art and altruism are only sex. The universe is only matter. Matter is only energy. I forget what I said energy was only."[31] When rational reduction becomes a habit of mind and a way of life and, particularly, when it becomes a way of understanding other people, everything a person encounters is melted down and homogenized.[32] Frost tells Mark in *That Hideous Strength*, "'I must ask you to be strictly objective. Resentment and fear are both chemical phenomena. Our reactions to one another are chemical phenomena. Social relations are chemical relations.'"[33] Even religious experience comes to be explained as suppressed erotic drives. Lewis does not deny basic ingredients, but he rejects their use as fully explanatory. For example, he recognizes, in *The Four Loves*, that the erotic has a role in religious life, but he by no means wants religious life reduced to it. He also does not want the experience of joy, as he describes it in *Surprised by Joy*, to be reduced to erotic terms.[34]

Whether by abstraction, which absorbs the particular interests of people into large, impersonal categories, or by reduction, which dissolves complex states of response and desire into their components, modern social science is, for Lewis, a fertile location for the disenchantment of the world. While, again, it does not seem that for Lewis the social sciences are necessarily committed to such acts of abstraction or reduction, the character of Mark in *That Hideous Strength* suggests that Lewis is not hopeful that the social sciences have within them self-critical or restraining factors that would keep them from leading people to relate to others with attitudes of detachment and eventual disdain. And the absence of such inner restraints in the context of a culture unable to provide them creates a situation that seems inevitably to carry disastrous consequences.

Max Weber saw the disenchantment of the world as institutionalized by that epitome of rationalist authority and power, modern bureaucracy.[35] Lewis clearly agrees. The two most evil structures that Lewis describes are both bureaucracies: N.I.C.E. in *That Hideous Strength* and the "lowerarchy" of hell in *The Screwtape Letters*. As we can see in Mark's gradual assimilation by the ethos of N.I.C.E., bureaucracy, because it is governed by efficiency and rationality, by abstraction and generality rather than particularity and actuality, bypasses the question of value and goal altogether. It is a structure of means. It creates an environment where people who are driven by pride or by the desire to expand their power and to exercise their ambition to control other people can thrive unchecked. And hell, in *The Screwtape Letters*, is a place where people are reduced and even devoured by the insatiable need of the bureaucracy to pursue its own interests at the total expense of those exploited and devoured by it.

Those who drain their world of value and project their own interests on it, while at first making themselves exceptions to this process, eventually also become its unwitting victims. They end not as elevated above or immune from but as subject to the reduction and devaluation that they perpetrate on others. For there is nothing finally by which the value of the self can be sustained. The self cannot hold out as an exception to the otherwise universal identification of all entities and events with their most basic and minimal ingredients and with states of inherent worthlessness. As Lewis says, "While we were reducing the world to almost nothing we deceived ourselves with the fancy that all its lost qualities were kept safe . . . as 'things in our own mind.' Apparently we had no mind of the sort required. The Subject is as empty as the Object."[36] The self cannot retain its own value when it is reduced and devalued by the views of others.[37] Those who turn the world into something to be exploited or dominated must also, as we will see, suppress their own genuine desires. For these desires suggest the possibility of a larger and more significant world, a world more important and primary than the one constructed by the self for itself. Such longings find fulfillment not by means of subjugation and control but by relationship and incorporation. The disenchantment of the world, which is undertaken for the sake of self-enlargement, ends with a withering of the self.

III

The question now arises as to how, according to Lewis, the world can be reenchanted. This is a task that cannot, for people with moral and religious concerns, be sidestepped. A person who does not first understand the basic relations in which he or she actually lives will not be able to understand the kinds of relations of which religion speaks. This is especially true of Christianity. To paraphrase the Johannine epistles, one cannot love God, who is unseen, if one does not first love other people who can be seen. As Lewis puts it toward the end of *The Four Loves*, "If a man is not uncalculating towards the earthly beloveds whom he has seen, he is none the more likely to be so towards God whom he has not."[38] He goes on to say that moderns do not stand so much in danger of loving the world too much as of not loving it enough.[39] To put it yet another way, religion cannot be called on to create relations between people and other people and the larger world in which they find themselves. What Christianity can do is to offer a differing, more truthful and satisfying understanding of what kind of relations they are, can, or should be.

If the world is to be reenchanted, the first thing that must be done is to house rational and scientific forms of analysis in larger, cultural terms. Lewis does not agree with C. P. Snow and his thesis of two cultures.[40] The problem is not that modern rational and scientific interests form an alternative culture in competition with literary culture. Rather, the problem is that moderns, in their disenchantment of the world, in their eagerness to use rational and scientific forms of analysis to explain the world and their place in it, treat their own culture as though it were not a culture. Moderns hold previous and other cultures in disdain not so much because of the assumed superiority of their own culture as because they imagine themselves basically to be unaffected by a culture, to be fundamentally free of its restraints. This notion was introduced already in the sixteenth century. Francis Bacon, whose models of inquiry set the standards for the Royal Society, thought that attention to natural facts and processes could bring the inquirer to a position prior to language. This assumption that scientific inquiry is able to secure a vantage point free from language and culture creates the impression that language and culture are secondary and even gratuitous.[41]

When Weston stands in the epitome of Malachandran culture, the isle of Meldilorn, in *Out of the Silent Planet*, he expresses disdain toward what is going on around him. This is not because he values his own culture above that of the Malachandrans but because, while trying to analyze what is going on around him, he assumes that he stands outside of culture. His swagger, his patronizing stance, and his attempt to penetrate behind the practices he sees to what "really" is going on are all the signs of one who counts himself as not impeded by any culture of his own. The distinguishing mark of the Western mind is its putative ability to determine what things really are or what is really going on behind the appearances of culture. Culture, the assumption goes, should be stripped away, allowing the facts to stand revealed.[42]

While Ransom the philologist and Weston the scientist may appear to represent the two cultures that C. P. Snow contrasts, they represent instead what happens when scientific interests break away from the constraining and directing value system embedded in or conveyed by the culture that Ransom embodies. Ransom's linguistic, literary, and historical interests sufficiently relate him to human culture so that he is able to engage and increasingly to understand the culture of Malachandra. He ventures to understand the language of Malachandra, for example, because his linguistic training tells him that there are structures to language shared even by languages that are separated by planetary space. Ransom is a moral and spiritual force in the novel not because he is in any way, as yet, a spokesperson for religion but rather because he places rational and scientific analysis and hypothesization within the context of cultural value and practice. His cultural location does not close him to new discoveries and experiences. Rather, he is able to apprehend them because he draws on the resources of his own cultural tradition. Weston, who has divested himself of such resources, is both dangerous and comic in his failure to understand where he is and what is going on.

Lewis rejects the notion that culture is optional. Even the scientist is located in a culture and has roles relative to it, and culture carries moral directives and goals relevant to the well-being of other people and future generations. When people, including scientists, imagine themselves to be free from the directives of culture, they can easily mistake their own interests for those of the larger world and dismiss those whom they see to be culturally located as hopelessly limited and parochial. This gives rise to arrogance and disdain for the larger world—attitudes epitomized by Weston as he stands before the Oyarsa of Malachandra.

What is also needed for the gradual reenchantment of the world, in addition to recognizing one's location in a particular culture, is a kind of pulling back. There needs to be a willingness to count characteristic forms of modern inquiry and analysis as at best partial and strategic, as designed to produce specific and limited results. The world is not coterminus with our abilities to understand and control it; it contains, rather than is contained by, our minds and techniques. What is needed is an attitude that allows both nature and other people to be what they are instead of what we want them to be in order to analyze, know, and control them. We must not define the world, especially other people, in terms primarily of what we can understand and control or devalue or repress what in our world we do not understand or control. Backing off does not guarantee the world's reenchantment, but it is the only way to begin; reenchantment depends on it.

The third thing needed for the reenchantment of the world is the recognition that we have value and significance not at the expense of or in isolation from the world of things, events, and people but in relation with them. Personal identity is not forged by means of individuation and even less by means of opposition but by means of relationship. As Paul Holmer, summarizing Lewis, puts it, "the self is a relation, not a thing. The personality is neither godlike and truly original, nor simply an effect and made only by externals. It is both made and maker, debtor and giver."[43] Indeed, acts of attention to other people, things, and events in the world are necessary counterparts to acts of inquiry and analysis.

Recognition that other things are more interesting, important, and valuable than we are ourselves is indispensable to all knowledge. This, I believe, is why Lewis continues to value scientific methods of inquiry and analysis. Scientific interests offer the possibility of recognizing, as the scientist is trained to do, that what is being examined is primary and takes precedence over any notions about it or intentions toward it that the scientist may have. More than many others in the culture, scientists have a sense of the cosmos as immensely complex and beautifully balanced; it is a distortion of science to think of it as subservient to our interest in reducing the world to human control. As Lewis says, it is the "little unscientific followers of science" who think that objects stripped of qualities are by virtue of that stripping more real. Such objects and a world constituted by them are not real but "an artificial abstraction."[44] Neither science nor its strategies of analysis constitute the problem. Trouble begins when the methods of the scientist are elaborated into a general account of the world and of our relation to it and to one another. This extension is increasingly common and now is poised to become the ideology of the modern self.

For Lewis, we are related to the world around us not only intellectually and physically but also by our feelings. In *The Four Loves* he addresses various kinds of relations that we have with one another and with nonhuman objects, such as nature and nation. He sees the various forms of love—affection, erotic desire, and friendship—as locating people in relation to others who are considered to be important and valuable in themselves. Our loves provide a significant basis for our sense of the value and meaning of the world of which we are a part.

Lewis's attention to human relations points to the fact that such relations are internal and not merely external. Our tendency is to construe our relations with other things and even other people as marked by difference and distance and to understand our identity as prior to and independent of them. We should, however, understand relations and identities as based on what we share with other creatures and on what we receive from them. As we shall see more fully in the chapter on pleasure, relations for Lewis are reciprocal, and our basic attitude toward our world should be one of both expectation and vulnerability.

For the world once again to be enchanted, therefore, we must recognize (1) that we have a cultural location, (2) that our characteristic methods of analysis are partial and strategic, (3) that the larger world has a real or potential value and meaning which must be recognized, and (4) that as individuals and groups we have value not primarily in isolation from or opposition to others but in relationships with them. In addition, we must recognize the relation of particular things in our world to our sense of the whole. Any particular object of study, of desire, or of devotion becomes distorted when it ceases to be part of some larger temporal, spatial whole. This does not mean that particulars become tools to reach a larger goal. Rather, the value or meaning of a particular thing or event is positively related to the value and meaning of the whole.[45] Recognition of the universal potential of particulars and of the particular qualities of the temporal, spatial whole serve, in complementary ways, to enlarge the world and to affect the way a person relates to it.[46]

Finally, the reenchantment of the world requires the revaluation of the language of poetry and imagination and of language in the service of celebration and gratitude. Because of its evocative and culturally resonant character, poetic language can convey a sense of the importance of particulars and of the particularity of kinds of relationships and of kinds of unity. Poetic language also, more than the language of analysis and inquiry, carries the culture forward, clarifies and tests values, and counters the alienating effects of rational and scientific strategies of analysis. More, poetic language, in contrast to the languages of philosophy and science, is able to bring us out of ourselves and to place us in possible worlds such as those provided by fictional fantasies. This power of poetic language allows us to participate in worlds not governed by our own self-interests.[47] Such uses of language alter not only the world but also the self in fulfilling and reconstituting ways. The world and self thus created conform more fully than their disenchanted alternatives to what we most deeply desire the world and our role in it to be. In the modern world, poetic and imaginative work often compensates unfortunately for the disenchanted world by creating fantasies of personal satisfaction, situations that counter reality in order to flatter the self. Lewis sharply distinguishes between acts of imagination that confine or distort and those that free, correct, and expand: "We long to go through the looking glass, to reach fairy land. We also long to be the immensely popular and successful schoolboy or schoolgirl. . . . But the two longings are very different. The second . . . is ravenous and deadly serious. . . . There are two kinds of longing. The one is . . . a spiritual exercise, and the other is a disease."[48] The diseased imagination is really an extension of the modern self's desire to be increased and to find its fulfillment in its own terms, that is, in itself. The creative imagination does the opposite. It corrects the tendency of the self to subject the world to its own interests by placing the self in larger, more significant situations.

IV

Every self-understanding and deportment implies an account of the world; a person and his or her attitudes are inseparable from that implicit account. Weston and Uncle Andrew do not realize that their lives are structured by a set of postulates as to what is real and valuable and what is not, or that these postulates form an implicit narrative of destruction both of others and themselves. A person and a person's implicit account of the world, while not the same thing, are closely intertwined. A good indication of who I am is the account of the world and my place in it that I take to be adequate.

Freed from the need to control and discount them, a person will find that the world and other people become more complicated, intriguing, and valuable than his or her accounts of them. For Lewis, accounts of the world are never adequate. They will always fall short of the value and significance that arise for a person in his or her relations to and within the world. This means chiefly that if we let the world, especially other people, be significant and if we are willing to listen to and be open toward it, the world will not only become significant but also will speak in edifying ways to our desire and need for fulfillment. To put it another way, we know that arrogance and disdain, when recognized for what they are, are boring and injurious, and we should be cautious concerning assumptions, attitudes, and acts (including religious and theological ones) that give space to them. Conversely, if we know that receptivity and respect increase the value of human life, then we should develop ways of attending to the world that will enhance them. An attitude or act that is not consciously religious or theological but increases recognition of the value of human life and its context is more helpful than religious or theological acts and attitudes that do not.

To live in an expanded world, a world that we treat as always more than we can take in, is nothing innovative or exceptional; we are always already living in such a world. When we look at anything, we are latently aware that it is part of something larger that we cannot see, and that it is significant not only in itself but in terms of that context. For example, when we see a building from the front we know that the facade that can be seen is continuous with an inside and with the rest of the building which cannot be seen and from which the facade derives a great deal of its significance. True, we know this from our experiences of the insides as well as of the fronts of other buildings. But it is also the case that we are always relating particulars that we encounter to something more, either temporally to the past or future or spatially to related or differing entities. The world is always more, and more important, than our encounters with it and our accounts of it, and encounters and accounts should be confirmations of that truth. The act of imagination that attempts to bring "all of our experience into a coherent synthesis so that the world is for us a whole"[49] is warranted not simply by the existence of our imaginative powers or even by the largeness and richness of the world. It is warranted by the mutually revealing and correcting relation between our experience and the world that our imagination illuminates. For people and groups who learn to live in the world in such a way rather than in the dominant, modern way, the world will increasingly become reenchanted and in ways that do not compromise rationality, exploration, and a sense of human advancement.

Americans who want to take on Lewis's project and apply it to their own context may face an even more intractable situation than that addressed by Lewis in the England of his day. American identity, far more than English, is closely associated with modern rationality, scientific analysis, and technological advancement. America's world prestige is not based on its cultural richness but on its power, a power tied very closely to an entrepreneurially fueled science and technology. Furthermore, our imaginative life is heavily influenced, if not dominated, by market values continually reinforced by advertising that directs desire toward consumption and uses enchantment to control. The American scene seems not unlike the disenchanted world that Lucy enters when she moves from the wardrobe into Narnia, a place under the spell of the wicked witch who brings only winter and never Christmas. And the religious life of Americans, rather than ameliorate these tendencies, seems actually to abet them. What is needed is not, first of all, more religion. America is not lacking in religion. What we lack is a culture that can check and direct the power of reduction and abstraction. We need to ask if we are wholly without cultural resources for reawakening a sense of the world as not utterly controlled by the cold hands of technological reduction and market abstraction. Is there still a culture available to us that can begin to thaw the deadly effects of the witch's spell?

3

· · · · · · · · · ·

HOUSES

While considering acts of retrieval, we pondered our relation to the past. In our discussion of the disenchanted world we inherit from modernism, we focused our attention on present time. Now, as we turn to houses and other spatial language that Lewis uses to frame his thoughts on religion and culture, we will look to the future. Before asking why houses direct attention to the future, we should look briefly at the place of spatial language in Lewis's work.

Since Lewis's academic position was based primarily on his role as a historian of literature, it may seem strange to claim that his work is controlled more by spatial than by temporal modes of thought. This claim does not slight the fact that he had a very good feel for earlier periods, especially for the Middle Ages and Renaissance, and for ancient cultures. Lewis also had clear ideas about modern history, especially about the changes that occurred in English culture from the beginning of the nineteenth century to his own time. However, his historical interests, though strong, were subordinate to his use of spatial language. In his historical work, for example, he tried to convey a sense of the world as a whole in which people once lived. In *Surprised by Joy* he narrates his own life as having, according to the book's subtitle, a "shape," and the sections of his autobiography are determined by various locations. In his fiction he transports readers to other worlds. Although his fictions contain many events and actions, temporality serves primarily to expose readers to the qualities of the worlds made available to them. Finally, Lewis was especially fond of using spatial imagery to suggest what it is like to live in a world that is understood religiously, and the task of giving a Christian account of things produced a more spatial than temporal construction. It is not surprising, then, that houses and housing provide recurring images for his understanding of the world and that houses, as he says in *Surprised by Joy*, are almost characters in his life story.[1]

A central image in Lewis's spatial language is of a child living in a house. He grounds this image in *Surprised by Joy* on the experience of the house to which his family moved when he was seven years old. The size of the house, its configuration, and, especially, its attics provided Lewis a stimulating context for the imaginative adventures in which he and his brother engaged. Lewis also describes the house of his mother's aristocratic cousin. He always felt welcomed there, and it confirmed the role of houses as both accommodating and stimulating to his sense of possibility.

The role of houses in Lewis's early years suggests that they are relevant particularly to the past and useful for giving structure to early memories. As we shall see, a leading theorist of spatial images, Gaston Bachelard, argues that our early memories are arranged not chronologically but spatially and that the house (or houses) in which we lived as children provides the framework for that arrangement. However, Lewis uses spatial imagery primarily to direct attention not to the past but to the future. This is especially clear in his use of locations in the space trilogy. Interplanetary travel is something that the reader entertains as a future possibility, and the last of the three novels clearly projects future, dystopic conditions. But it is also true that his central image of a child living in a house is oriented not to the past but to the future. A child lives in a house in terms of possibilities—exploration, a setting for make-believe, and a sense of both enticing and forbidding locations. From the standpoint of a child the house is related not to the past but to the future. The house offers space that the child can alter and enhance by acts of imagination. The various places in the house have both present and potential significance for the child. The house encourages the child's future.

Gaston Bachelard points out, in his *Poetics of Space*, that even adults imaginatively project their futures in terms of a kind of abode.[2] We relate a certain life for ourselves to appealing accommodations and project possible futures by imagining other types of housing. Indeed, life for many people seems to be a quest for just the right house, either by modifying the one they inhabit or by looking at different homes and imagining themselves into them.

This is the core of Lewis's interest in spatial language and images generally and in houses specifically. He has in mind the sense of possibility, of a future, the kind of desire that prompts the child to explore and make believe and that brings adults to consider adding a room or to look for a house that will better satisfy their yearnings. It is that sense of possibility that lies at the heart of what he means by giving an account of one's world, of taking seriously the world in which one lives. In effect, he asks his readers, "What kind of world-house are you living in? Is it adequate to your needs and desires?" He then invites them to compare that world-house with the kind that a Christian account offers. He contends that a Christian account provides a world-house that is more commodious, more satisfying, and more edifying than secular alternatives.

I

Houses in Lewis's work are large, have many rooms, contain surprising and intriguing nooks and turns, and have spacious attics. To a child, of course, a house will always seem larger than it would to an adult. For a child, too, the house is a haven from the complex and often difficult outside world of interactions with other children and adults, and the attic is a retreat from the vagaries of domestic life. While there may be other hideaways and places of retreat, a space behind furniture or a closet, the attic is an expansive, alternative world, a spacious exception to the rest of the house. The attic, moreover, where the framework of the house, the alignment of beams and braces, is visible, has a geometrical quality that makes going up to the attic an elevating and edifying movement, with rational and imaginative potentials.[3]

The house excites the imagination not only because it invites exploration, provides refuges and retreats, and comprises differing kinds of spaces. It is also comprehensive. A large house, especially for a child, is an inclusive space, a world large enough to be inexhaustible but not so large and various that it outstrips a sense that it constitutes a whole. For the child the house is not, as it may be for an adult, a possession that speaks of achievement but a potential world that receives the child. When a child and an adult say "my house," they are expressing quite different kinds of relationships. While it may be too much to say that the child belongs to the house, it can certainly be said that the child does not think of the house primarily as a possession. For an adult the house is a commodity. For a child the house accommodates, releases the imagination, and holds inexhaustible significance.

The house also sustains the child's imagination because the child deposits treasures within it. Such treasures can be, by normal standards, trivial: a box or drawer containing pictures, bits of string, stones, a cast-off piece of jewelry. Gaston Bachelard argues that there is a moral and spiritual dimension to this storing of items that are perceived as valuable and are hidden from others, including family members. It conforms to the development of the child's personal worth, to a value that is inviolable and to which the child can retreat in difficult times.[4] The treasure stored in some secret place of the house constitutes a kind of Fort Knox that validates the growing social currency of the child's activities. He contends that children are so interested in little boxes and in keys and locks not because of their protosexual significance but because children are fascinated by the idea of securing treasures, of placing their most valuable things in a location inaccessible to outside interference.

A striking example of the sustaining power of hidden treasure is provided by Elie Wiesel in his autobiographical narrative, *Night*. The young narrator turns, amidst the horrible deprivations and physical and psychological torture of the concentration camp, to the reassurance of remembered treasure. He and his father recall the fact that they hid family valuables in the basement floor of their house before their eviction. Now, under terribly dehumanizing circumstances, they have some sense of continuing worth because of the attachment, however distant and irretrievable they may be, to precious, personal things hidden in their house.

Lewis also uses houses to allow children to relate their world to animal life. The child thinks of animals as feeling in their beds, nests, and dens in ways similar to how the child feels when at home. The habitats of animals are so intriguing to children because they recognize immediately and intensely what it means to have a house and what being at home feels like.[5] In the Narnia Chronicles the children often encounter the talking animals in their homes. They relate strongly to the animals in terms of the warmth, hospitality, and relative safety that homes provide the animals, as well as to the horror of a home invaded and destroyed, as in the raid by the wicked witch's secret police of Tumnus's house in *The Lion, the Witch and the Wardrobe*.

Houses play other important roles in the Narnia Chronicles. For example, the action of *The Lion, the Witch and the Wardrobe* begins in the professor's large country house, to which the children have been brought for their protection during the war. Lucy moves from the upper story of the house through the wardrobe and out into Narnia. That movement is stimulated by the exploration of the house in which the children engage. The role of the attic is particularly elaborated in *The Magician's Nephew*. There the geometry of carpentry is suggested by the mathematical calculations made by the children. There, too, Polly keeps her little box of treasured items. The edifying, even idealist qualities of the attic are suggested by the fact that it runs uninterrupted above the divided houses below, allowing the children to pass from one house to another. In both of these narratives, entry to alternative worlds is stimulated by the houses that the children explore.

Houses in Lewis often take on maternal qualities. We may see in this some lingering effects on Lewis of his mother, who died when he was very young. That trauma, the loss of a sustaining world, may suggest why Lewis's houses take on maternal qualities, as houses often do for children. This seems especially possible for someone like Lewis who grew up in a home in which his father was associated primarily with the outside world and his mother with the domestic. Houses do have maternal qualities for him. True, a male professor presides over the house in *The Lion, the Witch and the Wardrobe*, but it is a house cared for by four women, and it provides shelter for the children. In addition, Digory, in *The Magician's Nephew*, is living with relatives in London because they are caring for his ill mother, and Digory, during his adventures in Narnia, thinks of her often and acts on her behalf. Lewis also underscores the maternal qualities of houses by the name he gives to the future house of culture in *That Hideous Strength*, St. Anne, the name of the Virgin Mary's mother.

In Lewis's work, then, a sense of being at home in a house, particularly as true of a child, serves as a metaphor for living in a world that is structured by a Christian account of things. All that we have said about living in a house can be transferred to the larger and vastly more complicated location of the world. One can live in the world that, like a house to a child, invites exploration, excites the imagination, and calls out our potential by its edifying effects. There can be a sense of being included, of participation. One can feel stimulated to imaginative elaboration. Specific places can be invested with personal treasures. And one can have an understanding of what other people's lives are like. One can even have some sense of rapport with animals, by extending the relation that exists between a person and his or her sense of placement in the world to the lives of other living creatures.

By making living in the world akin to living in a house, Lewis does not shrink the world or shape it to the interests of personal space. He does not domesticate the cosmos, which would be narcissistic. Indeed, the mistake that can be made at this point reveals again how close together for Lewis truth and distortion lie. No, by establishing a relation between the personal sense of living in a house and the larger and far more complex and ambiguous matter of being in a world structured by a Christian account of things Lewis expands and complicates the personal. He challenges the individual and private by means of the public and inclusive. One's house is in the larger world. The world does not become a private realm in which the Christian, let us say, holds pride of place. Lewis means that we know from our experience of being housed as children something of what it would mean to live in a world opened up by a Christian account of things. Both are marked, above all, by a sense of relationship, of being included. This feeling of incorporation within something larger and more significant, something that invites the mind to explore, complicate, and enhance it, is basic to his sense of what it means to be in a world. A Christian account of things fails from the outset if it does not release and validate such a sense. The opposite of what Lewis advocates would be an account of things that conforms the world to the interests of the Christian, that makes the Christian central within it.

II

St. Anne's, the house in *That Hideous Strength*, exemplifies the relations that Lewis draws between the metaphor of houses, a Christian account of things, and human culture. While world, Christianity, and culture have temporal qualities and are ongoing and developing, they are experienced primarily as spatial. As a historian, Lewis's goal was to make texts in the tradition available and useful to contemporaries, to work against the tendency of modern culture to treat the past as distant from or even as irrelevant to the present. St. Anne's is a house of culture or culture as a house, and the very ancient and the modern are accommodated side by side within it. There is something not only spatial but habitable about culture. Like the many books that crowded the house of Lewis's youth, the cultural past is present to a person in the texts that stand on the shelf ready to read. A culture, like a house for a child, is always already there. A person is born into and placed within it, becomes aware of it, explores it, and is affected by it. While it is encountered as a complex and commodious whole, the particularity of its various parts are not for that reason in any way compromised. Textuality provides, with equal force, the awareness both of interrelatedness between texts and of their arresting particularity.[6] Finally, relating to culture like inhabiting a house does not denote passivity. A person also rearranges and adds to the house of culture. A person within a culture is not a spectator in a museum but is a participant in an ongoing enterprise.

Unfortunately, moderns do not live in their world that way. They do not feel related to it, supported and challenged by it. They do not explore its many and varied parts and eagerly renovate and add to it. Rather than live in that kind of world (or in their world in that kind of way), moderns tend to live in a world defined by means, by machinery, tools for communication and transportation, and money. This is because they understand their culture and their lives as measured and determined by technological developments and by the increasing powers such changes provide. These changes consign the past to the outmoded and superseded.[7] Because outmoded machines no longer are useful and have value only as curiosities and because modern life is so conditioned by machines, moderns tend to treat all that belongs to the past as displaced by the present and relegated to quaintness. Moderns live not only in a greatly reduced and confined world but also in a world determined primarily by what is useful. This changes the metaphor from house to workplace, laboratory, or market. For Lewis, that way of being in the world is bound to be constricting and unsatisfying. He posits, instead, a large, furnished house of culture with its surprising nooks and crannies and its many evidences of brilliant and inventive former inhabitants who, both by what they did and what they failed to do, invite contemporary inhabitants to augment or rectify.[8]

Lewis's use of houses as metaphors in his work is not eccentric. By emphasizing relations both real and possible that moderns may recognize and renew with the past, he creates a more sharable world than the modern period provides. In fact, Lewis seems, by these efforts, to be more at home with postmodern than with modern thinking. This can be seen not only in his stress on living in the world as though in a textual house but also in his spatial language and orientation. As Fredric Jameson puts it, "it is at least empirically arguable that our daily life, our psychic experience, our cultural languages, are today dominated by categories of space rather than by categories of time, as in the preceding period of high modernism proper."[9]

The language of place and space in Lewis is prominent in his narratives. He creates memorable fictional characters, but they are usually arrivals to or inhabitants of places that they discover, explore, or represent. His plots, while marked by action and change, are usually journeys to and within places that are both threatening and intriguing. For Lewis, exercising the imagination is very closely tied to the act of placement, of imagining an alternative world and imagining it as a whole. What makes a garden or a model village so pleasing is that it grants that sense of an integrated whole that the imagination provides.[10] What he most likes about fictional narratives is that they allow one to live in a different world or to be placed in the familiar world differently. What for him is intriguing in stories about pirates or Native Americans, for example, is not the action or even the characters so much as it is the world in which they are set and of which they are an almost natural part.[11]

Alternative or fictional spaces provide Lewis with the potential for altering the attitudes that alienate us as modern people not only from the historical dimensions of our culture but also from the larger cosmic context of our lives. In his space trilogy he counters modern notions of space, namely that it is inhospitable and forbidding, with the contrary notion that space is stimulating and inviting. Ransom discovers that space has surprisingly supportive qualities, and it causes him, despite unfamiliar surroundings, quickly to feel at home: "He had thought it [space] barren: he saw now that it was the womb of worlds."[12] Ransom's hostess on Perelandra lives in her world as though in a house. "'Come,' she said, with a gesture that made that whole world a house and her a hostess." When Ransom suggests that they go to her home, she asks, "'What is *home?*' 'The place where people live together and have their possessions and bring up their children [Ransom replies].' She spread out her hands to indicate all that was in sight. 'This is our home,' she said."[13] Lewis's language of house or home, the prominence of settings in his fiction, his understanding of culture as textual, and his affirmation of the natural world as the arena of human life conspire to invite the reader to feel, in William James's words, "at home in the universe."[14]

These associations with place and home are crucial in *Till We Have Faces*. The revealing difference between the narrator and her sister Psyche is that the narrator is unable to see the new home that Psyche now inhabits. Here it is not seeing that is believing but, rather, believing that is seeing. Her inability to see the house also reflects the differing trajectories of the sisters' lives. While the narrator is possessive and self-oriented, Psyche has lived in her world outwardly. Her new house is the context of a realized future, the fulfillment of her hopes and desires. While the narrator is put off by the mysterious and even forbidding qualities of Psyche's new location, Psyche has the confidence to be included and fulfilled by it. Her life in her new home is an extension of her earlier disposition toward the world.

Till We Have Faces also makes clear that Lewis, while he associates maternal images with feeling at home, does not define living in the world primarily in static terms. The emphasis does not fall on security and comfort or on return. While much needs to be retrieved that has been lost, feeling at home itself is progressive, just as, for the child in a house, there is not only familiarity and reassurance but also discovery and challenge. The house does not confine; it expands. Nor does Lewis, by relating the cosmos and our place in it to living in a house, minimize the complexity of the world or reduce its vastness to manageable size. Indeed, as the child does not minimize but expands the house, so a person feels at home in the universe not by reducing it to his or her own size but by affirming it as inexhaustibly expanding and including. "Home" is not primarily a state of arrival, mastery, or contentment; it is a state of enlivened imagination, a sense of something more, of advancement and growth. A house has, for the child, unexplored and even frightening parts, but it is no less enticing and desirable for that.

To live in the world as if in a house is to feel related to it, to be excited and intrigued by it, to be both intimidated and supported, surprised and illumined by it, grateful and responsible for it. Feelings of what Rudolf Otto called the numinous, the feeling of the uncanny, can also occur in the house.[15] But those feelings are possible because they are housed within a larger sense of inclusiveness, a sense of being at home, of being in a state of primary relations with the human and nonhuman location and context in which one finds oneself.

III

It is not surprising, then, to find Lewis treating Christianity, too, as a kind of house, as in his preface to *Mere Christianity*.[16] Indeed, one begins to have some sense of what Christianity offers only when one recognizes what it would be like to live in the world or in culture as though in a large and many-roomed house. Christianity offers, for Lewis, an account of the world that is more accommodating and stimulating than alternative accounts. Nobody lives in the world in some kind of raw and immediate way. All live in the world as a construction. If that is the case, it becomes possible to argue that religion generally and Christianity specifically provide a more inviting and commodious house than do their main modern rivals, the constructions of materialism and narcissism.

Christianity offers a house to which those who have left it should return; conversion is a kind of homecoming. Christianity is like a house because it not only offers an account of the world but also makes clear how one can feel related to and accommodated by it, how one can be in the world the way a child is in a large and complex house. Christianity places us rightly in the world. Materialist accounts are less commodious because they relegate spiritual and moral matters to the status of epiphenomena and consequently alienate large and significant potentials of our lives from their surrounding context. Narcissist accounts are confining because they reduce the world to the self or expand the self to include the world.

In addition, Christianity is sufficiently expansive to allow place for contraries such as the material and spiritual, the particular and the universal, the past and the future, the ephemeral and the lasting, the self and the other. Christianity has room for cosmic as well as for personal matters, for sophisticated and simple interests, and for daily life as well as ultimate ends. It all fits together, makes sense as a whole even though particular parts may, in themselves, seem odd or perplexing. And, like a house, it has its forbidding and off-putting places.

The image of Christianity as a kind of house, as a capacious and inviting account of the world and of our place in it, does not convey as much finality or completeness as it might seem. The account of our world that Christianity provides is sketchy; a Christian account is a kind of framework that is constantly in need of being filled out. As Lewis writes, "I claim that the positive historical statements made by Christianity have the power, elsewhere found chiefly in formal principles, of receiving, without intrinsic change, the increasing complexity of meaning which increasing knowledge puts into them."[17] Christianity in its account of things always becomes involved with particular, culturally dictated interests, although it should not be permanently associated with them. If that happens, a basic distortion can occur: Christianity is relegated to the role of validating the interests of a particular culture or group, thereby becoming subordinate to those interests. Consequently, while it is to be expected that someone, let us say, with political interests would construct relations between Christianity and political issues and strategies, those constructions, while legitimate, remain partial and temporary.

Christianity is not so amorphous and insubstantial that it is completely altered by differing situations and times. Christianity also has an intractable continuity or skeletal stability that, to extend the metaphor, people in various times and situations and with particular gifts and needs build on or flesh out. The accounts of the world that various Christians articulate allow not only for specific applications of Christianity to differing situations but also reveal the continuity between them. What is subject to change in Christianity and what endures is revealed by the dynamics of continuity and discontinuity characteristic of human temporality. One can be certain, in other words, that there will be similarity between differing Christian accounts without being completely sure of what that similarity will consist and where the differences will appear.

While grieving the death of his wife, Lewis contemplated a more radical position on Christian accounts and their lack of permanence. Instead of the metaphor of framework and filling in, he chose a metaphor for starting each time from scratch: "However often the house of cards falls, shall I set about rebuilding it? Is that what I'm doing now? Indeed, it's likely enough that what I shall call, if it happens, a 'restoration of faith' will turn out to be only one more house of cards."[18] While I do not deny the validity and force of this radical metaphor of a "house of cards," I think that the other understanding of the Christian house as a more durable framework that needs in each new situation to be filled out is more consistent with his overall project. Lewis tends to take mediating positions on alternatives, and one can infer that his position is to affirm both the continuity of Christianity and its changing and diverse articulations. The "house of cards" metaphor emphasizes the temporary or insubstantial aspects of the construction, aspects that at points in a person's life, particularly painful times, can become more noticeable than the construction's more durable or sustaining aspects.

It is crucial, particularly in the face of some present-day theological interests, to stress that the house of Christianity is not an independent, separate, or substitute world. Rather, Christianity opens up the world in which people actually do or can live. The affirmations of Christianity reveal the size, structure, and complexity of the world. One affirms Christian statements not by retreating into them or even by assenting to them but by living in the world that is actualized by them. I find dissonance between Lewis and some of his American devotees at this point. They seem to recruit Lewis into a sharply focused set of affirmations believed to provide, in a culturally complex society, a sharply differentiated and separated identity. Lewis, in my opinion, tended to see theological and dogmatic statements not as marks of identity or battle cries in some kind of cultural conflict. They are, instead, articulations of the kind of world in which a Christian lives, statements that can be thought of as providing a framework for a constructed account of the world that clarifies relations and provides habitable space.[19]

When Lewis posits what he refers to as "mere" Christianity, that is, basic and shared Christianity, he is not proposing an essence in the way that fundamentalist or radical reinterpreters of Christianity do, as a core of central, identity-granting ideas. A Christian world is not Christian by virtue of some tenets that the person who inhabits it tries to impose on it. The tenets are recognizable extrapolations drawn from a Christian world or are templates for testing what is right about the world and a person's place and role in it. Christian identity is not first of all a way of being different or a matter of adhering to certain beliefs or doctrines. It is a way of being in the world or having a certain sense of the world, a sense that for Lewis is marked, above all, not by estrangement or opposition but, rather, by incorporation and relationships, by feeling "at home."

The metaphor of Christianity as a large and complex house also serves to accommodate the variety within Christian practices and beliefs. Differing Christians can be seen as furnishing and inhabiting the many rooms of the house, a house that allows diversity amidst an inclusive wholeness. Some of these rooms may seem quite strange or even discomforting to a particular

Christian who feels far more at home in some other part of the house. It is not too much to add that in some ways other religions, too, can be thought of as having their places within that house as antechambers and vestibules.[20]

Finally, it is not too much to say that the whole world is in the house as much as the house is in the world. Christianity as an account of the world and of our place in it is not limited to specifically Christian doctrines. It also comprises broader affirmations concerning the nature of things and our comportment among them that Christians share with people of other religions. As one can feel at home in the world articulated by Christianity, so one can feel at home in a world shared by diverse people and cultures. Its size and complexity make the world in which the Christian lives unexpected and at times frightening. Christianity's "anfractuosity"[21] has its counterparts both in the sort of surprising parts of a large house that constitute exceptions to an overall symmetry and in the admixture within our world of what is familiar and what surprises.

Moderns have debarred themselves from being at home in the universe by defining their own history as a disinheritance. Moderns think their world has been transformed from something within which humans formerly had a place into something that is contrary to human interests and needs, a hostile "Waste Land" inhabited by "hollow men." Increasingly isolated from their environment, moderns feel homeless in the world. As a consequence, the houses that they build or buy for themselves are mere possessions without larger significance, except to the extent that their identities become synonymous with their possessions. Houses as commodities, no less than the personal identities that living in such commodities confirms, stand as radical alternatives to living in a world as though in a house. Outside their own houses and the identities warranted by them, modern people find themselves on cold and inhospitable terrain both socially and cosmically. Just so, the tastes, opinions, and beliefs that modern people have are treated as possessions that grant identity rather than responses and accesses to a large, inviting, and complex world outside themselves. Christianity, if offered to people with such modern habits, will become, as it often has, merely another possession and form of self-identity. It is crucial to see that Lewis, by likening Christian beliefs and practices to living in a house, is countering the modern uses of houses and religion as possessions and self-articulations.

Because the world that moderns construct and imagine themselves living in is inadequate to their need for significance and their orientation to possibility, it allows vague and frustrated desires to haunt their lives. People satisfy the desire to feel at home in the world by accumulating property, joining one group after another, leaving their television sets on most of the day, or pursuing now this and now that fad. But quest for the new and different, even when it takes an outwardly religious form, cannot satisfy the need. What people really desire is not to gather the world to themselves, to possess it. What they desire, as *Till We Have Faces* makes clear, is to be invited into it, accommodated within it, and oriented to the future significance that the exploration of a house suggests. Moderns think that Christianity imposes confinements and that rejecting Christianity allows one to move out into a larger world. But the world they enter is either strange and cold or it is confining because it is owned or subjected to self-directed goals.

While most moderns flee from a world grown cold and hostile into the comforts of their own, self-affirming abodes—whether actual houses or some set of identity-confirming ideas or practices—some also flee into the church as an alternative world. Supportive and symptomatic of this move are theologies that identify Christian doctrine and practice as confined and relevant to a specific setting or community.[22] These theologies either imply or aggressively prosecute an oppositional relation between Christian identity, language, and practices and those of the surrounding culture. One provocative aspect of Lewis's work, in the face of this major trend in contemporary Christian theology, is that he refuses, despite the negative currents of modern culture and the trauma and devastation of wars, to turn the larger world into hostile terrain. Where others want to place the church, Lewis places the house of the world structured by Christian beliefs, filled in by a viable culture, and open to reality. The two locations are very different; a deployment of Lewis in the contemporary situation cannot involve the identification of his house of culture with a house defined as an alien church, isolated from the rest of the world.

IV

Lewis's use of housing as a metaphor for an adequate sense of the world and of one's relations to and within it, like the work of Gaston Bachelard, which I have used to help explicate Lewis, depends heavily on certain social and economic conditions. Not everyone lives in a house with a basement, an attic, many rooms, and intriguing nooks and crannies. It is legitimate to complain that Lewis assumes some childhood feelings to be natural and universal that are actually culture and class specific. He grew up not only in large domestic spaces that were available for exploration but also in places crowded with books. His vision of house as a metaphor for culture and for the textuality of the world is a part of his particular upbringing. The cultural capital of his family seems to have dictated his imaginative play and his curiosity about the wider explorations available to him in the books that walled his home. Are Lewis's uses of housing as setting and metaphor and of being at home in the world wholly subverted by their dependence on his particular social and economic conditions? Do they constitute an ideology that normalizes class status by joining a normative feeling about the culture, the cosmos, and a person's place within them to a privileged cultural and economic standing?

Here is one of many points where it becomes clear that Lewis's work cannot be taken uncritically and redeployed. The questions raised by his use of a certain kind of house as a metaphor for being in the world should not be lightly dismissed. However, I also think that the sense of place and space that is advocated by his work and, particularly, the sense of being in the world as like living in a house commends itself strongly. It does so particularly to readers who have grown indifferent to places and to space, who are highly mobile, who treat places as commodities or conveniences, and who look at their environments primarily as resources to be dominated or exploited.

Damaging attitudes toward place and space are epitomized in the demeanor and language of Weston and Devine as they encounter the world of Malachandra in *Out of the Silent Planet*. Whether intellectually (Weston) or materially (Devine), their interest is to dominate. Rather than adjust to a new and larger world, they subject what they encounter to the interests that they brought with them from earth. Their attitudes are contrary to the sense of place and space that for Lewis is necessary to feeling incorporated by means of Christian faith within a world larger and more important than one's own world or one's self.

The challenge is to find ways of talking about human place relations that will not covertly posit the authority of a particular social class. Pierre Bourdieu's ideas about how people create homelike places reflecting their values can help us arrive at a less class-specific understanding of domestic space.[23] It may then become possible to say that children will make something significant of the places in which they find themselves, however different they may be from the houses that Lewis had in mind. Lest this become a way of condoning the conditions of deprivation in which many, perhaps most, of the world's children grow up, it must be emphasized that children need better housing not just for their physical well-being but also for the well-being of their spirits.

The feeling of being at home is not confined to a house but can occur as part of other place relations. Lewis also associates a sense of incorporation in a larger world with landscapes and open vistas. This is basic, for example, to

Lewis's description of the experience of joy in *Surprised by Joy*, to Ransom's sense of inclusion within and exploration of other planetary worlds, and to the inclusion in and exploration of Narnia by the children who are summoned there.

Just as important for Lewis as a sense of being drawn in by or at home in open landscapes is the feeling of inclusion by or of being at home in social space. Perhaps his fullest depiction of accommodating and stimulating social space is found in *Out of the Silent Planet*. The society that Ransom encounters on Malachandra is one that has entered the last stages of its existence, but this is due not to its evil, since there has been no "Fall" on Malachandra, but to age. Indeed, Ransom uses the society as a model because, in contrast to it, he becomes newly aware of the distortions and evils of earthly societies. What he finds is a complex social space comprising three types of creatures who have differing gifts and interests and who work or have their place in the whole of the society in ways appropriate to their strengths. The three groups are respectful and affectionate toward one another, although individuals of each kind have strong ties with their own kind and treat others somewhat at a distance and with some lightheartedness. The three kinds of creatures depend on one another and respect the contribution that each makes to the whole. Social space on Malachandra also has not dominated or distorted natural space; it is difficult for Ransom to decide where the landscape has been altered by the Malachandrans and where it is natural. All the members of the society live at peace with one another because they are not in competition. They think of the whole society as much as they think of their own group or of themselves. Their peaceful ways allow them to experience much more continuity than modern Westerners feel between their social relations and their personal or intimate relations. This means that Malachandrans require less from their intimate relations. In addition, they have a firm sense of continuity, along with difference, between themselves and nontalking creatures on one side and angelic creatures, the eldila, on the other. Finally, they do not make sharp distinctions between religious, aesthetic, and practical interests. The island of Meldilorn is a cultural as well as a religious center.

Ransom feels at home in the social space of Malachandra, and he recognizes that societies on earth are marked by opposition and exploitation. However, while feeling accepted by the society, Ransom does not minimize the differences between himself and his hosts and does not try to remain on Malachandra with them. While he does not theorize as to how earthly societies could be brought into greater similarity to the social space of Malachandra, he seems to recognize that the three kinds of creatures that constitute the society of Malachandra stand as positive contrasts to the negative relations that exist between the three visitors from earth. Devine holds a roughly parallel position to the *pfifltriggis*; Weston is a rough parallel to the *sorns*; and Ransom has much in common with the *hrossa*. A sharp contrast appears when the relations of the three groups of Malachandra's society are compared with those of the three visitors from earth. The comparison suggests, among other things, the central, mediating role that could be played in rectifying earth's social space by the position and skills that Ransom represents. Like the *hrossa*, the philologist stands between those who work with physical material and the intellectuals of the society, mediating the distance between them. That mediating position is analogous, as we shall see later, to the role of the "heart" or "chest" in Lewis's anthropology. The part of human life that mediates between physical drives and the mind parallels the role of the *hrossa* in the social structure of Malachandra. Ransom's attention to and appreciation of Malachandran society reveal the possibility, in Lewis's understanding of human spatiality, of feeling at home not only in intimate and vast spaces but also in diverse but structured social space.

A social space that seems for Lewis to stand constantly in a negative relation to the possibility of feeling at home is the city, particularly London. He seems to have found little positive place for London in his spatial evaluations.[24] For example, in *The Magician's Nephew* Digory lives in London, but he thinks of it as a "beastly Hole"; he is from the countryside and much prefers it.[25] Digory's adventures and explorations are not in the city at all but in the attics of the house in which he is living and in other worlds. Later we learn that the "cabby" is also from the country and that while living there he sang in the church choir, something that he does not do in London. His horse, Strawberry, also from the countryside, thinks of London as a "hard, cruel country."[26]

It is not clear why London is for Lewis a negative social space, indeed, an almost evil place. Despite their many common interests and values, he differed with Charles Williams on this point: "Williams was a Londoner of the Londoners; Johnson and Chesterton never exalted more than he in their citizenship. On many of us the prevailing impression made by the London streets is one of chaos; but Williams, looking on the same spectacle, saw chiefly an image—an imperfect, pathetic, heroic, and majestic image—of order."[27] In *The Great Divorce*, hell is a city, while heaven is not, even though in the New Testament the eternal space is projected as urban (Revelation 21:2, for example). Perhaps Lewis connected with the view of urban space expressed in Joseph Conrad's *The Secret Agent*. Conrad depicts London in a resolutely negative way. The principal characteristic of London in Conrad's novel is that authority and power have taken on an almost wholly bureaucratic form. Bureaucracy, as we have seen, is the typical form of authority and power in the modern world, and it is tied by Max Weber very closely to modern Rationalism and to the disenchantment of the world.[28] Lewis relates bureaucracy to the structures and power of evil. It is not at all surprising, then, that the sinister characteristics of the academic and political world that form much of the setting in *That Hideous Strength* are also bureaucratic, and that the authority structure of N.I.C.E., like that of hell in *The Screwtape Letters*, has an explicitly bureaucratic shape. This also suggests, one could conclude, why Oxford and Cambridge do not stand for Lewis as celestial counterparts to the hellish social space of London.

If London and Oxbridge cannot stand for Lewis as normative contraries to stabilize spatial evaluations, we cannot conclude that other locations do. While Lewis affirms the importance of social spaces that accommodate and stimulate the potentials of persons and grant to persons a sense of being at home, he offers no realistic models of social space equivalent to those he gives for personal spaces and open landscapes. We might say that he anchors the evaluation of social spaces in his work not by Oxbridge and London but by hell and heaven. While the importance of these "locations" for Lewis should not be overemphasized (he does not think, as we saw earlier, that one becomes a Christian in order to gain the one and avoid the other), they stand like logical extensions of social spaces in which we find ourselves in this world. They appear to operate for him as stabilizing and normative social spaces. London, however negatively described, and even N.I.C.E. are not as bureaucratic and not as evil as the dominion of the Father Below in *The Screwtape Letters*.

Although Lewis relies on the ultimate, spatially stabilizing locations of hell and heaven, he seems not to need the anchoring that an ultimate beginning and ending, Creation and Final Judgment, would give to history. His generally evolutionist ideas of time are less dissonant with those of the dominant culture than are his spatial theories and beliefs. He writes, for example, "With Darwinism as a theorem in Biology I do not think a Christian need have any quarrel."[29] He seems tacitly to agree that it is not disruptive to temporal orientation to be uncertain as to a precise beginning and ending. This means that Lewis is able to move, as late modernism or postmodernism do, to a more spatial rather than a more temporal way of articulating location. He also avoids the kinds of uncritical orientations toward space that mark so much of modernist and postmodernist spatial theory. Because Lewis locates his spatial preoccupations between the ultimate value contrasts of heaven and hell he is free to affirm and to criticize various locations as more or less conducive to the possibilities of feeling at home. Places that are accommodating, outwardly directing, and humanly inclusive invoke heaven. Places that are alienating, reductive, abstracted, and self-oriented direct attention to and find their consummation in hell.

Feeling at home, whether in intimate places such as one's house, in social groups, such as with friends and colleagues, or on open terrain, directs a person toward the home that only can be projected as fully available in heaven. What that means above all, it seems to me, is that the feeling of being at home is the feeling of a new self being born. Heaven is not for Lewis a continuation of states of comfort as we know them but, rather, the culmination of the process by which human beings exchange a self they construct and own for a self that is given them. One receives a self, in other words, only and finally when one feels welcomed as though into a home.

Americans inherit several tropes that allow them to live in the world as though in a house. The sense of this country as a refuge, as a new home for people by which, as the words of Emma Lazarus's "The New Colossus" engraved on the base of the Statue of Liberty suggest, they are gathered in, especially people who have been rendered homeless or disenfranchised by persecution or poverty, was a strong invitation to emigration. The exploration of the West was also an irresistibly enticing project that inspired the imagination and enlarged the spirit, however much it was also a venture defined by economic and political interests. John Sears has pointed out that many natural locations in this country, such as Niagara Falls and Mammoth Cave, became pilgrimage sites because they were thought of as edifying buildings, cathedrals that, unlike their European counterparts, had the distinction of having had God as their architect and builder.[30] But increasingly Americans think of spaces and places as resources to exploit, property to own, or in other ways as occasions for and evidences of their own identities and power. The American quest for physical security, personal power, and psychological comfort has soured the sense of living in the world as though in a house, and houses have become signs of the self's substitute of a place of individual pride for a space that is shared. This means that heaven, too, for most American Christians very likely becomes a place of self-fulfillment and self-congratulation. The "dwelling places" promised by Jesus in the Gospel of John will likely sound to American ears like the dream houses of a "gated" suburban development.

We shall have to ask whether or not we have available to us a culture that will still structure and support a sense of ourselves in the world that resembles living as though in a house. Are there rudimentary, sharable, and flexible outlines of a space that we can both personally and collectively affirm, that contains us and helps to actualize our potentials as individuals, groups, and a people engaged, in at least some significant respects, in a common enterprise? However daunting it may be, that is a question to which at the end we shall have to return.

4

· · · · · · · · · ·

CULTURE

Lewis believed that religion, especially Christianity, allows people to give an account of the world that is more adequate than accounts sponsored by secular attitudes and norms. We should look now at what he means by an account of the world. We should see, first of all, that Lewis gives culture a crucial role in the formation of such an account, and we should ask why he does that.

Lewis implies that an account of the world has three distinguishable but inseparable components. At one end, so to speak, there are our encounters with events, things, and people and our awareness of them that comes under the heading of reality and our experience of it. An account of the world responds to and illumines our experience of reality. At the other end are the stable beliefs and norms that give structure and continuity to an account of the world. An account of the world brings beliefs and norms into relation with experiences of reality. This relation, for Lewis, is mediated. The middle, mediating factor in an account of the world is culture. Lewis gives a great deal of attention to culture. He does so not only because it is a crucial factor in giving an account of the world but also because the nature and role of culture were, he believed, being neglected and even damaged by the attitudes of people in his own day, attitudes, I would add, that continue in our own time. By placing a chapter on culture between what we have been considering thus far and what lies ahead, then, I am trying to make graphic the centrality in Lewis's work of the nature and function of culture in a Christian account of the world.

Culture stands between our experiences of reality and the structuring principles of belief, and culture is the means by which a Christian account of the world is fleshed out in particular locations and times. Christian accounts of the world, therefore, vary. Lewis would agree with Kathryn Tanner that, "What it means to be a Christian should not look the same from one cultural context to another. . . . One lives a Christian life differently depending on the cultural materials with which one has to work and the challenges to the Christian faith specific to that context."[1] As Lewis himself says, "Though we ought to imitate the procedure of Christ and His saints this pattern has to be adapted to the changing conditions of history."[2] One can see embedded in this statement of Lewis the three components of a Christian account: the "pattern" at one end, the "changing conditions of history" at the other, and, between them, the adaptation—culture, that is—playing its mediating role.

Lewis's view that culture is indispensable to relating norms and beliefs to experience and reality implies an alternative to the "knowledge and revelation" or "nature and grace" question, as this issue traditionally has been identified.[3] Lewis posits, without explicating or defending his position, a dynamic interaction of challenge and confirmation between three, rather than two, parties in the formation of a Christian account. It is not that one of the three determines or interprets the others. The three clarify, validate and challenge one another. A Christian account of things, while basically affirming continuity between the three, does not always succeed in articulating that continuity, and it does not establish the reasons for that continuity as a separate doctrine of faith.

Lewis seems to support his belief in the central role of culture as mediator between religious beliefs and everyday life from his understanding of medieval thought. He makes the point that the medievals, under the influence of Plato, tended to think that it was not possible to join two things together without a third to mediate their relation to one another. This is why, he argues, they were always building bridges. "The medievals are always supplying bridges, third things, between reason and appetite, soul and body, king and common."[4] Lewis is fascinated by the prevalence of these triadic structures in medieval thought.

Lewis's view of culture as a mediator between reality and belief also seems influenced by the deeply rooted relations of English culture to Christianity. The challenge is to restore the openness of English culture to, even its dependence on, moral and spiritual belief and desire. He sees the influence of English literary culture to be rapidly eroding. While it may be attentive to reality and human experience, it tends to marginalize moral and spiritual needs and beliefs. This neglect means that literary culture is losing its central, mediating role in the formation of English life.

While Lewis may give culture such a central role because English literary culture is deeply implicated with Christian beliefs and forms of Christian living, his position also has a basis in what he believes cultures actually do. If it is the case that English culture is beginning to give up its relation to the moral and religious life of people, it is becoming not only different from English cultures of the past but also different from non-Western cultures of the present. Other cultures retain their moral and spiritual content, he observes. If modern English culture continues to lose its relation to moral and spiritual beliefs and norms, it eventually will not be a culture at all.

Lewis assumes an interdependent relation between religion and culture. Religion requires a viable culture, if it is to be fleshed out, and culture requires religion for its completion, if it is not to be limited to one side of its mediating position, namely, relating people to what can be taken as reality. Culture's central, mediating role is lost if it is closed to either side, either to reality or to religious belief. Indeed, if either side is closed, culture becomes distorted and distorts.

The growing separation, even antagonism, between English culture and religious belief consequently threatens both religion and culture. Indeed, to the degree that this separation already has occurred, the culture functions increasingly as no culture at all. Religion, meanwhile, falls into disrepair either by being conformed to the reduced culture around it or by becoming abstract and irrelevant to its present context. The problem that this creates is grave. For Lewis it becomes very difficult to advocate a Christian account of things in the absence of an adequate or viable culture. Christianity can provide the structuring principles for an account of the world and can add some crucial, unique items to it, but it cannot itself provide a culture. The first task for reviving the prospects of a contemporary Christian account of the world and of our places in it, then, is to locate and amend those aspects of modern culture that close it to and separate it from religious belief. As Paul Holmer put it, "It is as if there are plain, primary, first-order ways of thinking and speaking that have to be restored to people before they can make any sense of the Christian literature."[5]

It is important to keep in mind that when Lewis addresses the problem of culture he does not separate high and popular culture from one another. There are for him differing levels of sophistication and learning, and those levels should not be underestimated or subverted, but there are continuities between them. He points out, for example, that a child's story ought to be one that an adult could read with profit and pleasure.[6] Culture both accommodates differences and clarifies commonalities, and it cannot become either a way by which some people separate themselves from others or a way by which people become indistinguishable from one another.

The task of addressing the question of modern culture and the relation of Christianity to it is problematic enough, but Lewis recognizes an additional hazard. It is difficult to address the question of one's culture without destroying by that very attention what culture actually is or should be. Culture is not primarily a conscious product of construction or an object of attention. Any attempt consciously to address, restore, or alter culture carries inherent risks. Lewis recognizes this problem because of his more general point that ordinary, daily living has primacy in relation to conscious awareness. Human living suffers when it is subjected to conscious control, and consciousness can assume primacy only in unusual circumstances. As we shall see, the seat of culture in a person is not consciousness but the heart or "chest." So also, the moral content of culture is not identical with conscious concern for and construction of culture. Those who hold that it is are people who live in a disenchanted world, a world that privileges consciousness. Culture is, rather, an ongoing, one could say living, context and medium of communal or shared life.[7] Lewis suggests that it is characteristic of modern culture not only to give primacy to consciousness but also to assume that culture is a conscious construction.

Lewis does not share, then, in the work of some of his contemporaries who, concerned about the plight of modern culture, became its self-appointed creators and guardians. For him, when culture becomes a focus of conscious intention it will inevitably become an extension of private interests. The resulting culture will be one that supports what its advocates take to be important. As Lionel Adey observes, Lewis, especially in his essay "Lilies that Fester," "derided the concern for culture that Leavis and Eliot had inherited from Arnold."[8] While Lewis shares the judgment that modern culture presents serious problems, he does not join those who distinguish themselves from and elevate themselves above others in the attempt to rectify them.

Lewis has the same reservations concerning self-consciousness when it comes to religion. Self-conscious religion is no less problematic than self-conscious culture. As he says, "A 'faith in culture' is as bad as a faith in religion; both expressions imply a turning away from those very things which culture and religion are about."[9] Indeed, the three components of a Christian account of things— reality, culture, and core Christian beliefs and norms—are not either in themselves or in their relations consequences of conscious construction. *A fortiori* they are not bases of separation and group- or self-elevation.

Self-consciousness keeps culture from doing what needs, above all else, to be done. Culture's essential role is leading people to recognize things outside themselves and beyond their own interests as of great, if not primary, value. A healthy culture will allow entities and events, especially human beings and their actions, to point to some larger end. Culture, if it is what it should be, counters self-centeredness, self-interest, and even self-consciousness. When culture becomes the object of conscious interest, it becomes subjected to the self and thereby dissolves.

We can now see one of the bases for the interrelations that Lewis assumes between reality, culture, and religion. All three can and should direct the attention of a person outward, leading a person to recognize that there are things outside the self that are more important. The mediating role of culture is crucial; if people are led by their culture to be self-centered, they will take that habit into the way they understand religion and all of reality.

Lewis implies, therefore, that an unhealthy culture contaminates religion. People who relate to their world in terms of a culture that makes them self-centered will find either that Christianity makes no sense at all or that it offers another way of giving power and importance to the self. So, in hell, which for Lewis stands as the culmination of the cultural distortions and evils that we see now around us, Screwtape fails to understand what "The Enemy" is up to and reads what "The Enemy" does as an expression of self-interest. As Screwtape misunderstands the attitudes and actions of divine grace, so people affected by the turn of modern Western culture toward the authority of the self will misinterpret and misappropriate religion.[10] Both culture and Christianity stand in danger of becoming ways by which people count themselves as different from and superior to others, ways by which persons talk more highly about themselves than they otherwise would be able to.

I

Lewis is critical of his culture not only because it fails to point beyond itself to religious norms and beliefs but also because, at the other end, it fails to relate people adequately to reality. While modern culture appears to be attentive to reality and our experiences of it, it fails, Lewis thinks, to validate actual relations with reality. It fails because it has broken experiences of events and entities into separate, unrelated components, objective facts and subjective understandings and evaluations of them. In addition, it has encouraged people to focus on themselves as distinct and independent. Modern culture, therefore, encourages self-centeredness in people. As Lewis says, "It is impossible, in this context, not to inquire what our civilization has been putting first for the last thirty years. And the answer is plain. It has been putting itself first."[11] Modern culture does this by positing human beings as basically unrelated to anything or anyone outside themselves.

A culture that functions properly militates against self-centeredness by directing the attention of people to things outside and beyond themselves that are there before they arrive, into which they are educated as participants, and that are more important than their own interests. Widespread self-centeredness is a sign that modern culture has not functioned as a culture, since a primary consequence of culture is to direct attention outward.

A second major doctrine of modern culture, one that Lewis sees as a correlate to the doctrine of individual autonomy, is materialism, the belief that only that to which the senses grant access is real. Materialism has both a refined, philosophical form and a vulgar, commercial form. The two, while very different in their locations and roles, support one another, primarily in that a general air of philosophical materialism legitimizes in subtle but powerful ways vulgar or commercial materialism. The two produce similar results: they sever the relation of material reality and sensory experiences from our evaluations of them. Evaluations are secondary, are add-ons to reality and our experience of it.

Lewis sees these two doctrines of modern culture as abetting one another. They are doctrines attached to the opposing walls of the canyon opened up by the cultural separation of objective and subjective or fact and value from one another. Under the influence of materialism all matters of value and meaning are relegated to private status. Materialism, having garnered the real, implicitly relegates value and meaning to internal locations. Individual selves become not only the sources of value but themselves the only value. Values, then, are projected onto things and, in one way or another, are self-serving. When the primary relation of values to reality is denied or sundered, values lose not only their groundings but also their public valence. They easily turn into personal whims or identity articulations. Culture in this way forfeits its relevance to shared life as well as its relation to reality. Values that are severed from reality and are not shared will begin to appear unstable and gratuitous. As Lewis says, "Either there is significance in the whole process of things as well as in human activity, or there is no significance in human activity itself. . . . If the world is meaningless, then so are we; if we mean something, we do not mean alone."[12] A culture separated from reality soon begins no longer to function as a culture.

Self-centeredness and materialism aggravate and reinforce one another and conspire to destroy culture. Reality is stripped of meaning and value, and meaning and value, perceived as subjective, are stripped of their claims on events and entities.[13] Self-centeredness and materialism make the self the exclusive source and object of value and subject the world outside the self to brute objectivity and mere utility.

Lewis responds to this situation primarily by arguing against the assumption that values are subjective. It sometimes seems that in these attacks he is arguing that values are objective, as, for example, in *The Abolition of Man*.[14] However, I think that it would be a mistake to conclude that value theory for Lewis is primarily based on objectivism. Rather than taking a stand against subjectivism and for objectivism, Lewis makes the case throughout his work that a viable culture is relational, one that clarifies and corrects the internal relations of people with the events and entities of reality. What he calls for is a restoration of a sense of relatedness between internal and external, subject and object. Value is relational. Lewis both as cultural theorist and Christian apologist is intent on rejecting a basic underpinning of modernity, namely, the assumption of gaps between mind and body, subject and object, value and fact, culture and reality.

One of the defining functions of culture is to create, define, and maintain right relations between internal states and their external counterparts. Consequently, the two major characteristics of modernity, self-centeredness and materialism, depend upon and confirm a separation that is not, and cannot be, true. When culture fails to retain the relations between internal and external or between meaning or value and entities or events, both are distorted. Lewis's principal aim is not to argue against subjectivism and for objectivism. Rather, he argues for the primary relation that exists between people's beliefs and values and the entities and events that constitute reality, a relation that always already exists because of culture.

One way in which Lewis argues against the subject/object split is by reference to the Romantics, particularly to their interest in the sublime. The experience of the sublime, as it features in Romantic theory, constitutes a moment, Lewis believes, in which one cannot separate an event or object from the human evaluation of it. Moments of the sublime become for him normative for reaffirming culture as that within which appropriate relations between entities or events and our sense of their importance and value are maintained and inculcated.[15] For all his interest in medieval and Renaissance cultures, Lewis's reference point is not so much the premodern period as the Romantics. For Lewis, the principal turn of or break in culture was not in the sixteenth century but in the nineteenth.[16] The main characteristic of this break is the erosion of culturally sustained relations between things or events and the responses of people to them and a final separation of these two factors. For more than a century, Lewis believes, modern culture, rather than do its proper work, has sponsored the separation of entities and events from our shared sense of their significance and value. This makes modern culture unique, an anomaly, among human cultures. Other cultures and Western culture until quite recently assume that there is a relation between people and the events and entities around them. The culture maintains, clarifies, and challenges those relations.

Since it is the proper purpose of culture to confirm the relations of people to what stands or occurs outside them, it becomes possible to see that modern educators and representatives of modern culture actually oppose culture. Modernity assumes that culture itself is dispensable or at best optional. This assumption is supported by the belief that when people are free from values they can see things as they actually are and make judgments about them that are true. This belief, which is basic to scientific interests and methods, has become definitive of modernity. The educational goal of dissociating entities and events from our responses to them is defended because it appears to create people who are free, who are not under the authority of preexisting assumptions about relations between things and their significance. The attack on already existing relations between facts and values is defended as creating a situation in which people can make up their own minds, can ascribe their own values to things rather than be subjected to those of others. Lewis objects to this because it subjects culture to consciousness, disenchants the world, and warrants the centrality of the self.

Lewis's response to the reasoning behind these educational theories is complex. He seems to see the claim that one can examine something more accurately when it is divorced from feeling and value as a strategy appropriate to some kinds of study, especially science.[17] Indeed, the rapid pace of advancement in scientific knowledge and the reliability of that knowledge are dependent upon this strategy. But when that act of suspension becomes not simply a particular strategy but a general attitude toward the world, it has damaging results. Scientific knowledge and its technological fruits are so impressive and, indeed, so definitive of modernity that the methods basic to them are carried into the culture, attached to and validated by their striking and powerful results. The illusion is created that moderns are people who, unlike people in other or former cultures, stand in no real, culturally stabilized value relations with the entities and events of their world. The illusion is created that people are therefore free to make of the world anything that fits their purposes.

Lewis more fully rejects the other rationale for dismissing culture, namely, that by so doing individuals become free from the tyranny of others' opinions and are able to choose values for themselves. It may seem credible that, in the classroom, severing the ties between entities or events and their values frees children from the sway of dogmatism and enables them to make up their own minds. But the notion of freedom implied by such a program is without content or direction. Children trained in such an environment are more and not less subject to authority and its manipulations because teachers do not have to acknowledge that they are working within a structure of assumptions, values, and interests. Teachers can pretend that they are simply presenting things as they really are. When value-free facts are secured, the truth question presumably has also been settled. Values are then relegated to a secondary position dissociated from the primary quest for truth. In addition, if teachers do not have to acknowledge the values they bring into the classroom, they can impose their beliefs undetected and unrestrained. When culture and education are separated from the sense of shared values and when teachers and students do not stand under a set of shared rules, power becomes the principal, indeed the only, factor. This is why Lewis can argue, in *The Abolition of Man*, that an education that divorces people from nature in order to exert power over nature easily turns into the exercise of power by some people over others or by a few over the many. "For," as he says, "the power of man to make himself what he pleases means . . . the power of some men to make other men what they please."[18] In addition, "man's power over Nature turns out to be a power exercised by some men over other men with Nature as its instrument."[19] The attempt to let children develop their own values and to dissociate value from entities and events dissolves culture and produces relations based only on power. This means that those with great power simply dominate those with less, since they have no other basis for relation with them.

II

Lewis locates the deficiencies of culture on both ends or sides. It fails to point to religious beliefs and norms, and it fails to relate people to reality. Lewis wants to retrieve and affirm English culture as a stabilizing and unifying order of shared knowledge, values, and judgments. A viable culture is related at one end to religious beliefs and norms that it both supports and challenges and, at the other, to reality that it both defers to and determines. A viable culture gives rise to public discourses that house the institutions of society— its schools and research centers, its commercial and economic interests, its political structures—in a shared context. This context prosecutes and questions what is best for human life. Culture, in other words, is a form of shared social identity, whose role is roughly analogous to that of character in the life of a person. It provides continuity and stability as well as large degrees of diversity and change.

The first question that arises is whether such an understanding of culture can stand up today, that is, in an academic situation that has been so shaped by theorists who subordinate culture to social, economic, and political dynamics and structures. For example, is it not the case that "culture," as a shared world of discourse, serves an immoral purpose, namely, to conceal differences that it is in the interest of some people, particularly those in positions of privilege, to keep hidden? Lewis seems to think that people of greatly different positions in English society can feel included within a common set of values and have a shared way of discussing them. People can be related by recognizing values that precede or transcend individual and group interests. He seems to have in mind a context that allows for meaningful relations, for example, between homeowners and their cooks and gardeners, such as existed at his home, the Kilns. The question arises as to whether a view of culture as a kind of house in which people with unequal resources share a common life too easily discounts social and economic differences, concealing hurtful injustices.

In my opinion, Lewis was not as aware of this issue as he ought to have been. We can say, however, that cultural theory may err in placing too much stress on the differences between people. The reason for this overemphasis is that current cultural theory rests on the assumption that human beings are basically in states of separation and potential conflict with one another. If one so believes—and it is a belief—then anything that suggests continuity and relations between people is bound to be judged incompatible with reality.

The suspicion that affirmations of cultural commonality conceal injustices does not necessarily arise, therefore, only from a desire for greater social, political, and economic equality. It depends as well on the belief that humans are basically pitted against one another in a deadly zero-sum game. This belief subjects culture to the struggle for power and to conscious control. The belief can become self-validating. It creates and aggravates differences and conflicts because it assumes that they are always already there, forming the inevitable, perhaps natural, ground for human identity and relationships. Lewis is not willing to concede that belief, and his resistance has merit. While Lewis could hardly be cited as a champion of social and economic justice, I would agree with him that the quest for justice need not depend on a theory that posits difference and conflict as basic to the relations of people to one another.

Lewis's stress on the shared should be treated cautiously, but it holds no more potential harm than its opposite, the stress on difference. For every instance in which the disclosure of concealed difference serves the cause of justice, an instance could, perhaps, be cited in which human well-being would be advanced by uncovering some shared value which would enable the discussion of differences and perhaps the redressing of wrongs. Lewis recognized the most fruitful assessment to be one in which an admixture of the shared and the differing is recognized. The trouble is that there is no way to predict what will constitute the shared and the differing or how much of either there will be. One must simply assume that both are present.

Furthermore, an emphasis on culture as something shared need not suggest that what is shared is necessarily good or unchangeable. The suspicion that marks current cultural theory may be a reaction to an overemphasis on culture as stabilizing and warranting the status quo. But Lewis is as aware of culture as the means by which norms in a society change as he is of how culture creates order and maintains continuity. Although conditions after the First World War, when he developed his theory of culture, seemed to call for a stress on continuity and stability, Lewis allows ample room for change. What in *The Abolition of Man* he calls the "Tao," that is, the specifically moral content of human culture, changes. And if the specifically moral content of culture changes, it follows, *a fortiori*, that for Lewis changes can occur in other aspects of culture as well.[20] Values endure, but they are not eternal. Culture does not only allow for change; it calls for change by virtue of the mediating role it plays between beliefs and various, changing life situations. Continuity and change are both part of culture.

Lewis understands culture as not only carrying forward values but also providing the terms by which disagreements about values can be aired and resolved and by which particular configurations of values can be formed. In *The Abolition of Man* he implies that in the absence of culture, or when culture is devalued, there is less difference of opinion about values and less diversity of value configuration. In the absence of shared values, the values of some people are imposed on others by force. This, Lewis believes, is precisely what is happening in English education; and the construction of a value-free environment results not in education but in social "conditioning."[21]

A second question suggested by Lewis's interest in and conception of culture is whether, by creating commonality within a complex society, such as that of England, the common culture does not inevitably repress local cultures. Although Lewis does not disparage local cultures and traditions, it is impossible not to privilege standard culture when one focuses on the need for

shared values in public life. This is another question that Lewis does not sufficiently address. His implied answer is that in theory there should be no conflict between what is of human value in local cultures and what is of importance for a culture shared by the entire society.

Lewis does not recognize the force of this question because he does not
take sufficiently into account that cultures are attached to and generate
power.[22] It is possible, perhaps even inevitable, that the culture of people with
less political and economic power will be suppressed or absorbed by the culture of those with more. This occurs not only in the relation of common
English culture to local cultures in England but also in its relation to cultures
in weaker or developing countries. The kind of inclusive culture that Lewis
favors sets him apart from such literary people among his contemporaries as
Thomas Hardy and D. H. Lawrence, who championed local cultures. It stands
under judgment, as well, from the ample evidence that English culture was
forcefully imposed on the subjects of colonial rule.

Lewis would reply, I think, that the larger culture that some of his contemporaries resisted in the name of local cultures and the Western culture criticized by historians of imperialism and postcolonial theorists is radically deficient or is even no culture at all. It is modernity with all its abstractions,
reductions, and suppressions. Modernity, for Lewis, is not only defective; it
largely militates against viable culture. The mark of a viable culture would be
the value it placed on, and the continuity it would have with, other cultures,
both local and distant. The suppression of other cultures is not the work of a
true culture but rather of power divested of culture. For Lewis, culture by def-
inition arises from, nurtures, and corrects relations between people, and it follows that it does not suppress other cultures. Lewis maintains, in his appendix
to *The Abolition of Man*, that the values of English culture find counterparts in
other cultures. He does this not to discount the integrity of those other cultures but to recognize their health. There is no reason to assume that he would
think differently about the relation of a shared English culture to the particular local cultures of England.

The third question to ask about Lewis's project regarding culture concerns the effects of culture's broad dissemination. How can its dissemination
be distinguished from the means by which that dissemination is accomplished? Can an inclusive culture be thought of as separable from the means of
communication and transportation, without which it cannot be inclusive? Indeed, is it the culture or the means of its dissemination that unifies the society?
Is a complex society unified by its railways, radios, telephone lines, and newspapers or by what is conveyed by them? The question becomes more complex

when we bear in mind that these powerful means of communication are not neutral with respect to meaning. The means of communication and transportation determine what is conveyed. Only some kinds of messages can be widely broadcast, and the means by which they are made available are absorbed along with the content.

Lewis's theory holds some potential to address this problem. At the heart of his critique of modern society is his resistance to its habits of abstraction, to modern culture's general disregard for particulars, especially for particular people. Abstraction, because it denies primary relations, destroys culture and creates external relations between people based on power. The means of communication and transportation are forms of power, and they need to be housed within and directed by culture. Because modernity is to a considerable degree not a culture, modern people have become more interested in the means of transportation and communication than in the places or information and the wider kinds of relationships that they make available. Because people have lost their sense of primary relations with other people and the world around them, they have formed primary relations with secondary things, such as the tools of communication and transportation. These tools draw attention to themselves and to the power that they grant to people to control their worlds. It is a measure of the culture's disease that the *means* of communication determine value and even themselves become the value. When technology is not housed and directed by a viable culture, it becomes itself a substitute culture that, rather than serve human relations, determines them.

However, I also think that this is not a problem that Lewis fully recognized. He did not take adequate account of the shaping influence that modern means of communication and transportation can and do exert on culture. While he himself eschewed driving an automobile, for example, he did not seem to consider the implications of having himself, toward the end of his professional life, conveyed by car between Oxford and Cambridge. He also used the BBC to spread his views to people in disparate local settings. And, as Walter Hooper points out, Lewis published articles in newspapers, although he did not himself read newspapers.[23] An inclusive culture depends on the means of its spread, and it is difficult to prevent the culture from being supplanted by those means or the means determining what cultural content is disseminated.

The final question to be raised about his theory of culture is that the culture with which Lewis is most fully identified is difficult to distinguish from "culture" in the more restricted or high sense.[24] His understanding of culture seems characterized by the difficult texts, leisure time, and prestigious institutional associations to which Lewis, but by no means all in the society, had access. True, Lewis advocates (as in his preface to Screwtape's Toast appended to *The Screwtape Letters*) equal access for all to the resources of high culture, but the difficulties involved in that proposal are hardly broached.[25] Meanwhile, those with such access are able to augment their social and economic strength with cultural capital, thereby justifying their positions of economic advantage by tying them to custodianship over the values of English culture.

This problem loses some of its force when we distinguish between culture as that which draws the attention of people to what of value lies outside of themselves and culture that is intentionally designed as an extension of self- or class interests. Culture, as Lewis understands it, is an inclusive set of shared values that arise or grow more than they are constructed and projected. This is why Lewis was willing not only to advance culture and its criticism in the society's most prestigious centers of privilege and cultural capital but also to address a general audience outside the confines of Oxford and Cambridge. He may not have extended his reach into every corner of society, and he may not have cast his net wide enough to include all economic and social levels. Indeed, he may have been deceived about the continuity between some of his interests and those of ordinary people. However, his work in popular genres and his efforts to communicate effectively in all the genres he employed with the largest possible audience place him in a mediating position between the more and less sophisticated poles of the culture.

Lewis tried to embody in his own career, in other words, what he took to be the central, mediating position of culture. This is not to deny that by calling attention to the value of English culture Lewis at the same time advocates values that conform to or support particular interests. But he was intent, I believe, as much as possible to avoid those dangers. He believed that culture should militate against the tendency to call attention to self. In his dispute with E. M. W. Tillyard, he calls this "the personal heresy." Critics, he contends, should not call attention to authors and even less should they call attention to themselves; they should concentrate on that something else or something more to which all can look and which it is the business of the critic to help locate and clarify.[26] The promulgation of the culture must be carried on with a lack of self-consciousness, with a sharply focused critical eye, and with an orientation to what of value lies outside of particular interests.

Lewis, to my mind, does not give adequate attention to the issues identified by these four questions, and any attempt to imitate his work in our own time and place cannot simply duplicate him. I believe, however, that these questions do not completely discredit his understanding of the nature and role of culture as mediating relations between beliefs or norms and reality or experience. I would say, indeed, that his project alerts us to the fact that there always are values and goals that people in a society share. The question can always be raised, then, as to whether or not they are the values and goals that people should share. It is always an urgent matter to surface shared values, to question their consequences, particularly for other people, and to know how to challenge values and goals that are inadequate or potentially destructive. Finally, it is always to the point to ask critics of culture what understanding of shared or common life is implied by their criticism. It is not only the advocates of culture but also the critics of culture who are vulnerable to fashioning their work in the shape of their own interests and advantages or of that group with whom they identify.

III

Now that we have looked at culture more directly, we can ask how for Lewis it is related to Christianity. We should see first of all that the central, mediating position that Lewis gives to culture implies some provocative assumptions about religion and Christianity.

The first, perhaps obvious, thing to say about the understanding of Christianity implied by Lewis's project is that it puts him outside the circle of Christians for whom faith and human cultures are unrelated or even opposed to one another. Lewis sees a positive relation between Christianity and human cultures, and that understanding implies a stronger doctrine of Creation than is characteristic, for example, of Barthian or evangelical theological positions. Lewis has a stout theological anthropology. He sees redemption as a strategic and enabling intervention rather than as an intervention unconnected with what already exists in the post-lapsarian human world.[27]

Having said this, it must also be stressed that while for Lewis there is continuity between Christian faith and human cultures, there is a discontinuity between Christianity and many prominent features of modern Western culture. Although Christianity potentially has positive internal relations with human cultures, it has contrary relations with dominant characteristics of modern Western culture.

Christian faith cannot be related to modern culture to the degree that modern culture fails to perform the principal functions of human culture. Those functions, as we have seen, are to direct the attention of people to values that lie outside of themselves, to establish right relations according to those values with the entities and events of reality, and to generate and maintain discourses by which those right relations are challenged, corrected and/or confirmed. Since modern culture largely fails to perform these functions, persons conditioned by it either will be unable to understand or will distort a Christian account of the world. A Christianity articulated and practiced by people so conditioned is bound to contain misunderstandings and distortions.

However, the deficiencies of modern culture do not mean for Lewis that one can reject it and do without culture altogether. A Christian account needs human culture to occasion it and flesh it out. It needs a culture to mediate its relation to the realities that people daily encounter. Christianity does not itself constitute a culture. It provides basic beliefs, norms, and practices, and Christians in differing cultures and times resemble one another because of that provision. But Christians cannot live above or apart from culture any more than they can live above or apart from the reality composed of entities and events. People who attempt to establish Christianity as something independent of culture are people who have been conditioned by modern culture's habits of abstraction.

This does not mean that religion is dissolved into or dominated by culture. A viable culture is open at one end to religion as it is open on the other end to reality. Indeed, what culture mediates, namely, religious beliefs and experiences of actuality, are more important than culture. Culture must be open to religion because without religion it will be reduced to matters at its other end, namely, the relations of people to the events and entities of their concrete worlds, and will eventually allow those relations to degenerate as well. While religion generally and Christianity specifically needs culture, culture also needs religion. Lewis is critical of culture when it fails to defer either to everyday life or to the transcendent to which religion directs it. Religion speaks of that to which culture points, and culture requires the completion that religion provides. While at one end culture opens out to the sense of a reality that outstrips culture, culture also opens, in an upward direction, so to speak, to that which challenges, corrects, and directs human moral and spiritual beliefs, desires, and potentials.

Readers who object to Lewis's position on the positive and even indispensable role of culture in relation to Christianity very likely mistake the incompatibility between religion and prominent aspects of modern culture for a basic incompatibility between Christianity and all human cultures. They think that modern culture is what any human culture inevitably will become. In other words, they accept modern culture's self-assessment. They assume that culture is necessarily self-serving and that a religion related to it will be self-serving, too. Lewis would agree that this is largely the case with modern culture, and in his fiction he gives several examples of clergy and theologians who use Christianity to further what are actually self-serving personal and group interests. Especially in *That Hideous Strength* we find examples of Christians who have compromised and distorted Christianity by subjecting it to the norms of modern culture.

Despite the negative characteristics of modern culture, human culture can have a positive relation to religion, and such a positive relation is needed by both. Christianity is not necessarily distorted or compromised by being related to human culture. On the contrary, it is by means of culture that Christianity is related to the particulars of people's everyday lives. Cultures are needed for their enabling and preparatory effects for a Christian account of the world, and cultures grant Christian accounts of the world their specificity, their variety, and their relevance to actuality. It is a sign of the disease of modern culture that attempts to relate Christian beliefs and practices to it result in compromise and distortion.

IV

We have looked at the role of culture as mediator between religious beliefs and the entities and events of ordinary experience. We have also looked at those aspects of modern culture that Lewis thinks militate against its functioning as a culture. We now ask what he sees as viable in the present cultural situation.

For one thing, despite the official line against the relation of events or entities to values, there are matters that we continue to agree upon as to their value. We can recognize acts of courage, for example, and we judge them as admirable. We also continue to have complex responses to experiences that the Romantics called sublime. We recognize, as well, some things and actions as inherently ugly, abhorrent, or evil. Lewis points out that there is a remarkable agreement among cultures about such relations. Cultures historically or geographically distant from one another not only recognize that there is a relation of events and things to human judgments about them but also agree widely as to what those relations are. These remnants of culture that remain with us are crucial for our ability to relate positively to other cultures, those both in other locations and in our own past.

It is not fashionable to argue, as Lewis does, that there are matters of continuity between cultures. There will be little agreement in today's academic world that there are things that people in a culture evaluate in common and much less agreement that evaluations are shared across cultures.

This resistance is due to the pervasive relativism in current cultural theories. But that relativism is slowly moderating. Even Barbara Herrnstein Smith, a notable relativist in matters of value, acknowledges that there are always operating for persons and groups beliefs in some values as noncontingent.[28] Indeed, it seems indispensable to the stability of persons, institutions, and societies over time that not everything should be open to question or up for sale. Smith would not explain such beliefs within a culture as arising from relations that necessarily exist between certain events or entities and human responses to them, but there is growing room even among relativists for recognition of nonrelative, shared beliefs and relations. Indeed, the projects of morally informed social criticism and actions, such as those undertaken on behalf of oppressed people in other cultures, depend on such an affirmation. Situations and events in differing cultures can be judged oppressive because they actually are so and not simply because people, given their particular culture, happen to think they are. That belief is implied by the United Nations' Universal Declaration of Human Rights.

Lewis's argument about cross-cultural similarities has increasing credibility in contemporary postcolonial theory. Until recently, a main point of postcolonial theory has been that the Western assumption of a common human nature allowed colonial powers to impose on non-Western people changes dictated by specifically Western ideas that were mistakenly assumed to be universal.[29] When Western culture assumed that human nature was the same regardless of differing cultures, cultural imperialism went unquestioned. Western ideas about human nature produced violent consequences for the lives of people whose differing cultural beliefs and behaviors were discounted by their colonizing intruders. Postcolonial theory, therefore, has understandably emphasized the differences between cultures. But theorists are beginning to recognize a violence that is a counterpart to the construction of the Same, namely, the construction of the Wholly Other. When we judge people of other cultures as people with whom we have nothing in common, we are free from having to take a genuine interest in them, from caring about their well-being, or from questioning our treatment of them. Distancing and excluding people under the construction of the "Other" is potentially as violent as their inclusion under a construction of the "Same."[30] The lines of similarity between cultures that Lewis draws in his appendix to *The Abolition of Man* may seem somewhat superficial or arbitrary, but they suggest a salutary recognition that other peoples are not only different from but also like us. Similarities as well as differences should be assumed between us and our culture and people distant from us, even though those similarities, both in their nature and extent, cannot be predicted.

The question of the relations of cultures to one another is quite simply answered when one chooses either to say that cultures differ from one another all the way down or to say that differences are relatively superficial, are ways by which people differently believe or differently perform essentially the same things. The result of arguing for a position somewhere between these clear options seems murky and unworkable. But we frequently find ourselves placed in this kind of position, and we seem to handle it rather well. A noteworthy example concerns how we adjust to the relation of difference and continuity over time. When we see someone at a reunion, let us say, someone we have not seen in years, we enter a conversation with that person with the awareness that in many respects the person before us is the person we knew many years ago and in other respects the person is different. There are similarities, I am suggesting, between the perennial problem in the philosophy of time created by change and continuity and the problem of difference and similarity between cultures. What makes the problem vexing in each case is that we can assume that there is both continuity and discontinuity, but we know beforehand neither how much of each there will be nor in what things the similarities and in what things the differences will be found. As with the person we see at a reunion after many years, so with someone from another culture, we must determine, during the conversation, how the question of same and different sorts itself out.

The question of how a person from a differing culture is like and is unlike us is precisely the question that Ransom faces as he deals with his hosts on Malachandra. He recognizes the great differences between them and himself and, even more, between their culture and the one that he left behind on earth. But these differences, while major, do not prevent him from understanding and appreciating much about the lives of the Malachandrans. Indeed, he is able to see that in many respects their ways of doing things and their attitudes toward their world are enviable compared with his own or with those of the culture that he left behind. In my opinion, Lewis gives his fullest answer to the question of the relation of cultures to one another in this narrative. Ransom enters his conversations with the expectation that there are similarities, that he will be able to understand creatures who clearly differ greatly from him. But he does not enter the conversation supposing that he knows where the points of similarity and of difference will arise and how much of each there will be. Furthermore, I think that Lewis would say that Ransom's relations with the *hrossa* on Malachandra, while extreme, are in this respect continuous with our relations not only with people of other cultures but also with our neighbors. In our dealings with people, even when they are close to us, we are always confronting the question of the same and the differing, and that makes our relations with people both difficult and enriching. Perhaps if I were to take more seriously the differences between myself and my neighbor, I would be better prepared to take more seriously the similarities between myself and a person from another culture. In every encounter with another person, but especially in encounters with persons of differing gender, ethnicity, or religious identity, one is engaged in dynamics of shared and unshared, different and similar.

We can return now from the question of the relation of cultures to one another to the question of the role of culture in an account of the world, particularly to the mediating role culture plays between the norms and beliefs of a person and people and their concrete experiences. This mediating role can be illuminated, perhaps, by seeing how some theorists are trying recently to turn particular communities into substitutes for culture. A typical and striking move of this kind has been made by Stanley Fish. Fish understands an interpretive community, particularly one formed by a profession, to constitute an ersatz culture. The functions that Lewis ascribes to culture Fish ascribes to professions. If we look at what Fish says about the professions, particularly the legal and literary professions, we can see more clearly what Lewis is saying about culture.

Fish militates against an "anything goes" attitude toward the interpretation of literary texts, attitudes sponsored by some kinds of postmodernist theories and apparently justified by his own reader-response theory. He counters such attitudes with his theory of interpretive communities generally and of professions particularly. He argues that it is never the case that "anything goes" because interpreters of literary or legal texts operate in a context of received norms regarding how texts are to be read and interpreted. The guild is really, for Fish, a condensed or substitute culture. The guild provides directives concerning what is to be entertained as a possible interpretation of a text, and it provides criteria for how the interpretation of a text can be challenged and defended. There are rules governing that process, and it can never be true that at any time "anything goes." Indeed, the guild even provides the means by which it does and can change its rules. The basis for Fish's trust in a professional community to handle effectively such perennial problems as constancy and change, or unity and diversity, is not, as it would be for Lewis, culture but the human mind. He extends the trust he has in the human mind to professions.[31] And he elevates professions to paradigms for interpretative communities within the wider culture.

Lewis would not share Fish's confidence in the hierarchy here established, which starts at the top with the human mind, moves down into professional and academic communities, and moves outward from there into the wider culture. Lewis believes and places more trust in a shared culture and in the processes by which families, schools, churches, and other settings bring children to awareness of and participation in it. He believes that the evaluations that people make of things they encounter need to be sharpened, challenged, and/or altered, and the professions, for Lewis, serve the larger culture by being more concentrated settings for these cultural processes. The literary profession, far from enclosed and operating by its own rules, should be influenced by and responsible to that larger culture.

Lewis would contend, I think, that Fish neglects the special relation of literary studies to the language of a culture. Literary studies has this public function because culture principally mediates relations between beliefs and reality by means of language generally and of literature particularly. Lewis would read Fish, I think, as short-circuiting the mediating role of the literary profession in favor of a model that relates literary studies to the culture only incidentally, if at all. Such a model makes the literary profession self-enclosed. Lewis would find that position, in my opinion, irresponsible and self-serving, and I am inclined to agree with him.

Out of the Silent Planet, as I have suggested, gives us quite a full exposure of the central role of language, literature, and literary studies in Lewis's theory of culture. Ransom is a philologist as well as a historian, and on his visit to Malachandra he is fascinated by its language. He assumes that the creatures he encounters, since they could communicate, have a language with rough similarities of structure and dynamics to his own. Of the three kinds of creatures he encounters on the planet, Ransom has most to do with the *hrossa*, who are the poets. The *hrossa* stand, as custodians and developers of language, in a middle or mediating position between the *sorns*, who are the intellectuals, and the *pfifltriggi*, who are the miners and artisans. Language and literature, therefore, are the means by which the mundane and the rational are related. Literature is the way by which the relations between mind or knowledge and experience or reality are clarified, refined, and challenged. It is also the means by which language is changed and improves its capacity to articulate the attitudes and evaluations implicit in the relations people have with one another and their experiences.

Language is, then, for Lewis not only the way by which we talk about ideas or beliefs and experiences, but it is also their mode. As Ransom learns the language of the Malachandrans, the language opens his eyes to the world around him and allows him to recognize it. He sees things when he has the words for them. Language relates ideas or beliefs and reality to one another in mutually revealing ways. Persons consequently reveal the kind of world in which they live by the language that they use. Poetic uses of language seem most important because they illuminate forcefully and meaningfully the relation of people to both their beliefs and their surroundings. Language does not simply provide a way of talking about our world; it is the way we are in our world. Language enables us to have and discover right relations between ourselves and what lies, so to speak, around us (our experiences with people, events, and things) and above us (our norms and beliefs).

Lewis grants to human language the potential for conveying something shared between human cultures and simultaneously the potential for making human cultures distinctive and particular. Languages are the source both of our understanding and our not being able fully to understand people who are different from us. As he says, "A language has its own personality; implies an outlook, reveals a mental activity, and has a resonance, not quite the same as those of any other. Not only the vocabulary—but the very shape of the syntax is *sui generis*."[32]

Literary culture, then, is the primary site for conveying, reinforcing, and changing the relations of people to their worlds. It does this in two ways or for two reasons. First, literature can record right relations and responses of persons to things and events, thereby challenging the reader to judge or respond to them in that way. This is the more lyrical side of literature's contribution to the validation of relations between internal states and external events or things. Second, literature allows the reader to enter a world and to undergo certain experiences by which assumptions about things and their value are tested. Literature, that is, provides models of actions and experiences that reveal the consequences of beliefs and attitudes. This contribution to the culture is made by literature's more narrative modes.

The culture derives its complex unity and its moral content primarily, then, from its stories and songs, and these operate both to confirm and to challenge relations between people and between people and their worlds. Scientific and technological language lacks the resources to provide that content and directive. It should, therefore, operate within a culture defined primarily in literary terms. The moral content of literature forms a tradition and offers direction in which the other interests and activities of the society find their places and accept challenges and corrections to their excesses and errors. This does not mean that science cannot affect literature and contribute as well to change in the culture. Indeed, it should and does. But the rules within which change and transformation can occur and which govern it are inherent to literary culture.

Lewis's work also implies a close tie between literature and religion. As scientific and technological language must look upward to the language of song and story to provide moral direction, so the language of Christian belief must look downward to literature for actualization. This is not surprising, given the fact that literary culture in England is so closely tied to Christianity. It is a literary culture that is marked by moral inquiry. Literary culture can acknowledge ends or goals as well as means. It can recognize things beyond the boundaries of self-interest as of principal importance. It can articulate primary relations between people and between people and their worlds. It can posit language as the principal medium of those relations. And it can place and interpret things in relation to what is believed to be higher and more edifying.

However, literary culture need not necessarily be Christian to do such things. It need only create a situation in which Christian beliefs can be articulated as providing the framework for a viable, even satisfying account of things. That viability lies in Christianity's capacity to take what is adumbrated in culture and to complete it, to provide that to which it looks. It also is positioned to expose the culture's deficiencies, especially when the culture begins to generate attitudes and assumptions that militate against the transcendent or to relegate religious belief and moral concerns to the margins.

What are the consequences of Lewis's stress on the basic role played by literature in and for the culture, the church, and the Bible? First, we must keep in mind that the church will always be affected by its culture. It requires culture as the means by which its beliefs are fleshed out and by which its beliefs are related to the entities and events that make up what we refer to as reality. The simple fact is that an inadequate or diseased culture will negatively affect the church. So, the Reverend Straik in *That Hideous Strength* is carried along by the ideology of N.I.C.E. and reduces Christian doctrine to terms that support its enterprises. The program of the institute claims to pursue the betterment of human kind, even eventually to provide deliverance from death. Straik finds no difficulty in subsuming Christianity under those goals, arguing that what Christianity foretold is now being transposed to and fulfilled in the agenda of the institute and its goals.

Let us suppose that a spokesperson for the Church were to avoid Straik's mistake by moving in the opposite direction, namely, to condemn the culture and isolate the church as much as possible from it. We have already seen that this would largely be impossible. But more important, it would be a move that depends on modern culture. It would be a move that defines the church and its culture in a negative relation, and thus adopts the culture's assumption of external relations and identity by opposition. Nothing is more like the culture than acts of taking exception to it, than acts of self- and group distinction. The act of rejecting modern culture cannot be dissociated from what is rejected or from the culture's high estimation of identity by opposition.

The church requires culture, but it is not subservient to it. People generally and believers especially have the responsibility to be aware of what the culture makes available and how the culture exerts influence. The church is the community of those who actively examine, clarify, and try to articulate the right relations between Christian beliefs and the language of their culture.

What has been said about the complex relation of church to culture can also be extended to the Bible. Reading the Bible is not for Lewis a practice exceptional in relation to reading other texts. Reading, including the Bible, is a process of making oneself receptive, a process that "can be described either as an enlargement or as a temporary annihilation of the self."[33] Reading the Bible in the same way one reads other texts does not mean that the Bible and reading it are the same as other texts and what it means to read them. No text and no reading are the same. If one is receptive to reading *this* text, its particular, even unique, qualities will become available. I infer from what he says about the relation of the Christian story to other stories that what one receives in reading the Bible is this: what one longs to be true in reading other stories is clarified as true in the reading of this story.

The core doctrines of Christianity are conclusions and extrapolations drawn from reading the Bible. In the Bible they are inherent to particular literary genres. Biblical doctrines and beliefs are affected by various and changing cultural conditions. Because literary traditions expose human needs and desires, they anticipate Christian beliefs or reveal Christian beliefs to be viable languages for the articulation of those needs or desires and their fulfillment. Literary traditions prepare for and reinforce the authority of the Bible. We have a sense of the Bible's force and significance because, despite the distance of our own culture from those of ancient times, we have been prepared for reading it by the poems and narratives of our own literary culture.

Lewis, unlike so many theorists of culture, does not see humans, individually or in groups, as passive and helpless in their relation to culture. He thinks that it is possible for people to question what the prevailing culture is leading them to believe, how it is asking them to behave and why. Culture, however powerful and pervasive it may be, need not displace the person. Indeed, Christians, having access to norms and beliefs of Christians in other cultures, can test their own culture by judging if and why those norms and beliefs are excluded or distorted by it. There exists both actually and potentially a mutual, interactive relation between persons, especially religious persons, and their culture. As we shall see in the next chapter, culture and character must be taken together. The aspects of modern culture that resist and distort religion, although powerfully entrenched, can, for Lewis, still be resisted by people generally and by Christians especially. That should be done in two ways. First, Christians should reveal that narcissism and materialism, the extreme, contrary articulations of the subject/object, value/fact split, not only do not, either separately or together, offer adequate accounts of the world but also conspire to destroy culture. Second, they should seek out and advocate what in the culture remains viable, what serves to enhance and to evince right relations between people, between people and the events and entities of their world, and between people and what speaks accurately to their moral and spiritual needs and desires. Lewis addresses his readers as potential co-agents in the work of resisting the negative and affirming the positive aspects of modern culture.

Can we, as turn-of-the-century American readers, appraise our culture as in any way still viable enough to do, even partially, the kind of work that Lewis asks a culture to do? I am not certain of the answer, but I do believe that there are remnants of a culture analogous to what Lewis tried to retrieve and redeploy, remnants still within our reach, however attenuated and scattered they may be. But the time of their availability may rapidly be slipping away. The challenge placed before present-day readers of Lewis is that they become co-agents in gathering and redeploying those remnants of our culture that are still available to us, primarily in our literature. We will have to say what those remnants are, where they can be found, and how they suggest incipient values and relationships. It is hoped that such remnants will be seen as a sharable resource with which to articulate the basis for improved, even edifying relations to things and events around us, other people, and the source of human good.

5

· · · · · · · · ·

CHARACTER

By giving the topic of character a separate chapter, we risk the danger of dissociating character and culture from one another. That is something that we, as moderns, tend to do. Our thoughts are governed by the assumption that a gap exists both between internal and external aspects of a person's life and between the individual and society. Indeed, not only do we think that they are separated, we also tend to think of society and the individual as opposed. Much of the literary culture of the twentieth century documents this sense that individuals, like Willy Loman in Arthur Miller's *Death of a Salesman*, are victims of a society that opposes them, that is hostile to their well-being.

Lewis, as we saw in the last chapter, militates against the idea that there is an inevitable gap or even enmity between individuals and society. Once we have absorbed the belief that there must be such a gap, we begin to construct our world accordingly, fleshing out the belief in all kinds of ways. The results are bound to be bad, because the belief is wrong. While there are differences between the individual and the social, even tensions, they nevertheless exist in reciprocity with one another. Who I am and what other people expect, need, and enable me to be, while by no means being the same thing, are intertwined. Indeed, as we shall see, Lewis draws a parallel between the structure of public life and the parts of a person's internal makeup. As culture mediates relations between norms and beliefs and the entities and events that constitute our experience of reality, so, for Lewis, the parts of a person's internal life, the intellect and instincts, are mediated by something that corresponds to culture which he calls the "chest," or heart. The three-fold structure in which culture plays a central and mediating role corresponds, therefore, to the three-fold structure of the individual's life, in which "chest" or heart plays a mediating role between mind and body.

Lewis tends to avoid the terms we generally use to talk about these matters. Lewis talks more about culture than about "society," and when he looks at persons he tends not to speak of the "individual" but of character. Both "society" and "individual" suggest something formal and without content. Lewis does not like to talk about people that way. We saw that culture has content. Character does, too. "Character" identifies the person as a moral and spiritual being, as engaged in a process of formation, and as in a constant dynamic of conformity and resistance with both other persons and the surrounding culture.

After all that we have said about culture and its crucial role in structuring and mediating the relation people live out between their beliefs and the realities of daily life, it might seem that for Lewis culture is far more powerful and significant than character. The fact of the matter, though, is that Lewis takes the person, character, to be primary. One might think that here again Lewis is revealing his indebtedness to the Romantics. But the basis for Lewis's affirmation that the person is of greater importance than the culture is not Romanticism but Christian belief.

Lewis stated the basis for his choice between culture and character clearly in a famous sermon, "The Weight of Glory." Culture, even in the form of its most magnificent monuments, such as Oxford with all its architecture and learning, is of secondary importance when compared to the nature and destiny of persons. Toward the end of the sermon he says, "Nations, cultures, arts, civilizations—these are mortal, and their life is to ours as the life of a gnat. But it is immortals whom we joke with, work with, marry, snub, and exploit—immortal horrors or everlasting splendours."[1] Culture is a part of all that someday will pass away; but the person is part of what will not. Lewis is primarily concerned with character not because he is an individualist or a Romantic. He treats character as primary because he believes that is what Christian faith requires.

The principal result of viewing character in a religious way is that a person is thought of not only as a moral and spiritual being but also as in relation with others. It is only by a rather odd, though at times fruitful, exercise of abstraction that we can think of the person in isolation. A person is related to the force and significance of what we think of as reality, and a person is related to other persons. A person is also related both to culture and to him- or herself.

All of these relations and their content as well as the tensions they generate are included, for Lewis, under the topic of "character."

The relation between culture and character is complex and dynamic. There are both continuities and discontinuities between them. This means that for Lewis the relation between them can be one neither of total conformity nor of total dissimilarity. Culture and character contribute to and correct one another. No person can contain the whole of the culture, and the culture does not, indeed cannot, wholly determine or absorb the potentials of character. Consequently, while they are similar and mutually affective, neither exhausts or contains the other. The advancement of culture and the formation of character are, therefore, interactive processes. When they are not in that kind of reciprocity—and, if the literary testimony of our century is heard, they have not been—something is terribly wrong. The culture has become repressive and resistant, the person has abandoned a sense of relation to and responsibility for the culture, or both.

This interaction between character and culture, a process that is complex because there always will be both continuities and discontinuities between them, is further complicated by the fact that both are always changing. This is important to keep in mind because the terms "character" and "culture" tend to suggest what is stable and continuing. There are good reasons why we tend to associate these terms with what is unchanging. We saw in the last chapter why "culture" tends to be associated with what is stable. An emphasis on culture is generally taken to stress what conserves, what counters change. Character plays a similar role, and the stability or continuity of character relates to modern philosophical debates about personal identity. The problem, to put it simply, is how it can be said that I am the same person that I was several years ago. I change, but people still know who I am and refer to me as that same person. This problem was set forth by Locke, who located personal identity in consciousness, and it is addressed by many who follow or dispute him, Butler, Leibniz, Hume, and Reid, to name a few. The problem is so central to the modern period because in the seventeenth century it became difficult to argue that the "soul" was the seat of personal identity, that it was the soul that did not change while the body and other aspects of a person's life did. While Lewis's understanding of the person arises from his Christian beliefs that a person is destined not only for time but also for eternity, he does not try to locate the soul as the unchanging seat of personal identity. Nor does he locate personal identity in consciousness, as Locke did. Personal identity for Lewis lies in character, the continuity of moral practices, attitudes, and right relations that marks a person and of which a person may not be fully aware. Character is a kind of second or acquired nature. When people refer to me, then, they are referring first of all neither to my body and my outward circumstances, important as those may be to who I am, nor to my ideas or beliefs, which are largely internal. Rather, they are referring primarily to this second, acquired, and mediating nature, to my character.

Locating personal identity in character relates the person to his or her culture. Characters are affected by the influences, for good or ill, of the context of their lives. Primary among those influences are other people, family members first of all, but many others as well. Indeed, a person, especially in youth, is involved in a truly amazing complex of imitating and resisting, as well as being accepted and rejected by, other people. In these, and in less direct and pervasive ways, character is formed in relation to culture.

However, Lewis relates the formation of character to other things as well. First of all, he ties it to the person. This may seem obvious. But it is truer to say that a person *has* a character than that a person *is* a character. This does not mean that Lewis gives primacy to consciousness. Rather, it is that for him there is always something mysterious about a person, something of the unexpected, something that is all potential. This is because a person has the capacities of will, reason, and imagination that are able to intervene in the relation of that person to the culture, to initiate alternatives to that relation, or even to project alternatives to the culture itself. Another way of saying this is that a person is and can be creative and responsible. It is from the person that the genuinely new or unexpected can come. This means that a person is not wholly determined by the culture. We cannot simply blame the culture when a person does something bad or give a person no credit if he or she does something good.

Lewis finally relates character to faith. The formation of character yields to what, in theological language, is called sanctification, that is, the process by which a person can become more and more Christ-like. These two, the formation of character and becoming more Christ-like, while they are not identical, are continuous. We shall have to see later how and why this is so. It is enough now simply to say that there is for Lewis an analogy between the relation of a viable culture to Christianity and the relation of character to becoming Christ-like. As Christianity requires the presence of a viable culture, sanctification requires character.

I

The topic of character is first of all tied to the question of personal morality. That creates difficulties because we tend to restrict personal morality to the practice of obeying moral laws and conforming to social standards of conduct. In addition, we think of moral laws and social mores as contrary to what people want to do, so that there is conflict between morality and a person's desires. To think of moral law as imposed on people and to think of law and human nature as in conflict with one another are characteristically modern ways of thinking. In contrast, Lewis thinks of morality as the way in which a person, to borrow a line from the TV commercial for the army, can "be all that you can be." Morality is the way by which the potential particularity of a person is actualized. While moral rules are relevant, even indispensable, to the process, they are not sufficient. Moral rules are general, even abstract, articulations of moral practices that help secure human well-being. They guide the process by which a person's unique potentials are realized. But the processes by which human well-being and personal character are advanced are not wholly subject to rules. Morality is not primarily a matter of conformity and repetition; rather, morality is marked by creativity and discovery. Guidelines and directives relate ambiguously to creativity and discovery.

If it is true that for Lewis morality is not first of all a set of rules that a person follows, it is even truer for him that morality is not imposed arbitrarily on a person's life. Lewis does not assume that there is a necessary, inherent conflict between what a person wants and what that person is allowed or required to do. For Lewis, there is continuity between what a person ought to do and what a person most deeply wants to do. In *The Screwtape Letters*, for example, we find that people end up in hell not only by failing to do what they ought to have done but by not doing what they really wanted to do, and even by doing what they really did not want to do.[2] Moral law, in other words, stands to human well-being a little like the set of instructions enclosed with some new gadget stands to its best functioning. As Lewis says, "In reality, moral rules are directions for running the human machine. Every moral rule is there to prevent a breakdown, or a strain, or a friction, in the running of that machine."[3] Moral law, then, stands to human beings as though prefaced with some such statement as this: "For the most trouble-free and effective life of this human being, the following instructions should be observed." But the potential of a gadget for its many uses is not exhausted by guidelines. Morality as a set of rules is a general guide to how people can most fully actualize their potential as human beings, but morality and character are by no means exhausted by moral rules and conformity to them. The purpose of the rules is not to shape humans into them but to provide guidelines for nurturing their flowering.

Not only is it typically modern and, for Lewis, mistaken to think of morality as conformity to a set of rules and as in conflict with human needs and desires; it is also modern and mistaken to think of morality exclusively in terms of the relations of persons to other persons. Moderns tend to think that way because they assume that there is a conflict between the interests of a person and the interests of other people. This is why, when we think of personal morality, we tend to think of it as rules that govern and limit our relations to other people. This encourages us to think of morality negatively, as something that keeps us from doing what we would like to do because some behaviors would harm other people. As we tend to think that morality inhibits personal needs and desires, so we also think that morality inhibits our behavior toward other people, because the rights of other people would be violated if we were to pursue our interests freely. Other people, we tend to think, constitute and expose the limits of our self-interest and largely account for moral restraint.

But the relation of a person to other people, important as it may be for Lewis's moral theory, is only part, and perhaps not the most important part, of the moral story. He places equal stress on two other aspects of morality: the general direction of a person's life and the relation of a person to him- or herself, the internal makeup of the person.[4] When personal morality is treated positively in terms of character formation, these other two aspects of moral life, the internal makeup of a person and the direction or goal of a person's life, become very important. As we already have seen, value, significance, and human well-being for Lewis are relational, are matters of right relations. But right relations can only arise for a person who is morally constituted, who has character, and character is a matter of the right relation not only between a person and other people but also between aspects of a person's life and between a person and his or her goals.

It appears that by stressing personal morality Lewis is minimizing the moral importance of social, economic, and political factors. Questions of social justice, economic equity, or acceptable forms of political order are not central to Lewis's thought. But this is not because they are unimportant or unrelated to morality. Rather, they are too variable, specific, and complex to be addressed in a general Christian account of the world and of a person's deportment within it. They are matters that must be left to the particular occasions when Christians are required to assess their social, political, and economic situations, to make choices regarding them, and to work for changes in them. They are also matters that Christians with expertise in these areas should be asked to address. As Lewis says, "Christianity has not, and does not profess to have, a detailed political programme for applying 'Do as you would be done by' to a particular society at a particular moment. It could not have. It is meant for all men at all times and the particular programme which suited one place or time could not suit another."[5] Every Christian is committed to pursuing the well-being of others, including distant people and strangers. But how the Christian should enact that commitment or responsibility toward others in terms of social, political, and economic policies is something that Lewis addresses only in very general terms.[6] Furthermore, social morality is a topic largely housed for him under the category of culture, since, as I have said, culture is for society what character is for the individual. This makes Lewis more interested in the moral and spiritual values shared among people than in the, so to speak, physical or material way in which they are structured. There are exceptions, such as his identification of bureaucracy as the form of human relations most suited to hell and advanced forms of social evil, and his insistence on democracy as a counter to human pride.[7]

Lewis's reluctance to speak directly to questions of social morality may vex some Christian readers. Christian spokespersons are justifiably alarmed when Christians withdraw from their responsibilities to alter unjust conditions and lift burdens of oppression. I do not find Lewis on this point to be wholly indefensible, however. I think a Christian account of the world always carries incipient social, political, and economic beliefs relevant to particular situations. I also think it very likely that many Christians fail to reflect on and apply these beliefs to their own circumstances. But I also think that theories and strategies for creating a more just society seem most effective when they are deployed in particular situations and not in some uniform and universal way. There is something limited and even distorting in an approach to people and events that is consistently political and politically consistent. We all know people who become tedious and ineffective by translating every situation into political or economic terms and always into the same terms. We react that way to such people because their assessments slight the particularity, complexity, and variety of human situations. Lewis, for that reason, resists viewing people and their relations through the lens of a theory. Finally, he may also be seen, I think, as wary of modern social, political, and economic theories and programs because they are largely based on doctrines of negative, external rather than positive, internal relations. Such theories and programs are bound not only to be inadequate but actually to aggravate the problems they are designed to correct.

II

The topic of "character," then, turns our attention to behavior relevant first of all to a person's internal makeup and to the actualization of that person's particularity. Although this aspect of morality is only partially covered by moral rules, the person is not left to his or her own devices in developing a moral life. It is not as though each person must improvise particularity from scratch. There are, of course, moral codes that serve as directives for everyone. But more than that, there are examples made available by the culture, examples both from the past and in the present, of people who in their own ways have tried to live morally and have actualized their particularity in that effort. Such examples cannot be applied to another person's life like a pattern to be copied, because this would damage particularity. However, we see how such people acted in difficult situations, draw inferences from their actions as to why they responded as they did, sense why their responses were morally admirable, and interpret a relation between that person's life and our own.

The models of moral behavior that culture can provide are more important than rules because they are more complex and vital. It is not that human models draw their legitimacy or authority from their conformity to rules; models of behavior have a vitality and particularity that rules lack. It is incumbent upon a culture to provide especially young people with a wide variety of models whose lives can be taken as in one way or another admirable. A culture with very restricted models is not only itself very restricted but blocks the access of young people to the range of potentials within them. Culture should provide young people with evocative models, that is, with models that bring their potentials to awareness. These models can be both actual and fictional. The process of character development relies not only on imitation but also on imagination, on evoking as yet unrealized human potentials and directing them past markers already attained.

The provision of models, then, is not an imposition or manipulation. Children need and constantly look for models to imitate because models awaken potentials and stimulate desire. If models are not provided, children will seize on or create their own. While some of this is inevitable and good, as in the desire of children to resemble their parents or teachers, the process of model selection ought not to be left exclusively to children or to chance. That is particularly true for a culture that provides models not to admire in a moral sense but to envy in a greedy or competitive sense.

One can measure the inadequacy of the models our culture offers by the fact that young people tend to vacillate between slavish imitation of others and defiant rejection of them. They tend either to copy closely the styles of certain people, wanting their bodies, for example, to resemble those of models or athletes, or to rebel against the cultural authority of models. Character formation is a process that should largely be free from both copying and defying. It is a process marked by dynamics of continuity and discontinuity, similarity and differentiation. It relies primarily on interpretation, on articulating what is admirable and/or objectionable in the model and how that can be translated into the terms of the person's own character and situation.

For Lewis, education should include constant exposures to such examples. He is concerned about the state of education in England not only because it no longer is contained by a culture or dedicated to its continuation but also because education is no longer the setting for nurturing the growth of character. As we have seen, education apart from culture becomes training and at worst conditioning. Training tends to be rule based, to stress conformity. Children learn rules that are imposed on them and to which they must adhere, but they are not led to develop character. Character development, while related to rules, is not rule subservient. Rules employed for training and conditioning stress conformity and uniformity. While training creates conformity in outward behavior, conditioning creates internal conformity. It is control over thoughts and feelings. It is the truly sinister effect of modern education.[8]

It is very important to realize how easily people influenced by our culture mistake morality for training and conditioning. Lewis would want to distinguish sharply between the nurture of character and its modern substitute, social training or conditioning. The educational system, with its stress on training and conditioning, is able to develop skills of various kinds. Even personal relations are subjected to training in "social" skills. When training rather than nurturing character becomes the principal interest, value shifts from the particular person to the social whole. Skills begin to determine the worth of the person, and that worth can be abstracted from the person and exchanged for wages. As he points out in *The Abolition of Man*, training and conditioning are the tools and effects of power, of what is left in the formation of society and individuals when culture and character cease to be central.[9] This power reveals itself in the imposition of some determining and finally arbitrary regime over people's capacities to determine for themselves what actions or attitudes are proper in a given situation. Conditioning, which is the design of social and political power abstracted from a cultural context and separated from the particularity of persons, allows social power to displace the moral content of culture and the morality-producing capacity of the person.[10]

Lewis, in *The Abolition of Man*, calls the products of an educational system that has substituted training and conditioning for the formation of character people "without chests."[11] By this he means that the educational system in particular and the society in general have allowed human beings to be reduced to two, contrary factors, their drives and their intellects. Missing is the middle, relational factor, which he refers to as "chest."

Modern culture, as we have seen, tends to structure reality according to a dualism between mind on one side and events or entities on the other. The anthropology that modern education assumes is also dualistic. Children are taken to be combinations of two contrary factors: their minds and their emotions or physical energies. This anthropology leads to the assumption of conflicts between reason and desire, between a person's urge to do certain things and the force resisting those urges generated by the person's awareness of the mores and rules that structure social reality. For Lewis, something crucial is missing, namely, the chest or heart. By this he means a mediating factor that allows a person to create right relations between desires and mind. While always already present, the heart needs to be developed. When developed it allows the person to direct his or her life in ways that are good both for the person and for other people. This ability becomes a kind of acquired instinct or a second nature. This ability does not develop easily or without interruption. Morality involves conscious choices, painful decisions, and learning from mistakes. The ability to make decisions and to learn from mistakes develops in the doing. That process creates character, a morally marked continuity that is consistent with the actualization of a person's integrity and particularity.

For Lewis the role of "chest" or heart in the formation of character is analogous to that of culture in a Christian account of the world. Culture, as we saw, mediates the relation in public life between what people know and believe and the entities and events that constitute their experience of reality. Similarly, "chest" or heart is that aspect of a person's life that mediates between thoughts and beliefs and energies and actions. As culture gives moral content and direction to public life so the "heart" gives moral content and particularity to the life of a person. It is the seat of identity. It is what people primarily are referring to when they refer to a person by name.

Readers familiar with Plato's *Republic* will recognize similarities between Lewis and Plato on these matters. One such resemblance is between Plato's doctrine of the soul and the anthropology implied in Lewis's discussion of the internal makeup of persons. Further, Plato's belief that the parts of the soul and the political structure of the city resemble one another corresponds to Lewis's implied analogy between the aspects of internal life and the three parts of public life.

In the fourth book of his *Republic,* Plato describes the parts of the soul as, first, the appetites, second, the spirit or emotions, and, third, reason. Plato sees an important, perhaps even causal, relation between the three parts of the soul and the three-part organization of the city. In the city there are, first, those who are involved in production and economics. Second, there are the auxiliaries, who protect the city against enemies without and who encourage good behavior within it. Third, there are the guardians who, like philosophers, guide the city by virtue of their wisdom. The relations between the appetites of a person and the producers in the city, between the spirit or emotions of a person and the auxiliaries of a city, and between the reason of a person and the guardians of a city are quite direct, though more complex for Plato and for his interpreters than I am making them sound.

Lewis in general draws quite a bit on Plato, especially in *The Abolition of Man*. Plato like Lewis addressed the relation of the parts of the soul to one another, the relation of the person to the city, and the role of education in the internal lives of children and their formation as future citizens. However, Lewis also differs from Plato in these matters. In Plato reason holds the primary position in the structure of the human soul. Correspondingly, in the city state the primary position is given to the guardians, the philosophers or the wise. This reflects Plato's confidence that people desire the good and, when they know what the good is, will do it. Lewis grants primacy neither to a person's reason nor to the public role of intellectuals. Rather, he gives primacy to the middle or mediating factors, to "chest" or heart and to culture.

This difference in priorities arises, I believe, from Lewis's recognition that modern people, when they think about internal life, give adequate weight to drives and to intellect. And, when they think about public life they give adequate weight to ideas and to the events and entities that constitute engagement with reality. What moderns neglect or even repudiate is that each of these two sets of factors needs a mediator. Appetites and intelligence need to be related to one another by the "chest" or heart, and public beliefs or norms and reality need to be related to one another by culture. This also means that "chest" or heart needs to be related to culture. It is because moderns fail to recognize this, or even actively deny it, that Lewis gives primary attention not to reason but to "chest" and not to intellectuals but to literary culture.

This is apparent in the three-part structure of the society on Malachandra, particularly in the central role of the *hrossa*. They are, in the society, the poets. Lewis could not make the point more clearly. Right relations between the internal parts of a person's life, between the various aspects of public life, and between a person and society are all mediated by a middle factor. That middle factor is most fully constituted by language and most significantly exercised and engaged by the literary arts, by poetry and narrative.

Character formation is the process by which a person becomes more and more what the person is and, therefore, should be. Rather than marked by conformity and uniformity, a society constituted by people of character makes room for and values particularity and diversity. Cultures need always to be changing in order to accommodate the singular contributions made by differing characters. Cultures are not molds into which people must fit but living and changing organisms affected by the vitality and variety of the characters that constitute them.

It is a recurring theme in Lewis's work that the moral life leads to creativity and diversity, whereas the immoral life leads to repetition and homogeneity. To put it more theologically, God is the great diversifier and Satan the great homogenizer. This runs counter to common assumptions. We often think that morality means conformity, a limiting of one's own particularity, and that immorality means breaking with restraint and doing what one wants, being one's self. This is because we think of morality as rule governed and as conformity to social conditioning.

When morality is equated with conformity, evil looks creative; breaking rules appears inventive and heroic in contrast to keeping rules and conforming to the power of the regime. But for Lewis, God, as creator, releases persons to develop their own particularity; Satan, as parasite and devourer, absorbs persons and creates uniformity. Evil, while it at first may seem bold and groundbreaking, eventually becomes monotonous and obsessive. Goodness is creative and diverse, while evil is reductive and repetitive. As Lewis writes in *The Great Divorce*, "Good, as it ripens, becomes continually more different not only from evil but from other good."[12] The good life is marked by crossing thresholds, by growth, while an evil life is marked by crossing boundaries, by deviance. It is only because people have mistaken training and conditioning for morality and culture that they are led to regard immoral actions as creative and self-liberating.

In our culture we tend to substitute identity formation for character development. This substitution has two consequences. It fails to relate the formation of a person to moral content and direction, and, because the principal process of identity formation is individuation, it stresses separation and difference at the expense of relations and responsibility. These consequences encourage children, however tacitly, to discount the importance of moral examples for the formation of their personal lives. Their response to such examples will be primarily how to differ from them. Or, they will select as their models forms of behavior that are marked by opposition and rebellion. Our substitution of identity formation for character development and of society for culture are signs of the moral quandaries and sharp curtailment of human potentiality that Lewis detects as dangerous consequences of modern culture.

Culture, as we have noted, should provide stories that are vital to character formation. By reading and hearing stories, children live through various situations and learn how characters react and make decisions. This going-through process, which is basic to reading or hearing a story and is crucial to character formation, allows a person to negotiate between the situations encountered in stories and the reader's own life and between the character's responses and the reader's responses to situations of equal gravity or complexity.

Although some narratives are subject to rules and can be summarized by a moral—"The early bird catches the worm," for example—it is a serious mistake to suppose that the moral importance of narratives for children is limited to illustrating rules or morals. Narrative is more deeply instructive when the reader perceives that the decisions made and the actions taken turn out to have been good or bad ones, even though it may not be possible to say exactly what makes them one or the other. It is not always necessary to cite a rule in order to certify rightness. Participation in narratives produces a kind of moral intuition that cannot be fully translated into rules. Moral fiber develops from working through complex narrative situations with a character, reacting to challenges, making decisions, and suffering or enjoying the results. Rather than apply the narrative to his or her own life in a direct way, the reader or hearer of such stories tends to recognize his or her own life as also constituted by challenges, decisions, and consequences for which one cannot be completely prepared but which must nonetheless be faced and lived through.

III

The specifically moral content of character formation is for Lewis very much tied to virtue and the virtuous life. This interest in virtue arises from his training in classical philosophy, particularly Plato and Aristotle, and from his work with medieval and Renaissance cultures. Virtue delivers the discussion of morality from a captivity to which it often succumbs, namely, to the analysis of specific moral problems and to the act of making conscious moral decisions. Stress on virtue in moral theory has the consequence, among other things, of conveying a sense of continuity in moral training and behavior. Rather than atomize and isolate experiences and decisions, which are typical modernist moves, Lewis stands with a premodern emphasis on moral behavior as both arising from and reinforcing character, and character is nurtured and sustained by, although it is not subsumed under, tradition and culture.[13]

In his discussion of the cardinal virtues in *Mere Christianity*, Lewis does not make a special plea for the importance of any one of them. He lists prudence first, however, and it does seem to have a special place in his moral theory. For one thing, prudence is a virtue that carries suggestions of tradition and culture as sources of moral knowledge. But there is also another way in which "prudentia" seems crucial for Lewis's theory of virtue. Prudence comes into play whenever a situation arises that cannot be addressed by means of a rule, and such situations arise constantly. For example, suppose someone is on the way to perform an important task and encounters a neighbor in need. Should that person forsake the task for the neighbor or vice versa? The decision about which rule to apply—compassion, say, or responsibility to fulfill a commitment—is not itself rule governed. Narratives can introduce young people to dilemmas of this kind; in this way they learn that occasions can arise that will require them to decide which rule to follow, that will make clear that there is no rule governing the selection of the rule to follow, and that there are features of particular situations that may help in making the decision. Prudence is particularly productive in revealing the whole of the virtuous life, namely, that it is strengthened by exposure to complex situations, to making decisions in them, and by evaluating the results of those decisions.

The virtuous life is not repetitive or stagnant. Like tradition and culture, character develops. In this respect, morality is like a game. Games change over the course of time because players introduce new strategies or risks. Changes in a game are wrought neither by spectators nor by neophyte players but by those who know the game very well. Likewise, morality develops by morally creative persons. In order to illustrate this process, Lewis does not use the analogy of inventive players of a game but, rather, of a poet's relation to language. The poet, who knows language and is resourceful in using it, changes language and usage. It is not surprising, given Lewis's view of the role of literature in culture and in the formation of character, that his example is literary. He says, "A great poet, who has 'loved,' and been well nurtured in, his mother tongue, may also make great alterations in it, but his changes of the language are made in the spirit of the language itself: he works from within."[14] Indeed, one of the characteristics of admirably moral persons is that they have somehow changed the game or the language, perhaps even the rules. While Lewis is far from cavalier about the stability of rules and norms in moral theory, he does not make the virtuous life and the formation of character subservient to them. However, laws may be modified, suspended, or broken only by people who respect them, who recognize their generally authoritative status.

Lewis's emphasis on virtue in his moral theory allows him to stress the continuity between human action and human nature. This is why Lewis relates character formation to "natural law." He uses the concept of natural law neither to warrant morality by affirming that it is inscribed in nature nor to elevate a moral code by making it inclusive of all creatures. Lewis's theory of natural law underpins his conviction that character and virtue do not run counter to the natural constitution of persons as human beings and do not throw persons out of alignment with their environment. Morality reveals interrelations and continuities between a person's natural condition, a person's relations with other people, and a person's internal makeup.

Antagonism toward moral law, consequently, is not a natural but a socially acquired attitude. Rather than assume and promote a sense of relatedness between persons and moral behaviors, our culture largely teaches that there is antagonism between them. Such a belief, even dogma, is unthinkable apart from the separation created by the culture between internal and external factors, between mind and body, between consciousness (which knows laws) and energy (which knows none). On this model, human life, because it is basically in conflict with itself, produces turmoil and unhappiness. A person continually either denies his or her desires or breaks social mores or moral laws.

For Lewis the model is more complex because a middle, relational factor must be added, the heart or "chest." It mediates a relationship between bodily drives and intellect, and the person becomes both more moral and more him- or herself as that relationship emerges and is secured. Virtues are results of that relationship. When virtues develop they stabilize relations between physical and mental potentials that serve the well-being of a person by producing integrity and moral reliability. Lewis believes that persons can live in positive continuity with their worlds and that they can do so without necessarily having to repress their own potentials and desires. The two need not conflict. Moral acts need not create conflict between happiness and responsibility, between the well-being of others and the development of particular, personal gifts.

Finally, while moral laws should not be treated cavalierly, at times moral considerations can lead a person to depart from law. There may be ways of acting in a particular situation that are more moral than simply abiding by a rule. Situations, especially human relations, are not, for Lewis, wholly subject to rules; rather, rules are modified and interpreted in relation to situations. This does not mean that Lewis advocates a kind of "situational ethics," an approach to morality that was very popular after World War II both in Europe and in this country.[15] It is not as though rules for Lewis lack authority and must be derived from each situation. A person brings to every situation not only knowledge of moral rules but also a character that is trained in the difficult task of making moral decisions in complex situations. But situations call the person to practice the virtue of "prudentia," to make a decision about how to act in that particular situation. At times, this may require a choice between differing rules, the modification of a rule, or the suspension of a rule altogether in the process of making a moral decision or taking moral action.

Moral behavior or character formation is, therefore, always a creative, even heroic work. It is a process by which a person is strengthened to act freely and responsibly at the same time, to act in a way that allows both personal desire and situation to coincide.

It is very hard to counter the modern notion that moral behavior is uniform and dull. It is not made easier by the fact that the drama of moral decision-making is largely an internal one. Moral persons do look somewhat ordinary on the outside, consequently, while immoral people stand out because they seem to have the courage to defy conventions, to assert their individuality, and to create unexpected and provocative situations.

But for Lewis immoral behavior turns out to be not creative but monotonous. Immoral behavior becomes predictable: "Once a liar always a liar," as people sometimes say. Goodness has variety, innovation, and specificity. Evil creates only apparent unity between people because it dissolves their particularities. Goodness, however, from the outside looks ordinary or natural. It is something like the ability of a musician or athlete to do remarkable things with apparent ease, the ease concealing the fact that the ability comes only with years of concentration and practice. Evil stands out because it is arbitrary. It attracts the morbidly curious. It is analogous to the difference between sickness and health. Illness is more dramatic, more alarming, and gets more attention than health. This is why hypochondriacs need complaints; they need to make themselves more interesting to others and, perhaps, to themselves by feeling ill. The ordinariness of moral life is one of the things that endangers it. Like health we take it for granted and are tempted to discount it in relation to the apparent though illusory excitements of evil.[16]

Lewis had to face the problem of creating evil characters for his stories without making them attractive. He does this by making them ludicrous, like Uncle Andrew and Jadis in *The Magician's Nephew*, boring, like Weston and Devine in *Out of the Silent Planet*, or increasingly unhappy, like Mark in *That Hideous Strength* and Edmund in *The Lion, the Witch and the Wardrobe*. On the other hand, by keeping evil from being attractive, Lewis must also avoid making it trivial, downplaying its force and pervasiveness.[17] This he does by showing not only how widespread and damaging it is but also how strangely natural evil can become, how immoral behavior gradually dulls moral sensitivities.

Evil can be rationalized because it always attaches itself to something good. Evil is parasitic. It perverts the good. As a consequence, a case can always be made in defense of an evil. This also means that it often is difficult to distinguish between evil and good because the two will always, at least to some degree, resemble one another. Let us take only one example, the difference between a creative imagination and a destructive imagination.[18] The destructive imagination serves the desire for self-expansion, projecting situations in which the person can feel more important or experience more pleasure than in ordinary life. The creative or productive imagination, on the other hand, serves the purpose of enlarging one's world and giving a person a correct, more accurate sense of his or her place within it. While both types of imaginative act compensate for deficiencies and both can be exciting and pleasing, they radically diverge. Why? In the first the individual reduces the world to his or her own desires, making it a projection not only of self but also only of some part of the actual or potential self. In the second a person is placed in a larger or more complex world that calls him or her to be not less than but more than before. The difference between the two is an experienced difference and not one clearly marked by a rule. This is due to the dependence of evil on good. Evil always turns something good to destructive ends. And the point of divergence between good forms of something good and bad forms of something good is often difficult to detect.

While the moral life, the life of virtue, is an ordinary life, it is not dull. Character is always growing. As athletes and musicians are always trying to improve and diversify their performance, so a person works at personal development as a process of refinement and expansion. We are always encountering new challenges and always needing to judge what to do about them. We can recoil from these challenges and retreat to some kinds of habitual responses. Passivity and inactivity can look to other people very much like morality, but from within nothing is happening. Character arises not from avoiding evil or always doing the same thing; it arises from doing good, and doing good is innovative, is always a part of a concrete situation, and enriches both the doer and the doer's world.

IV

While predictability becomes the characteristic of the wicked person, reliability becomes the mark of character. True, they seem much alike, but predictability is monotonous and empty of content while reliability inspires trust and confidence. We are not always sure what a reliable person will do, but we are sure that it will in some way be the right thing to have done. Reliability has authority; it counts for something. When Professor Kirk questions the children about Lucy's reports, toward the beginning of *The Lion, The Witch and the Wardrobe*, he says to Susan, "'. . . a charge of lying against someone whom you have always found truthful is a very serious thing; a very serious thing indeed.'"[19] While the virtuous life is always growing, it is also constant and creates confidence in others.

Reliability has close ties with making and keeping promises, and this aspect of the virtue of justice is also very important in Lewis for character formation. Promises ought not to be made rashly, and once made they should be kept. It is by promising that a person projects a life and lives toward that projection. By keeping promises a person instills confidence in others as one whose word is consistent with performance.

Reliability is a form of moral authority. In fact, it seems implicitly to stand in Lewis's work as an answer to the question left by his rejection of bureaucracy as the characteristic form of authority in the modern period. It is a mistake, I think, to assume that Lewis, by rejecting bureaucratic authority, advocates either of the alternatives to it included in Max Weber's well-known typology. Lewis does not support either traditional authority, that is, authority that is passed down from generation to generation, despite his use of royal titles in the Narnia Chronicles. Nor does he promote charismatic authority, Weber's third type. The virtue of justice, primarily in the form of reliability substantiated by keeping promises, covenants, and contracts, may be taken, I think, as a fundamental ingredient in Lewis of moral authority and its social consequences.

One of the contexts for promising to which Lewis gives particular attention is marriage. He takes a strong stand on the inviolability of the marriage vow. His discussions of sexuality, romantic love, and Christian marriage, especially in *Mere Christianity* and *The Four Loves*, are very firmly tied to his sense of the importance of promises to the formation and continuity of character.

Lewis's belief in the importance of keeping promises deeply affected his personal life. Before they went off to serve in the First World War, Lewis and his friend Paddy Moore promised one another that if either one of them should die in the war the other would care for the bereaved parent, Lewis's father or Paddy's mother, who was separated from her husband. Paddy did die, and Lewis lived with and supported Mrs. Moore until her death more than thirty years later. This relationship was difficult and demanding, especially in later years, and raised questions for Lewis during his life and for biographers and students of his work ever since. Very soon after the death of Mrs. Moore, Lewis began his relationship with Joy Davidman, a married woman who later divorced. This relationship is well known from the stage play that was later made into films in England and in the U. S., *Shadowlands*. Joy Davidman became a close friend and collaborator with Lewis, and they married in a civil ceremony in 1956 so that she could remain in England. Despite the obstacle of marrying a woman whose former husband was still living, Lewis and Joy were united in Christian marriage the next year. My point in bringing up these two moments in Lewis's life is that they reveal something about character. First, they reveal Lewis's ability to adhere to his promises even when the consequences became very taxing, such as dealing with the demanding personality of Mrs. Moore and the sickness and eventual death of his wife, Joy. But also they reveal how he choose to ignore convention and even to suspend some rules of behavior in order to carry through on his commitments and promises.

Promising, it seems to me, provides for Lewis a connection between character formation, a general moral, human possibility, and sanctification, a specifically Christian one. There is a relation between keeping a promise and becoming more Christ-like. The willingness to keep a promise often means doing so when it is inconvenient or contrary to one's wishes. This means that promising and adhering to promises often involves self-sacrifice, and self-sacrifice is the process by which a person gives up him- or herself while also receiving a new self, a process, that is, of sanctification.

What has to happen before a person can think of his or her development not in terms of self-extension or self-enrichment but in terms of self-sacrifice? The ability to make that change depends, for Lewis, on faith, hope, and love, on the theological virtues. A person who makes and keeps promises is one who does not live primarily for self, and the theological virtues can emerge only in such a person.

Lewis gives so much attention to Christian marriage because it is the most common and the most fully involving form of promising in which people engage. It is only the Christian, that is, the person for whom the sacrifice of self can be a process entered into willingly, who should promise, he argues, to marry for life. In *Mere Christianity* he suggests that society should make available to nonreligious people the possibility of more limited or conditional vows.[20] The form of marriage that we now have is one appropriate to religious belief, and if the religious context of marriage dissolves, people should not, perhaps, be expected to adhere to a promise for the entirety of their lives or without regard to changing circumstances. Only a person of faith, he suggests, should be called on to make that kind of vow, since it will almost inevitably require substantial self-sacrifice. While I think that Lewis is only half-serious in this proposal, it does make some sense. There are many reasons why people live together without being married, but one of them may be an inability or unwillingness, as they say, "to make a commitment." It may be too much to ask individuals in a culture like ours in which self-interest is a primary value to make an unconditional and life-long commitment. For many couples renewable term contracts may be a sensible alternative to the present all or nothing status of the marriage bond.

Character formation and the process of sanctification are overlapping or continuous with one another, but they are not identical. Character formation issues into sanctification when a person becomes aware that self-actualization occurs not by retaining or increasing the self but by letting it go, letting it die. Lewis offers the keeping of promises, particularly marriage vows, as a clear and common way by which the process of character formation yields to the process of sanctification. The cardinal virtues, then, lead to and prepare for the theological virtues, and the life of sanctification arises from character.

As models of virtue, especially in narratives, are the best guides for character formation, so models are crucial to the process of sanctification. In *Mere Christianity* Lewis advocates the imitation of other Christians and of Christ. As with models of virtue, models for the process of sanctification are not slavishly copied. Rather, imitation is something like "getting the hang of it." He seems to have in mind, when he addresses imitation, Paul's invitation to the Philippian Christians that they imitate him as he imitates Christ, which primarily means the fundamental act of self-emptying (Philippians 2:1-11).

The relation between the cardinal and the theological virtues resembles the relation between culture and a Christian account of the world. As saintliness depends upon character formation, so a Christian account of the world depends upon a viable culture. As saintliness is something very different from character formation yet depends on it, so Christianity is very different from culture but also requires it. The relation of culture and character to one another, by which each affects the other in complex ways, is further secured by their mutual roles as preparations for and bases of the Christian life and a Christian account of the world.

When we turn to the question of what it would be like to attempt a project similar to Lewis's on American soil in this present, transitional time, we shall have to consider what prospects there may be for character formation in the American literary tradition. We shall have to ask whether the interest that Lewis took in character and virtue is an interest that we can pursue as part of our culture. It is my hope that we can find such resources within the culture, resources that can be retrieved and that will allow us to see moral character as a central concern of our literary cultural tradition. But we must also ask whether these resources are forceful and clear enough to counter the isolation and conflict that seem increasingly to mark the identity of people today and their relations to others, to their own constitutions and circumstances, and to their future.

6

•   •   •   •   •   •   •   •   •

PLEASURE

With all its stress on self-sacrifice, the Christian life may look at first glance like a pretty dour affair. But, despite his emphasis on the pain and sacrifice that the transformation of character requires, Lewis is very much on the side of pleasure. It is a recurring topic in his work. He says, for example, "We have had enough, once and for all, of Hedonism—the gloomy philosophy which says that Pleasure is the only good. But we have hardly yet begun what may be called *Hedonics*, the science or philosophy of Pleasure."[1] Screwtape gives us some indication of the importance of pleasure when he scolds Wormwood for allowing the "patient" to engage in several enjoyable activities.[2] Screwtape also thinks that one of the really solid achievements of hell was to convince Western culture that the Puritans were joyless.[3] Lewis discusses pleasure extensively in *The Four Loves*, but it receives its fullest treatment in *Perelandra*. We will gather the sundry points that he makes about pleasure and outline the incipient theory of pleasure in his work. We will then try to account for why pleasure is an important theme for him.

A corollary to Lewis's treatment of pleasure is his often expressed view that modern society, for all its stress on exuberance, is not a garden of earthly delights at all. Rather, it tends to produce the sort of austere and humorless world that N.I.C.E. creates in *That Hideous Strength*. His theory of pleasure leads him implicitly to claim that a Christian account of the world, despite its ascetic ingredients and its stress on sacrifice, gives greater place to pleasure, understands it more fully, and promotes it more effectively than do its secular counterparts.

There are three reasons why the topic of pleasure is consistent with Lewis's overall project. The first is that pleasure draws the attention of a person outward toward something external. It counters self-preoccupation. To take pleasure in something is to acknowledge and experience the value of something outside oneself. This is particularly true of unexpected pleasures and of pleasures that do not satisfy recognized needs. In *The Four Loves* he uses the example of being suddenly aware of a pleasant aroma.[4] But even need-based pleasures, such as the delight a thirsty person takes in a drink of water, orient a person outward. Even anticipated or expected pleasures can direct attention away from self toward appreciation for something beyond. Although we might think of pleasure as drawing attention to an inward state or response, it is most itself when it does not do that. Pleasure holds the potential for making us aware of our relation to a larger world for which we should be and are grateful. Pleasure is thus consistent with Lewis's larger project because he is eager to counter the tendency of modern people to be self-preoccupied.

Pleasure is also consistent with Lewis's overall project because it militates against the common assumption that there is a gap between us and what lies outside us, between values and facts, and between things and people's understanding of them. In moments of pleasure a person is aware of the continuity between his or her evaluation of something and its pleasurable characteristics. A thirsty person who drinks water does not think that the delight water brings is projected by the person on it. The person thinks that the water is a very good thing indeed. Experiences of pleasure, then, like the experiences of the sublime to which Lewis repeatedly calls our attention, cause the gap that we assume exists between things or events and our evaluation of them to disappear.[5]

The third reason pleasure is consistent with Lewis's overall project is that it allows for edification, for an upwardly directed and expanded sense of the world. The thirsty person does not think of the water in a detached or reduced way, as having a certain weight, volume, or molecular constitution, for example. Rather, the water becomes the occasion of refreshment and restoration. Because of the pleasure that the water brings, the person has a newly realized appreciation of the world.

We begin to see why the topic of pleasure is so important for Lewis. It would be difficult to find three interests more central to Lewis's project than these. He wants very much to counter self-preoccupation, to counter the idea that there is a gap between persons and what lies outside of them, and to counter the tendency to define things in ways that reduce and simplify them.

Since pleasure aids all three of these interests, it generates great force and significance in his work.

Now that we have seen the relation of pleasure to Lewis's overall project, we should look more closely at his theory of pleasure. First, we should see why pleasure is edifying. Second, we should examine the relation of pleasure to other positive experiences, especially to joy, to gaining knowledge, and to reading. Finally, we should see how and why pleasure is distorted in modern culture.

I

First, why are pleasures edifying? There are three reasons. To begin with, pleasures draw us into a larger and more abundant world. A person recognizes that the world supports him or her, is even fulfilling. This is why Screwtape wants his nephew to keep the "patient" from enjoying something for its own sake, precisely to keep him from thinking that there exists outside his own interests and needs a world of significance and delight into which he can be drawn and for which he can be grateful. A person who has been drawn into that larger and more abundant world may become vulnerable to religious attitudes.

Pleasures are also edifying because they provide occasions for a person to be more him- or herself. In moments of genuine pleasure a person has a richer sense of identity than usual because the occasion of pleasure awakens an unrecognized potential to appreciate the delight. Brought to the surface by a pleasurable moment is something that heretofore was only latent. The discovery in the moment of pleasure is double-sided; in pleasure there is at the same time both recognition of the external, pleasurable entity or event and of the internal capacity to recognize and benefit from it. Pleasure, rather than subjecting the internal to something from outside, allows the internal to be awakened and released in the pleasurable moment. Pleasure is a compound formed by the value of the external object and the awakened potential within the person to respond appreciatively to it.

Third, pleasures are edifying because they are not closed and self-contained. Pleasurable moments, rather, open outward to yet higher possibilities because they suggest even greater fulfillment. So, in the midst of a highly engaging and energizing conversation, one of the participants might say, "Oh, if only John and Janet were here, how they would enjoy this and how we would enjoy having them be a part of it." Such a statement does not express dissatisfaction, as though the occasion is deficient because John and Janet are absent.

No, it expresses a recognition that the occasion is on a kind of track that could be extended, that points outside the occasion to something more. Others, if the statement is on target, will not be offended, as if their presence left something to be desired, but will endorse the insight enthusiastically. They will say that yes, indeed, John and Janet would have enjoyed this occasion; they would have added something valuable to it, and it's a pity they are not here with us. Again, the observation in no way detracts from or threatens the enjoyment; rather, it recognizes the outward, expansive direction of the moment and celebrates the fullness of the occasion by indicating how it opens itself to something more.

Pleasures are edifying, then, because they direct a person's attention away from self and toward something outside, because they awaken a latent capacity in the person to appreciate the pleasure, and because they point beyond themselves to a yet more fulfilling and desirable pleasure. Another way of saying this is that pleasure when it is most itself is a gift. This could be put the other way around. Giving and receiving gifts carry the most potential for being occasions of pleasure. In contrast, pleasures that are planned, even more, pleasures that are controlled, tend to be less like pleasures, tend, indeed, to turn pleasure into something else.

II

Now that we have seen the constitutive ingredients of pleasure, we can compare it with several other positive experiences or moments in human life to which Lewis also attaches significance. One of these is "joy," which he addresses most fully in his autobiography, *Surprised by Joy*. Joy is the exhilarating moment when one is drawn out of oneself by the lure of something grander, higher, and elusive. Awakened by joy are deep desires and potentials in a person, of which the person was not previously aware. And joy also contains an element of pain, a sense that there is a level of participation in something more or something other that cannot now be attained or received. "Joy," a topic on which several readers of Lewis comment,[6] has a similar structure as pleasure but is a more specific and intense experience. Pleasures are more common, more precisely oriented, and more physical than are experiences of joy.

I think that it is both possible and important to follow Lewis's theory of pleasure in a contrary direction, that is, to less exceptional and engrossing experiences than joy. I think Lewis's scattered comments on pleasure suggest his incipient epistemology, a theory, that is, of knowledge and how we come to know things. Lewis, as we have seen, attacks dominant, modern epistemologies because they tend to assume a gap between minds and what lies outside of them. But Lewis does not offer an explicit alternative to the modern epistemologies that he in general rejects. While he is clear that he rejects the notion of a gap between internal and external, or mind and reality, he does not directly apply his relational model to epistemological questions. But if we take pleasure as our guide, we can infer what that epistemology would be like. I think we can conclude that for Lewis coming to know something is an event in which the nature and meaning of something and the person's capacity to recognize or comprehend them arise mutually and simultaneously. Knowing something is an event when the latent relation of subject and object is actualized. To put it differently, the event of knowing something is one in which the continuity between the subjective and the objective, a continuity that potentially is already there, becomes conscious and is confirmed. This is why learning and knowing are pleasurable experiences. Learning or knowing something is an event that affirms the fundamental relationship that we have with what lies outside of ourselves. Gaining knowledge expands both us and our world, and that expansion gives pleasure. Finally, gaining knowledge is pleasurable because it kindles our awareness that the world in which we find ourselves beckons us both to learn more about it and to be enriched by that process.

Joy, pleasure, and knowing have, then, similar structures. All three direct attention away from self, reveal the relation between something external to the internal capacities to know and appreciate it, and point beyond the occasion to something higher, something yet more significant and fulfilling. Pleasure, as a more general category of experience, stands between joy, which is more intense and infrequent, and knowledge, which is a more ordinary kind of experience. All have the potential of expanding human life by placing a person in a larger and more meaningful world. That world is one in which the person belongs and into which he or she is incorporated.

It is important to an understanding of Lewis to ask at this point whether his theory of reading is to be related to his theories of joy, pleasure, and knowing. In my opinion, it is. Remember that one of the pleasures that Wormwood's "patient" enjoys and which makes Screwtape so nervous is reading a book. Perhaps his theory of reading, lodged principally in his somewhat elusive *An Experiment in Criticism*, seems less important to Lewis than his theories of joy, pleasure, and knowing because he took it more for granted. Today reading has become the site of controversy in contemporary literary and cultural studies that it was not half a century ago. I think that Lewis's theory of reading provides an interesting alternative to the theories that constitute the present debates, theories determined by the subject/object split.

The first thing to recognize is that reading has for Lewis a relational quality similar to the experiences of joy, pleasure, and knowing. This means that
reading is not only something that the reader does but also something that
happens to the reader. As Bruce L. Edwards says, summarizing Lewis on reading, "literature consists of a transaction that occurs between the *literary* reader
and the offered work. The vital evaluative dimension of the literary world is
retained in the literary reader. Literature happens, exists only in this transaction," which Edwards later describes as "the interaction of the received work
with the literary reader."[7] In the transaction between the reader and the text,
the reader makes the first move by placing him- or herself in a vulnerable position relative to the text. As Lewis says in *An Experiment in Criticism*, "In love,
in virtue, in the pursuit of knowledge, and in the reception of the arts, we are
doing this [i.e., correcting the confinement of the self and healing its loneli-
ness]. Obviously this process can be described either as an enlargement or as a
temporary annihilation of the self."[8] This is strong language. It means that in
reading a person puts him- or herself as much as possible in a position of self-
and world-abjection. That move is crucial to the reception of and into a larger
world and a new sense of the self that reading can provide. Lewis continues,
"But that is an old paradox; 'he that loseth his life shall find it.'" Lewis uses not
just religious language but words from the Gospel to illuminate what he
means by reading.

Lewis's theory of reading, in my opinion, though not fully fleshed out, is
potentially more adequate than the theories that divide participants in recent
literary canon debates. Those largely fall into two groups. The first, usually
claiming to uphold the tradition, contends that the text determines reading;
the other, shaped by reader-response and relativist theories, contends that the
text is constructed by the act of reading it.[9] These alternative positions cash
out as contraries, the one objective and the other subjective, and current reading theories, despite disclaimers and refinements, find their homes on either
one or the other side of this divide. Lewis offers an alternative position, one
that I would argue is more consistent with the tradition of reading than either
of its present-day alternatives. It is basically relational, and both sides are required, the text and the reader. It is a theory that may carry possibilities for
avoiding the impasses that stymie the current debate.

The first thing to remember about *An Experiment in Criticism* is that it
does not begin with the modern assumption of a break or even opposition between subjects who read and the texts that they read. This lack of agreement
in Lewis with the assumptions that govern the continuing debate may explain
why Lewis's theory seems elusive. But once it is recognized that we are always

already in actual and potential relations with things in our world, especially with texts, we can see what a right reading is. Reading, as with Lewis's understanding of joy, pleasure, and knowing, is right when the force and significance of a text coincide with the reader's awakened capacity to recognize and be affected by them.[10] A good reading is one in which reading actualizes potentials in both the text and the reader.

There is for Lewis, then, a shared structure to such positive moments in human life as pleasure, joy, gaining knowledge, and reading. This shared structure is one by which a person is drawn outside the boundaries of self into a larger, more significant situation. The self is awakened in its capacity to recognize the significance of that situation and becomes aware that the situation stands open, so to speak, at its far end to yet more significant possibilities. This is why Lewis can begin the crucial sentence on reading with a catalog of positive experiences: "In love, in virtue, in the pursuit of knowledge and in the reception of the arts, we are doing this," he says; that is, we are countering containment within the self. All of these moments require the "temporary annihilation of the self."[11] As he also says, "The first demand any work of art makes upon us is surrender. Look. Listen. Receive. Get yourself out of the way."[12] And this initial stance is not trumped by the plea that one is actively trying to derive a moral benefit from reading. This also can come only when a removal of the self has first occurred: "Attention to the very objects they [novels and poems] are is our first step. To value them chiefly for reflections which they may suggest to us or morals we may draw from them, is a flagrant instance of 'using' instead of 'receiving.'"[13] The "temporary annihilation of the self" is an unavoidable part of a process by which an enlivened and expanded self arises.

Lewis's theory of these positive experiences, particularly since he uses recognizably religious language to describe them, may sound excessive. One may question whether Lewis, by attributing to intellectual and aesthetic experiences postures and transformations that resemble those associated with religious acts, is granting to reading, let us say, the kind of attitudes that should be reserved for prayer.[14] This question goes to the very root of Lewis's project. He posits continuity, a positive relation, between certain human experiences—virtue, love, joy, gaining knowledge, pleasure, or appreciation of a text—and loving God. And he can do that because he sees in all of them a similar structure, a way in which a person gets free of an old self or small world and receives a reconstituted self and a larger world. All, from the very lowest or simplest, like drinking a glass of water, to the very highest and most complex, like praying, reveal a similar structure. All reveal, as Lewis says, "an old paradox; 'he that loseth his life shall save it.'"[15] Lewis's answer to the question of whether he is giving too much importance to reading, making it look similar to acts of worship, would be, I think, that reading, like the other positive experiences it resembles, opens up on the far side. These experiences become substitutes for religious acts only when they are closed off. It is not possible, for Lewis, to think too highly of things or to enjoy things too much. Problems arise only when the things of which one thinks highly or enjoys are taken as self-contained and self-sustaining or when experiences of pleasure merely result in enhanced interest in one's self as the receiver of the occasioned enjoyment.[16]

Implicit in Lewis's theories of reading, knowing, pleasure, and joy is a confidence in the deep and often unrecognized needs that operate in people's lives often without their awareness. While it is risky to shift attention from the things that occasion pleasure to the desire for pleasure, we should note his affirmation of human desires. This repertoire of desires not only enables a person to recognize moments of pleasure but also directs the person outward in search of fulfillment to those desires. It is as though one has within a bank of receptors, like those that scientists have deployed in the hope of picking up messages from outer space, receptors directed outward in the hope of a signal. Although moderns have disenchanted the world, isolated consciousness from it, and defined themselves as exceptions to it, they still have a hope that they are not alone in the universe, that there is intelligent life out there. They deploy expensive and sophisticated equipment in the pursuit of confirmations of that hope. The desire not to be alone or abandoned but to be, as William James put it, "at home in the universe" directs attention to the possibility of rapport between ourselves and the larger world around us.

It is a damaging mistake to understand and to act on desires in ways that reduce them to something less than what they are and point to. Desires are also directives, and they direct a person outward toward potential moments of genuine pleasure, that is, toward moments of rapport, of a new sense of richness in both world and self. But desires can lead in other than edifying or transforming directions. Lewis is very aware of the tendency in modern culture to read desires as pointing to something less rather than to something more than themselves. As he points out in *Surprised by Joy*, the experience that he names "joy" will easily be mistaken for repressed or unrecognized sexual desire, although sex may easily be a component in experiences of joy.[17] To interpret the desire for a pleasure that is potentially spiritual as really a disguised desire for something solely physical is to distort and finally destroy the receptors that should always be directing us outside our immediate needs to something else or something more.

Lewis believes that modern culture conditions people habitually to reduce and even to discount altogether the significance of things or events that are seen positively and appreciatively. He describes the atmosphere of the schools in which he was educated as training young men in sardonic and ironic intellectual styles and personal attitudes.[18] Lewis is sensitive to such attitudes for several reasons. They lead people to discount edifying experiences and to distrust their own desires for and responses to joyful occasions. This accelerates the corrosion of the culture by draining it of any resources it yet may contain for directing the desires and potentials of persons toward what may be both worthy of and challenging to them. Such dismissive and reductive attitudes combine with forms of analysis, political and psychological, that treat what is edifying or directed outward in experience with suspicion, as concealing or diverting attention from something beneath that is more real and self-serving. This combination of popular attitude and scholarly method places a devastatingly negative burden on the culture, and the unavoidable result will be to erase the final vestiges of productive effects that the culture, in its last, present stages, is still haltingly able to produce. Strange as it may seem, a culture can be evaluated, perhaps evaluated most effectively, by how it defines pleasure, how much pleasure it provides, and by the pleasures that it prizes most highly.

When a person has been trained to interpret an occasion of pleasure as indicating something less rather than something more than itself, there can be no expansion of the pleasurable situation. A good example of those dynamics is Weston's sardonic attitude toward Ransom on Perelandra when he finds that Ransom has been alone with a beautiful, naked woman. Weston takes for granted that Ransom has taken advantage of this situation and has engaged in acts of sexual gratification with the woman. Ransom responds by saying that while the situation is certainly sensual, its pleasures are not to be defined in terms of sexual acts. Contained in Ransom's response is the suggestion that in a truly pleasurable occasion, specific desires and pleasures can be dissolved in and raised to more complex or higher states.[19] The reader is led to conclude that it would be anxiety or greed, the need to possess, that would propel a person to, so to speak, cash in on the pleasurable potential of such a situation by performing a sexual act. Ransom has not been compelled to do that because the situation has been reassuring and edifying. While being no less sensual for want of sexual acts, the situation has called from Ransom the ability to suspend the desire for immediate gratification and to enter a more rather than a less pleasurable state. That act Lewis refers to as "transposition."[20] Modern people are so filled with anxiety and distrust and need so much to compensate for that anxiety and distrust that they are quick to translate the potential for pleasure in any situation into the immediate reassurance and possession of physical gratification.

Lewis goes so far as to use the elevation of a sensual situation above a focused and physical sensual act as a metaphor for the resurrection of the body and the life of the world to come.[21] If, as moderns tend to do, we take all pleasures as finding their seat in physical pleasures, and all physical pleasures as focused on specific organs, then the notion of heavenly delights becomes foreign if not absurd to us. But the picture can be reversed. Physical pleasures can become momentary glimpses into larger and more enduring states of pleasure that can receive and sustain the person. If particular, especially physical, pleasures defer to larger and more intensely pleasurable situations, then moments of physical delight can reveal "the life of the world to come." The eschatological metaphors of the New Testament that present fulfillment as the marital union between Christ and the church and as a final feast (Luke 13:29 and Revelation 19:9, for example) provide the language for this transposition. Rather than collapsing spiritual into physical experiences, the physical acts of sex and eating are taken up into the language of the future and transcendence. When so directed, these acts become not ends in themselves but means by which eschatological fulfillment is anticipated.

It is because we are conditioned to look for the cause of desires as below or beneath them rather than as beyond or above them that we automatically interpret pleasures as less than they appear to be. Consequently, pleasure has the consequence not of securing our sense of relation to the larger, external world but undermining it and our confidence in it. When we are taught that our desires are not what they appear to be, or that they conceal interests which we want to deny, our potential for relatedness to the world and to something more beyond it is thrown into question. As a result, people turn to things and people around them with undisciplined, insatiable, and undirected desire. They disdain their world because they have devalued their desires and no longer treat what they encounter with anticipation and gratitude for its potential to raise desire to a genuinely pleasurable state. Because they have been taught to reduce and distrust their desires, to interpret them in purely physical, psychological, or political/economic terms, moderns accordingly reduce their worlds to those aspects of it that conform to this set of reductive terms. As their own desires have been stripped and reduced, so they also strip and reduce their world, exposing what they think of as its true nature but is really a projection of their own reduced sense of need and their own cynicism toward the possibility of need's fulfillment.

Moderns not only increasingly disdain and distrust their world; they also increasingly fear it. This is because they no longer treat their world as that to which they are related, as an arena of possible edification, or as able to draw and direct them to something more. Consequently, moderns, like people of Narnia under the reign of King Miraz, inhabit a smaller or more reduced world than do people in former or other cultures. They have grown distrustful of their capacities and willingness to have pleasure, to be drawn out of themselves into a world that they have not themselves provided. That distrust produces fear of what lies beyond the immediate boundaries of a world that a person subjects to his or her own reduced desires. Modern people are dogged by fear and anxiety, and it is due to the greatly constricted world in which they live. In *Prince Caspian*, the reign of King Miraz has fostered increasing skepticism among the population concerning the stories of Aslan and his sacrificial and redeeming act. This skepticism confines the attention of people to their immediate surroundings. They increasingly distrust anything that they do not themselves construct or understand. The result is a greatly reduced world. We find a similar result of skepticism and reduction in the first two narratives of the space trilogy. Ransom's characteristic and inhibiting attitude, one from which he must be delivered if the process of sanctification is to be engaged, is his fear. The academic culture of which Ransom is a part, because it fosters skepticism, places persons in increasingly confined worlds, and Ransom's journeys to other planets expand his sense of the world as they also reduce his fear of the unknown.

III

Modernity is so successful in reducing and distorting human desire and pleasure because pleasure, as Aristotle long ago made clear, contains the potential for its own distortion. In any culture, desire and pleasure can be corrupted. The destruction of the relation of desire and pleasure to the actualization of human potential is no uniquely modern achievement, although modern culture may outstrip others in the effectiveness of that destruction. The self-preoccupation, materialism, and desire for power prevalent in modern culture play directly into pleasure's potential for its own subversion. That potential is most apparent in the possibility of repeating pleasure and in the possibility of manipulating one's world to produce occasions for pleasure.

While on Perelandra, Ransom encounters many delightful things. One is the unexpected and unprecedented sensual delight he experiences in drinking from a gourd. "It was like the discovery of a totally new *genus* of pleasures, something unheard of among men, out of all reckoning, beyond all covenant." Ransom is about to repeat the pleasure, but he realizes that he would do so not because he was thirsty but because he wanted the pleasure again. "But for whatever cause, it appeared to him better not to taste again."[22] Ransom somehow recognizes that it would be better not to repeat it, and he goes so far as to suggest that repetition and the desire for repetition endanger pleasure and, perhaps, even constitute the root of evil. Ransom's decision not to repeat the pleasure implies that he distances himself from the distortions of pleasure by which moderns have been seized. For Lewis, we must conclude, repetition is a potential threat to desire and pleasure, while for moderns repetition is a principal, if not a defining, characteristic of desire and pleasure.

The thrust of Ransom's decision is this: to repeat the pleasure draws attention and value away from the object of pleasure. What becomes the value is the experience of pleasure, even more, the person's capacity for pleasurable experiences. There is potentially, for Lewis, a contrary relation between enjoyment and our consciousness that we are enjoying something: "enjoyment and the contemplation of our inner activities are incompatible," he says.[23] This does not mean that self-consciousness and reflection are necessarily bad; it is that they are potential contraries to enjoyment. This contrary relation between experience and our consciousness of experience must be respected in regard to pleasure. The tendency will be to shift attention from the outward occasion of the pleasure, which comes to us as a kind of gift, to the inner capacity for pleasure, which we can think of not as awakened by a gift but as self-possessed. "This, I say, is the first and deadly error, which appears on every level of life and is equally deadly on all, turning . . . love into auto-eroticism. And the second error is, having thus falsely made a state of mind your aim, to produce it."[24] When the state of mind or the capacity for pleasure becomes the focus of attention and the center of value, the orientation has radically shifted. Rather than being drawn into a larger world, the pleasure seeker begins increasingly to draw the world into self and to reduce the world to the terms of its pleasure-granting possibilities.

In addition, because the capacity to have pleasure is so valued, the person turns toward the world as the means by which his or her capacity for experiencing pleasure is reaffirmed and fed. Such a person, furthermore, becomes anxious as to whether this capacity may dwindle. The person looks for occasions—indeed, constantly tries to create them—that will test whether the capacity to have pleasure is still intact, occasions, that is, when the person will be delivered from the anxiety that the capacity may have weakened or disappeared. Repetition becomes obsessive because it must never end, can never be enough. The more pleasures a person experiences, the more important the capacity for having pleasure becomes and the greater the anxiety that the capacity may dwindle or be lost. That person is always trying to impose on the world his or her need of occasions to test the capacity for experiencing pleasure. Far from living in a world that is always surprising and expanding, far from being able to be edified, and far from being edifying oneself, such a person homogenizes and internalizes the entire world. It is not surprising, then, that the search for pleasure and the need to repeat pleasures are characteristic of a narcissistic culture and of people who turn their world into an arena of gratification of their need for pleasure. In such a culture, pleasure is no longer pleasure, no longer the moment when a person is drawn out of self to something more that is given. Instead, pleasure becomes the means by which anxiety is temporarily relieved, the fear, that is, that it may not be true that the self constitutes in and of itself a total world.

It is clear, I think, that Lewis is both alluding to Aristotle on pleasure and departing from him in his analysis of what pleasure is and why it goes awry. In the "Nicomachean Ethics" Aristotle treats the distortion of pleasure, as he does the distortion of all good things, in terms of excess and deficiency. For Aristotle a good thing is distorted when it is overdone or underplayed. Pleasure is distorted when it becomes excessive and when it is deficient. Excessive pleasure Aristotle refers to as self-indulgence, while deficiency in pleasure (which he says does not often occur) he refers to as insensibility.[25]

Lewis follows Aristotle's discussion of pleasure on two crucial points. First, he agrees with Aristotle in opposing both the excess of those who take pleasure to be the only or highest good and the deficiency of those who take pleasure to be dangerous or even bad.[26] Second, he agrees with Aristotle that pleasure goes bad when it turns into self-indulgence.

However, Lewis also differs from Aristotle at several points. First, Aristotle makes a clearer distinction than does Lewis between bodily and intellectual pleasures, and Aristotle relates bodily pleasures more directly to the distortion of pleasure than Lewis does. Lewis, if anything, is more attentive to errors and excesses of the mind than to those of the body. Second, Aristotle focuses attention on pleasurable activities, and Lewis shifts attention to the objects or occasions of pleasure. This puts the weight on what is received by the person in pleasurable moments rather than on what the person does to have pleasure. Finally, Lewis departs from Aristotle on the question of what makes pleasure go bad.

Lewis agrees with Aristotle that pleasure goes bad when it turns into self-indulgence. For Aristotle self-indulgence is bad primarily because it implies excess. This form of excess is not simple, not merely too much of a good thing. Other factors enter. First, self-indulgence is marked by the extraction of pleasure from the activity. When this happens—and for Aristotle it more often happens with bodily than with intellectual pleasures—the person "will come to value the activity for its pleasure instead of seeing the pleasure as dependent on the character of the activity."[27] Also, for Aristotle, the self-indulgent person becomes conscious and deliberate in relation to pleasure. The self-indulgent person justifies self-indulgence.[28] These two factors, abstracting pleasure from the activities that occasion it and indulging deliberately in excess with a sense of excess as good, certainly turn self-indulgence into something other than simple excess.

However, I think Lewis goes further and even changes course on self-indulgence. It is not, for him, something primarily about excess. Self-indulgence is pleasure to which something has been done, something has been added. The result is no longer pleasure but another thing altogether. Self-indulgence is the opposite of pleasure.

Pleasure is no longer pleasure when attention shifts from the object of pleasure to the self. When that happens pleasure turns into self-interest. Self-indulgence is not excessive pleasure, then. For Lewis, pleasure cannot easily be excessive. However, when attention shifts from the site of pleasure to the self as the object of pleasure, we are no longer talking about pleasure. Under the banner of pleasure, the self-indulgent person is drawing the world into the self and reducing the world to that aspect of the self that needs most to be gratified. Pleasure, in other words, has been replaced by power.

Pleasurable experiences are also distorted in modern culture because they are detached from and seen as different in kind from experiences in general, especially experiences involving other people. Our daily experiences of people are commonly marked by opposition because we live in a society that places persons in competitive relations to one another. The result is to view others with hostility. Life is a zero-sum game. What someone else gets is something that I forfeit. Since our relations to other people are marked not by pleasure but by threat, experiences of pleasure with other people are exceptional. They have no relation with other experiences. They form a separate category of experiences and have more relation to one another than to experience in general. On Malachandra, Ransom is surprised to learn that the *hrossa* engage in sexual activity rarely even though they enjoy it very much.[29] They do not engage in it often because the activity itself is much more integrated with their ordinary experiences and their daily relationships. Since their experiences with other people are pleasurable, they do not turn to distinctively pleasurable experiences as an alternative to daily life. On Malachandra, anticipation and remembrance also help to integrate pleasurable experiences into the everyday. That seems to be impossible in the world from which Ransom has come because human relations on earth are antagonistic. Moments of pleasure, especially sexual pleasure, are fetishized, are abstracted from ordinary life. They constitute a category that must be kept up to date. Ransom's life on earth seems to have been a lonely one, isolated from human relations or marked by relations that were merely external and competitive.

If it is the case that human relations are what Thomas Hobbes (1588–1679) called a war of everyone against everyone else, then moments of pleasure must be exceptional and, especially if they involve human intimacy, badly needed. As a result, such moments become extraordinary and separate. This tends to produce obsessive attitudes toward them. Added to culturally induced self-preoccupation and the need to control, these conditions contribute greatly to the distortion of pleasurable occasions and of our response to them. When pleasurable occasions, especially those related to human intimacy, become oases on a battleground of human antagonism, their force and meaning are changed. The recent and quite popular film and novel *The English Patient* provides a striking illustration of this. The setting of the story is provided not only by warfare but also by the north African desert, and the scenes of sexual intimacy are exceptional in relation to that setting both because they are separate from the war and because they are associated with water. When moments of pleasure have no connection with the rest of experience, they lose their significance as possible examplars or occasions when hitherto concealed aspects of life are revealed. Moments of pleasure are important for Lewis not because they are separate from other experiences but because they are related to them and expose ways in which other experiences are related to one another.

Lewis ties the desire for repetition of pleasure to issues of power. In this respect he joins a number of recent theorists.[30] A person in a pleasurable situation has the strong sense of being dependent on something outside, something that he or she does not supply. The pleasurable situation, then, holds potential power or authority, and the one whose desire has been awakened defers to it. The dynamics of such an event are fraught with danger because the person or people associated with it can exert that power, and the person whose desire has been awakened is vulnerable to subjugation. This possibility may trigger a contrary move; the person whose desire has been awakened can try to avoid a subservient role by subsuming the situation under his or her own power. The impetus to do that comes not only from the desire not to be subservient but also from the desire for repetition. If the person who desires has become anxious about the ability to have pleasure and needs that ability confirmed, it becomes paramount for that person to create and control pleasurable situations. Finally, control provides its own gratifications because control enables a person to transform what is outside into something inside, into his or her own image. Control, whether over others who desire or over situations that can be forced into conformity with one's own desire, furthers the narcissistic agenda which desire and pleasure can so easily be used to serve.

Lewis emphasizes repetition as a form of pleasure's distortion not, I think, because repetition is itself distortion. Reading, for example, is not something to be reserved for rare occasions. And Lewis also regularly participated in Christian liturgical and sacramental acts. Rather, repetition distorts because it is so easily related to power and to the desire to manipulate the world. When Ransom in *Perelandra* identifies repetition as the source of evil he remembers that the love of money has traditionally been described as the root of evil. But, he concludes, money may be tied to repetition.[31] And, indeed, it is. Money represents the power to subject situations to control. Money greatly expands our capacity to turn our world toward our needs so that our world will confirm our capacity to have pleasure as well as our ability to shape situations in such a way that we can take from them the pleasure that we need. The power of money becomes irresistible because it is driven by an anxiety that is cut loose from any possible source of its alleviation. One can never have enough power either to satisfy the need for occasions that confirm one's ability to have pleasure or the need for power sufficient to turn the world into a reflection of one's own desires.

The final state of pleasure distorted by anxiety, self-preoccupation, and power has some characteristics of what we would recognize as addiction, although Lewis does not use that word. Indeed, his description not only of distorted pleasure but of evil more generally often recalls addiction. Someone in advanced stages of pleasure-distortion manipulates his or her world to provide the experience that quiets anxiety by means of the familiar and now necessary feeling of pleasure. Such a person also thinks of every situation in terms of that possible yield. This results in a sharply reduced and focused interest and produces repetition as simple monotony. More and more of the person's interests become defined by and confined to the gratification of that need and nothing, finally, is too much to sacrifice to it. While the addict seems to be dependent on something else—alcohol, gambling, sex, being noticed, or power, let us say—he or she is primarily oriented not to something else but to the insatiable internal need to reconfirm and reinforce the self that has become the sole object of interest. It is not surprising, then, that the narrator of Perelandra refers to Weston, that incarnation of evil, as having an "intoxicated will."[32] We are also told that Mark, as he is more fully seduced by the evil empire of N.I.C.E. in *That Hideous Strength*, becomes more dependent on alcohol: "Luckily he now kept a bottle of whisky in his room. A stiff one enabled him to shave and dress."[33] And Uncle Andrew in *The Magician's Nephew*, who is absorbed by the prospect of the power that magic can bring him, is a closet drinker.

IV

How can we keep occasions of pleasure from turning our attention to our capacity for pleasure and to our need, born in anxiety, to confirm and reinforce that capacity? The first thing to say is that a pleasurable situation, if truly pleasurable, will be recognized as authoritative because it awakens desire and offers fulfillment; but its authority, rather than residing in itself, will be recognized as derived from something beyond it. Pleasurable situations point beyond themselves. One does not attribute the desirability of a pleasurable occasion to his or her own designs or even to the occasion itself, although designs and the occasion may be integral to it. A truly pleasurable situation will have characteristics that cannot be reduced to planning or the enumeration of its ingredients. There is something irreducibly gratuitous in a pleasurable situation. Attempts to repeat and to control pleasurable occasions deny this crucial ingredient. Even more, truly pleasurable occasions point beyond themselves to some greater possibility, defer to a higher level of delight—if only John and Janet were here! That is, the authority and power of a pleasurable occasion arise not only from its gratuitous quality but also from something beyond the occasion that is both a presence and a lack—"if only John and Janet . . . !"

It becomes clear, now, why moderns are so deprived of pleasure. There is little cultural support for recognizing that the direction of pleasure is outward and upward. The culture supports the direction of pleasure as downward and inward. To recognize the quality of pleasure, we have to counter the cultural habits of reducing occasions of pleasure, of defining them in terms of gratifying chronic needs, of using them to confirm the ability to have pleasure, and of controlling them in order to make them conform to self-interest and the desire to possess. There can be no pleasure, and, *a fortiori*, there can be no joy, true knowledge, or good reading for people conditioned by such habits.

One sees the end results of the modern distortions of pleasure in the behavior of Weston. On Perelandra Ransom comes upon Weston mutilating small, frog-like creatures. It is a behavior marked by repetition and control. Weston takes it as a pleasure that Ransom will find irresistible, and his conspiratorial grimace toward Ransom is an invitation to join in. But Ransom is not seduced into mistaking the kind of unity that Weston offers in this perverse pleasure for the shared world of participants in occasions of genuine pleasure. Weston's version of pleasure offers a unity determined by the language and dynamics of power, reduction, repetition, and homogeneity.

Another example is, of course, "Our Father Below" in *The Screwtape Letters*. He is the consummate narcissist, the one who wants to reduce the entire world to himself, who, indeed, wants to devour it. Hell, the great perversion of pleasure, is subjected to a single desire and power. And all who enter his domain and are finally absorbed by his insatiable appetite recognize that they have not only done what they should not have done but also what they did not desire. They have denied their own desires and allowed them to be directed toward the great maw. The narcissist who represses the desire for something fulfilling outside the self and tries to achieve fulfillment by drawing the world into the self is actually being devoured by the great, insatiable emptiness.

Genuine pleasure is received as a gift. Another way of saying this is that gifts are potentially the greatest source of pleasure. Unfortunately, most of our gift giving today is obligatory. It is marked by routine and troweled into our socially determined exchanges. We give because we think it is expected. But although our gift giving and receiving are housed within routines and schedules, we continue to feel excitement about the prospect of giving or receiving a gift. And the reason is that we have had the experience of receiving a gift that we did not know we needed or wanted until it was received. The gift awakened the need and desire. That moment of reception and recognition is a high pleasure. It is the kind of pleasure of which ultimately the Christian faith speaks. It speaks of and offers gifts of grace. Those gifts create or awaken in the recipient as no others can an awareness that all of the desires aroused before by pleasures find their fulfillment in a particular gift. We recognize for the first time what it was all along that we desired and what, finally, delights.[34]

It is not possible to move directly from a culture of self-preoccupation, of life as battle, and of power into the Christian language of gift and grace. If one were to attempt that, the language of gift and grace would become just another way of being important, being different, or being self-preoccupied.

What is required first of all is the willingness to receive, to acknowledge, and to defer to what lies outside the self—things, events, and people. It is in and through relations that a self is given. What is required first of all is a remedy for those habits that prevent us from wanting to be edified and from anticipating and appreciating pleasures as gifts. And the form that remedy can take is the recognition of the primary relations that we should have to the context of our lives.

That context in our own culture has three components. There is a relation with the so-called natural context of our lives, those events and entities that we take as constituting reality. There is our relation to other people, who, whether we like it or not, are different from us. And there is our relation to models of a more just and peaceful common life. When we live in terms of these primary relationships we can have moments of genuine pleasure. Only because we experience moments of genuine pleasure can we begin to understand the language of religion in general and of Christianity in particular.

7

· · · · · · · · · · ·

CELEBRATION

While considering pleasure we looked primarily at the gifts of grace and the states they create as they affect particular persons. Pleasure, as we saw, actualizes the potential in a person for uniqueness. When we turn to celebration the emphasis falls on the communal side of the gifts and states of grace. We shall have to see that the communal qualities of grace do not compromise particularity and that particularity anticipates a communal setting.

Celebration is mainly a matter of relations. The shadow sides of the relations that characterize celebration are difference, opposition, and antagonism. Such shadow sides are especially apparent in victory celebrations. We will have to examine the relation of celebration to competition, conflict, and warfare. Which of the two is more important? Is conflict basic to human life, and celebrations occasional and exceptional moments of respite in a constant situation of strife? Or is celebration basic, and warfare occasional and strategic?

Celebration may seem to play a secondary role in Lewis's work. Struggle, violence, and warfare are the stuff of his plots. Ransom tracks Weston to the fiery pit and, after a long, exhausting struggle, kills him in the name of the Trinity, crushing his head with a stone. Strong stuff! In *That Hideous Strength* the domain of N.I.C.E., which has strengthened its position by acts of public violence and internal repression, is finally overthrown by the forces unleashed from St. Anne's and the hidden powers that Ransom has contacted. Even the Narnia Chronicles, children's stories, recount many bloody conflicts. And these are not isolated moments in the fictions. They culminate stories that

begin in opposition and end in final battles. Confrontations between protago-
nists and their adversaries are central, and the only way to resolve these conflicts seems to be a battle to the death.

In these stories battle is often followed by a celebration. The most important characteristic of a victory celebration is that it occurs at someone else's
expense. After Peter defeats the wicked Miraz, a celebration breaks out: "And
so at last, with leaping and dancing and singing, with music and laughter and
roaring and barking and neighing, they all came to the place where Miraz's
army stood flinging down their swords and holding up their hands, and Peter's
army, still holding their weapons and breathing hard, stood round them with
stern and glad faces."[1] Things really get lively when Bacchus, Silenus, and the
Maenads join the party and begin dancing. It turns into "not merely a dance
for fun and beauty (though it was that too) but a magic dance of plenty, and
where their hands touched, and where their feet fell, the feast came into existence—sides of roasted meat that filled the grove with delicious smell, and
wheaten cakes and oaten cakes, honey and many-colored sugars and cream as
thick as porridge and as smooth as still water, peaches, nectarines, pomegran-
ates, pears, grapes strawberries, raspberries—pyramids and cataracts of fruit.
Then, in great wooden cups and bowls and mazers, wreathed with ivy, came
the wines; dark, thick ones like syrups of mulberry juice, and clear red ones
like red jellies liquefied, and yellow wines and green wines and yellow–green
and greenish-yellow."[2] Lewis spares nothing in elaborating the extent and
vigor of the celebration.

However, a victory celebration always occurs at the expense of someone
else, and there is something unseemly about celebration at someone else's expense. For good reason, coaches teach young athletes to refrain from celebrations that draw attention to the defeat of the opposing team or person. Celebration that is occasioned by the defeat of an enemy not only occurs at the
opponent's expense but also depends on having an opponent to defeat. Does
Lewis give such importance to enemies, conflicts, and victories?

I will argue that, for Lewis, celebration, rather than derived from and dependent on something else, is basic to the Christian life. Conflict plays, relative to celebration, a secondary and strategic role.

I

Celebration in Lewis refers to and is based on the relations anchored in Creation. These relations are inclusive. Celebrations are therefore not limited to
people; animals and plant life are also included. What are celebrated are the re-

lations that we humans have with one another and with nonhuman and even nonliving creatures around us. These relations are not superficial. And they are not occasional. These relations are always there, although sometimes, perhaps most of the time, they are occluded. These relations—and not defeat of an enemy—occasion celebration.

The relations that we have with other people and with the creatures and events of our world are not only inclusive; they are also basic, just as basic as our sense of being particular persons.[3] Our being particular persons and our state of being in primary relations with other people and with other creatures in our world cannot be divorced from one another.

Thirdly, the relations warranted by Creation are internal. That is, they are not simply contractual or constructed; they are relations of continuity, like those among members of a family. When Christians refer to others as brothers and sisters, this is no euphemism or hyperbole. Christians even refer to animals as family members—think of St. Cuthbert and St. Francis, for example. That kind of talk makes sense because of what Christians believe about primary relations with other people and creatures. Lewis assumes and affirms all of that.

Celebration is an occasion when particularity and relations with others, human and nonhuman, are seen not as contraries but as supportive of one another. We tend to think of celebrations as group occasions, and we do not take adequately into account how important particular people are for them. In fact, celebrations, particularly in the common form they take for us, namely parties, are occasions that are designed to dissolve the differences between people by subsuming individuality to some kind of group behavior. On college campuses the very genius of parties seems to be this loss of particularity. Students, who daily are exposed to comparisons with others and to competition for recognition and grades, seem to require parties where, primarily through intoxication, individuals are allowed to enter some state that resembles a least common denominator. In contrast, we have other celebrations at which a person or a few selected people are honored, such as birthday celebrations or award ceremonies. We immediately recognize celebrations of these two kinds, those that absorb particularity into the group and those that exalt particularity. But we are not accustomed to thinking of celebrations as occasions when both the potential of a person and of a group are simultaneously actualized.

In Lewis, celebration is of this complex kind because celebration, when most itself, is celebration of the Creation. It is because Narnia was created by Aslan that celebrations in the Narnia Chronicles actualize the potential of particular and communal at the same time. Positive, even harmonious, relations characterize Creation. Indeed, Creation in Lewis pertains more to relations than to origins. This is clear in *The Magician's Nephew* when the story of the creation of Narnia is told. Narnia comes to birth in response to music. This means that the structure of its relationships, despite the complexity of the structure and the many kinds of creatures that are related to one another, is harmonious. As Lewis writes, "All things are related—related in different and complicated ways. But all things are not one."[4] The contribution of each particular is crucial for the completion of the whole, and the whole itself is a particular that, so to speak, sings a certain song.

It is important to notice that Lewis depicts the creation of Narnia as taking place without a conflict. In this he is faithful to the Creation accounts in Genesis. Unlike the cosmogonic stories of many other cultures, the biblical Creation stories are not marked by combat. The waters that precede the Creation in Genesis could be seen as a kind of opposition to be overcome, a kind of natural resistance. But then look at Yahweh's description of Creation in the Book of Job. There the waters that precede the Creation are described as a kind of child that needs to be contained (Job 38:1–11). This text also validates Lewis's introduction of music during the Creation.

Because celebrations are based on the positive relations established in Creation, they are for Lewis not exceptions to the rest of life but epitomes of it. They bring into focus what is always the case, namely, that people are in relationships with one another and with the nonhuman creatures around them. To put it another way, celebration is a quality of all good and creative actions. For all of Lewis's stress on particularity and its actualization, there is an equal stress on or an equally important assumption of basic, substantial, and positive relations.

The stress on the relational quality of life seems to come to the fore gradually in his work. In *Surprised by Joy*, he emphasizes, as male autobiographers often do, the process of his individuation. Relationships are depicted as occasions toward greater individuation. This may also reflect the fact that Lewis worked in a philosophic tradition that stresses particulars rather than their relations. In *The Abolition of Man*, for example, he stresses moral training and the moral life primarily in individual terms, as, for example, aligning a person's energies and rationality or relating the subjective and objective sides of a person's experience to one another.

But it becomes clear that moral health is relational as much as it is particular. In *That Hideous Strength*, Mark and Jane come to recognize that the rejuvenation of their lives lies not in their competitive individuality but in the mutuality of their marital relations. More important, perhaps, St. Anne's itself, the community of people and animals, is a celebration waiting to happen. This is true even though those who make up the community are all quite different from one another. Lewis makes this clear when, using the analogy of a family to describe human relations, he says, "If you subtract any one member you have not simply reduced the family in number, you have inflicted an injury on its structure. Its unity is a unity of unlikes, almost of incommensurables."[5] In the Narnia Chronicles, community, in terms of the siblings who play the major roles, the cooperation of characters with one another, and the relations of the children with animals and plants, is also emphasized. Edmund's evils are not limited to the distortion of pleasure by his desire to have an unlimited access to Turkish Delight. More important is his betrayal of the other children. Reincorporation within the community is a sign of his forgiveness and restoration.

It is in *The Four Loves*, however, that Lewis addresses the relational character of human life most fully. He defines four kinds of relationships not only to distinguish them from one another and to establish their relative order but also to affirm human life as basically relational. He presents affection, friendship, and erotic love as recurring and beneficent forms of human relations that not only point beyond themselves to charity, a fourth kind of relationship, but find their fulfillment in charity; without charity, other forms of relationships inevitably go awry. Charity, a love that pursues the well-being of the other, is basic to celebration. Charity is not condescension but affirmation, not sacrifice but gift, not control but setting free. Charity counters self-preoccupation because it takes delight in and cares for the other as particular, not as a means but as an end, an end, however, that also becomes a means to find delight in the ultimate source of both self and other. Charity, then, is the recognition of a relation that already exists between a person and others.

Celebrations are like the tips of icebergs. They make us aware of a great deal that is under the surface of life, namely, the basically relational character of our being in the world. Far from being isolated, celebrations stand out because they relate to so much, they bring so much into view. They bring to awareness what we know and want to be true, that we are related. As Lewis says, "If you could see humanity spread out in time, as God sees it, it would not look like a lot of separate things dotted about. It would look like one single growing thing—rather like a very complicated tree. Every individual would appear connected with every other."[6] The doctrine of Creation is more a doctrine of relations than a doctrine of origins. Celebrations are celebrations, finally, of the Creator whose creative act is a great and complex gift of interrelationships.

The question to raise now—a question, I might add, that is as important as it is difficult—is whether celebration in Lewis refers not so much to Creation as to Redemption and Atonement. Some Christian readers of this chapter, if they have persisted this long, will have all along been raising an objection. They have been thinking, "No, what Christians celebrate is not the relations that are constitutive of Creation but the new relations that are established between some people, between them and God, and between them and the wider Creation by Redemption and Atonement. The original relations were broken by the Fall and had to be replaced or restored by new ones." I think this reaction would not be hard to find among Christian readers of Lewis.

This is the heart of the nature/grace question in Christian belief, and Christians disagree on it. This disagreement has been exacerbated during our own century. Many people, both religious and nonreligious, and many Christians, including artists and prominent theologians, were deeply influenced by the disillusionment of the period after the First World War that was further aggravated by the Second World War. People felt betrayed. They felt that the culture had failed to prepare them for the horrors of war, had deceived them about what people are capable of doing to one another, and had concealed the realities of the human condition. It was thought that now we see things as they really are, stripped of the illusions of a liberal or humanist culture. Graham Greene took a kind of delight in walking through bombed-out cities in England during the Second War, for he could see buildings with the fronts torn off and their rooms exposed. There was a sense that, like the facades of buildings destroyed by bombs, the facade of culture had been stripped away to reveal the realities of human life.

Even in the beginning of a new century, this attitude continues to determine many theological interests and debates. Although it is most fully articulated in what is often referred to as neo-Barthian theology, current Christian thought in general is strongly marked by the conviction that the language of Redemption and Atonement must be the first, strongest, and last word in any Christian account of things. The events of the last century, it is thought, have revealed humans and their relations to be broken and lethal. And the only response to this revelation is a language of grace that creates new and separate communities of people in newly created relations. Such Christian spokespersons feel antagonism both toward their surrounding culture and toward other Christians who want still to affirm the doctrine of Creation and the viability of human culture despite the effects of evil in general and the traumas of the twentieth century in particular. In other words, this is not only an important question; it is also a volatile one.

In my opinion, Lewis does not come down in support of neo-Barthians and culture-war evangelicals on the Creation/Atonement issue. I say this while remembering that Lewis served in the First World War, was wounded, and joined the Allied effort during the Second World War by addressing troops and, in enormously effective broadcasts, the English people. I also say this while remembering how important warfare and struggle are in his work. And in saying this I also want to insist that Lewis affirms Creation and culture without becoming, as it is sometimes put, a knee-jerk liberal and without resorting to sentimentality or nostalgia for an earlier Christian humanism that no longer is possible. Finally, I think Lewis's position is a very strong one, worth taking seriously into account. Which, I guess, is another way of saying that I largely agree with it.

First of all, there is no doubt about the importance of Christology in general or of the doctrine of Redemption in Lewis. The person and work of Christ and their redemptive and atoning force and significance are unmistakable, as are also Lewis's insistence on the extent and power of evil in the world. Evil is not something that human beings can overcome within themselves, in their relations with others, or in the world at large. The force of evil and the means to overcome it are most memorably depicted in the suffering and death of Aslan in *The Lion, the Witch and the Wardrobe*.

It is interesting to notice, however, that the children do not dwell on the sacrifice of Aslan. They know that it is grave, painful, and terribly significant, but they do not try to understand it. Although Lucy insists that Edmund should be told of the sacrifice of Aslan even though it will make him feel bad, Susan and Lucy are reluctant to share with him what they have seen. To put it another way, the event does not become the central theme of the Narnia Chronicles. The conclusion we should draw from this, I think, is that for Lewis the doctrine of Atonement, while basic, is not central in a Christian account of things.

There is something about all of this that is consistent with the Christian doctrine of Atonement. What I mean is that Christians have never been able to understand what the atonement was and entails. The doctrine of Atonement is basic, but the atonement itself, what actually was going on there, has always eluded Christians. As Lewis says, "The central Christian belief is that Christ's death has somehow put us right with God and given us a fresh start. Theories as to how it did this are another matter. A good many different theories have been held as to how it works; what all Christians are agreed on is that it does work. . . . Theories about Christ's death are not Christianity: they are explanations about how it works."[7] This means that Christians cannot construct their accounts of the world on an agreed-upon and clear understanding of the atonement. The doctrine is unstable. Some Christians, for example, have understood the Atonement as a set of events by which Satan, who had gained possession of human souls by reason of their sin, is paid off and the souls are ransomed by the sacrifice of Christ. Other Christians have followed St. Anselm, the eleventh-century bishop of Canterbury who, in his *Cur Deus Homo*, developed the theory that by the sacrifice of Christ a debt was paid not to Satan but to God. God's requirement that righteousness be satisfied was met by Christ's perfect sacrifice. There are also moral-influence theories of atonement which contend that the person and work of Christ are, in themselves, so powerful and significant that they can, through contemplation, participation, and imitation, have a transforming effect on the life of a person. This position is often traced to Abelard (1079–1144), although it has had many variations. Lewis, instead of choosing one doctrine of atonement, in one way or another, affirms all three. He is not trying, it seems to me, to be ecumenical and avoid taking sides on this question. Rather he is suggesting that the Atonement, while basic, is not something that we can understand. This means that it cannot be central to, cannot be the lynchpin of, a Christian account of the world.

The next question is whether the sacrifice of Christ and the doctrines of Redemption and Atonement should be central in Christian consciousness. If we cannot make it central to an account of the world because we cannot understand it, should we at least make it central to our consciousness, the way a certain inexplicable injury or terrible loss can burn into our awareness? I think the answer again is "no." I hope that I can explain why. An analogy may help.

It is a very good thing for children to know that the home their parents provide them does not simply fall from a tree. That home is the consequence of considerable effort, sacrifice, and love. Parents should not conceal that fact from their children. If children are not aware that it is not any easy thing to provide a loving and secure home, they will be unprepared to encounter those costs when they themselves set out to marry and have families. But more than that, the truth of the situation will have been hidden from them. They will live in an illusion. To conceal the truth from them is, in some important way, dishonest.

However, it would be mistaken and even cruel for parents to take every possible occasion to rehearse for the children all of the sacrifices and costs they have taken on to provide a home for them. Parents need not share with their children all of their difficulties—unpleasant people at work, the cost of a new roof, their own disputes and incompatibilities. Children need both to be made aware of the costs and to be protected from exposure to the full extent of those costs.

Another way to say this is that children, in their relation to their parents, ought neither to be ignorant of the fact that their parents sacrificed for the home that they enjoy nor should that sacrifice be a central or constant part of their consciousness. They should neither take the home for granted nor beat their breasts on account of their parents who, for their sake, have sacrificed so much.

What would be healthy is this: Children would show their gratitude for the sacrifices of their parents by enjoying and enhancing as much as possible the life of the home that those sacrifices have made possible. And indeed, good parents want nothing so much as that. Parents who support a child in college, to use another example, want that child neither to ignore what it costs them nor to dwell on it. They want the child to participate as fully and profitably in the college experience as possible.

Like the children in the examples above, there tend to be two kinds of Christians. There are those who take the world in which they find themselves for granted. They have a doctrine of Creation, but they tend to think of the world they enjoy as not having cost all that much. They take it, in that sense, as natural. Then there are other Christians who constantly dwell on the cost. When they think about themselves and their world, they think of the sacrifice, that the sacrifice was made for them, and that the sacrifice was undeserved and painful. They feel guilty about everything they enjoy in the world because they are thinking of the sacrifice, like children who cannot enjoy a trip to the zoo because their parents had to pay an entrance fee. The present state of things Christian, it seems to me, is that there are these two kinds of people. There are those who enjoy the world and affirm human life or culture in it but have little or no sense of sacrifice and atonement. And there are those who are so attentive to sacrifice and atonement that they reject the world and culture and retreat to isolated communities.

Lewis, it seems to me, offers a way out of this impasse. That way out is to affirm the basic standing of the doctrine of Atonement but, at the same time, not to make it central. As he says, "Even so, the image [of the Crucifixion] ought to be periodically faced. But no one could live with it. It did not become a frequent motive of Christian art until the generations which had seen real crucifixions were all dead."[8] The way by which one affirms atonement is to be aware of it, periodically to recognize the cost, and to be thankful for its benefits. But also, and more so, one affirms the atonement by enjoying and enhancing life in the world as much as possible, by affirming the Creation and human culture that the atonement assures.

Now we can return to our original question. Is celebration in Lewis celebration of the Atonement? The answer is both yes and no. Yes, in the sense that there would be no creation to celebrate if the threat to primary relations had not been undercut by the Atonement. No, in the sense that what is celebrated is the world that the Atonement makes possible for us, the world, that is, of the Creation, of our relations with other people and with nonhuman creatures.

II

The next thing we need to see is that Lewis, by positing celebration as basic to life, counters a major emphasis of modern culture. Put most succinctly by Thomas Hobbes, when he called human life a war of everyone with everyone else, and given putative scientific basis in the social Darwinism of Herbert Spencer (1820–1903), it is a recurring theme in modern culture that human life is intrinsically agonistic and competitive.[9] We tend to believe that we are basically in a state of actual or potential warfare with one another and that it is the principal role of law and government to keep that warfare from erupting or getting out of hand.

In recent years the stress on conflict as basic to life has been intensified. Perhaps because of the influence of such formative thinkers for postmodernism as Marx, Darwin, Freud, and Nietzsche, conflict is a prominent theme in postmodern theory. Jean-François Lyotard, a typical voice in such theory, understands all human relations as basically agonistic. He says, for example, "I place them [speech acts] within the domain of the agon (the joust) rather than that of communication.[10] And Michel Foucault sees power and the will to control as not merely inseparable from such cultural staples as language and knowledge but also as their determining base.[11] For all the emphasis on playfulness, pleasure, and freedom in postmodernist theory and styles, there is another, grimly dominant theme. We are in a perpetual state of antagonistic relations with other people and with the nonhuman extensions of our world. Under the influence of such theories, life becomes a zero-sum game: your gain is my loss. In this picture of human life, celebration can only be a distraction. The real business of life is conflict.

When life is defined as conflicted, celebrations occur at someone else's expense. They are primarily victory celebrations that depend on the defeat of a competitor or enemy. In this arrangement of things, not only does celebration become secondary and occasional; celebration becomes questionable, even unseemly. For good reason contemporary athletes who play in public arenas are often forbidden to engage in excessive celebration at their opponent's expense.

If conflict is seen as basic to life, celebration can itself be suspect as serving to conceal the real conflicts that lie at the base of society. We should view light-heartedness, play, and celebration as distractions from a more basic, conflicted state of affairs. All celebrations— personal, institutional, national, and religious —must be seen as other than what they appear. Take, for example, Christmas, which is so important in *The Lion, the Witch and the Wardrobe*. A case could be made that Christmas is a celebration intended to hide the political and economic differences, tensions, and conflicts that exist between groups of people in a society. The Christmas crêche, with its mingled shepherds and kings, it can be argued, has the effect of hiding deep economic and political inequalities and injustices and suppressing the possibly violent correction of these social wrongs. Christmas is so popular because it conceals social inequities and injustices. If human life is basically a conflict, celebrations like Christmas must be seen as occasions sponsored by economic and political victors to keep the losers from recognizing that the real situation is defined by unequal power and repression. Such an explanation can as easily be given to national holidays. The celebration of Memorial Day or Independence Day conceals the fact that mortality in combat is not evenly distributed between social, economic groups, and that freedom and justice are not equally available for all.

Applying these ideas to the Narnia Chronicles, we can ask if the many celebrations that occur are victory celebrations. Do they occur at the enemy's expense? And do they actually conceal economic and political tension and inequality? What is the relation in Lewis of celebration to conflict and the defeat of an enemy?

III

At first it may seem that Lewis agrees that conflict is basic to human life. One could argue that he differs from most modern social theory only in that he defines the nature of that conflict not as political and economic but as moral and spiritual.

I do not think that Lewis agrees that life is basically conflicted. Lewis does not separate moral and spiritual issues from material and visible ones. More important, he affirms that life is primarily celebrative rather than agonistic. It is conflict and warfare that are secondary and hide the real nature of human life.

There appears to be abundant evidence to argue against my assessment of Lewis. At a number of points he steps outside the dramatic needs of his plot to remark explicitly on the conflicted nature of human life. In his autobiography, reflecting on the tensions and conflicts of his school days, he says, "To this day the vision of the world which comes most naturally to me is one in which 'we two' or 'we few'. . . stand together against something stronger and larger."[12] As a schoolboy he retreated into the protection and relative peace of the library, suggesting that the culture of texts offers some place apart from the harsh, even brutal, realities of society. And warfare was the defining characteristic of the world in which he emerged as a young scholar and did his most characteristic and influential work.[13]

Not only the context but also the style of his work is marked by battle. Lewis was a consummate debater and polemicist, a person who relished a good argument. He seems to have really found his intellectual stride when engaged in verbal combat. Polemic and disagreement mark his work. Even his more purely academic studies are oppositional; for example, he writes against the modernist assumption that interest in medieval cultures is retrograde and that they are not worth taking with intellectual seriousness.

His advocacy of English literary culture is also marked by conflict. He mounts an outspoken campaign against current representatives of literary culture for what he takes to be their disregard for the care and perpetuation of literary value. He offers cruel caricatures of clergy as well, as in *That Hideous Strength* and *The Screwtape Letters*, suggesting that in the struggle to propagate Christian faith he at times feels unsupported by the church. His belief that the academic community was being taken over by scientific assumptions that increasingly were applied to human life and behavior and his accusations that the academic community was both elitist and bureaucratic put him on the margins of the literary and academic establishments. Both the church and the university were as much his opponents as his allies. With few exceptions his work was antagonistic, and conflict marks its setting and its thrust.

Let us return to a particularly graphic example, Ransom's conflict with Weston in *Perelandra*. What is striking is that the shift from verbal debate to bodily struggle is presented as a necessary progression. It becomes necessary for Ransom not only intellectually or verbally to resist Weston and reduce his influence on the Queen of Perelandra; it becomes necessary to wrestle with him physically and to kill him. This is because moral and spiritual enemies take on physical forms, a kind of inverse incarnation, and these forms need to be engaged and destroyed. The progression not only implies Lewis's justification of warfare and execution but also seems to imply that conflict is inevitable and fundamental to human life and that this conflict must eventually move from argument and debate to physical combat.

The conflicts and battles in the Narnia Chronicles are not child's play and are not included simply as a form of entertainment. The message to his young readers seems to be quite clear: Life is one conflict after another because human life is primarily a big war with occasional respites. During respites celebrations can break out, marking the temporary cessation of war and a partial victory over the enemy. Otherwise, celebrations conceal war or divert attention from it, and war is the primary characteristic of human life. As the children are summoned into Narnia because some campaign requires their help, so youthful readers are summoned to view their own world as chiefly marked by moral conflicts and battles in which they are not too young to join.

There seems to be ample basis, then, for conscripting Lewis into current, so-called culture wars or into the theological task of setting Christianity in total conflict with modern culture. But are we correct in aligning Lewis with those theorists, secular and religious, for whom conflict not only marks human life but also basically defines it? In order to resist such a conclusion we should look again at the relation between warfare and celebration in the Narnia Chronicles.

When we first enter Narnia in *The Lion, the Witch and the Wardrobe*, we find ourselves in a world under the influence of a wicked witch whose principal goal is to kill joy, to stop celebration. Her success is epitomized by the fact that in Narnia there is constant winter and never any Christmas. Later in the story, Edmund makes a significant move in his recovery from error when the witch turns creatures into stone in the midst of their festive meal. Edmund reacts strongly to her action. We are told that it was the first time that he felt sympathy for someone other than himself.[14] Nothing marks Jadis more than her antipathy toward celebrations. She and the evil she embodies are set against them.

The principal consequence of evil, then, is to destroy the conditions and finally the possibility for celebration. Evil not only perverts pleasure, as we have seen; it also is threatened by and counters celebration because celebration reveals primary relations. Consequently, the principal goal for those resisting evil is, for Lewis, to emancipate the conditions for celebration and to celebrate. The occasion for celebration is not the defeat of the enemy; celebration is not parasitic and does not depend on enemies. Nor is celebration a way to conceal or repress the tensions and conflicts of life. Celebrations articulate what life basically means and is. The purpose of warfare is to lift the evil siege of life that is constantly repressing or concealing the conditions and potentials for celebration. Celebration follows warfare in Lewis's stories because victory removes the obstacles to celebration.

Agents of evil, like Jadis, are threatened by celebration and try to prevent it because celebration is communal. Evil pits individual against individual and group against group in a struggle for power. In the empire of evil, one increases at another's expense. People lose their particularity and are absorbed by the collective. Celebration, in contrast, is a communal event, and in genuine celebration the particularity of participants is released. Celebration counters both individuality, defined as nonrelation, and collectivism, defined as the absorption of particular persons into some anonymous or homogenous whole. Celebration is an event that expands human life. It reveals relations between humans and between humans and the larger world. Celebration is the opposite of hell, therefore, which in *The Screwtape Letters* is marked by competition and absorption, by simultaneous stress on competitive individualism and mass collectivity. As the opposite of hell, then, celebration directs the attention of the participant and of the reader to heaven.

Celebration in Lewis is not only a human event. It also includes the nonhuman world. Animals and all of life suffer under the reign of evil and are liberated when its siege is lifted. Human life comes into its own when it begins to recognize not only the relations that exist between persons but the relations that exist between people and their nonhuman context. Animals are not alien to humans in Lewis's version of things, and they look to humans for their deliverance from the abuse and disdain that evil imposes on them. Lewis's lifelong campaign against the mistreatment of animals, particularly in scientific experiments, is only an example of the larger emphasis in his work on our relation with and responsibility toward the nonhuman world. Celebration is communal not only in its human inclusiveness; genuine celebration is all-inclusive.

We can see the principal ways by which evil cancels the conditions for celebration from the effects Jadis has on Narnia. Her acts are reductive (turning animals into stone statues), homogenizing (causing the constant winter), intimidating (deploying her Gestapo-like henchmen), and controlling. The conditions that make for celebration, then, are vitality, diversity, trust, and freedom. These conditions are not limited to human life. The right relation of human beings with animals and plants, for Lewis, is not one of control but of cultivation and release. Animals and plants are vitalized by Jadis's removal, and, as they suffered under the effects of her tyranny, they join in the celebration made possible when the spell of that tyranny has been lifted.

These dynamics and their significance seem to suggest that Lewis, in countering one modern assumption, may have swallowed another, namely, the notion that life is defined primarily by energy or vitality. But vitalism, whether in its Romantic or late modernist forms (Bergson, Shaw, and D. H. Lawrence), is not the point of it at all. True, Lewis would side with vitalists of various stripes against the political, social, and economic forces that reduce or abstract human life. His interest in the Romantics can be taken to include their espousal of spontaneity and freedom against the force of technology and social, political control.

However, while the Narnia Chronicles rejoice in celebrations and Bacchus features in them, it is not finally with some kind of vitalism that Lewis leaves us. For while Bacchus is released by the defeat of Queen Jadis in *The Lion, the Witch and the Wardrobe* and again by that of King Miraz in *Prince Caspian*, the celebrations are not bacchanalian. If they were, the particularity of participants would again be threatened by absorption, by another kind of homogenization, and by reduction, by becoming less than what they are. At celebrations Bacchus is present, but, more important, so is Aslan.

These are neither celebrations of vitality nor celebrations of achievements. They are finally not even celebrations of human life or of life in general. They are celebrations of Narnia, of a particular world, a world made possible by its creation and by that strange, painful business that averted the threat to its existence. What is celebrated is Narnia and all that it contains and allows, and celebrating Narnia is the primary way by which Aslan, as its Creator and Redeemer, is celebrated, too.

Lewis's theory of basic relations of persons to one another and their world is his principal point of difference from modern and postmodern views of human life. It explains why celebration, which is communal, is fundamental for him and why competition and conflict are at most occasional and superficial.

As earthly moments of celebration and edification reveal the Creation and direct attention to the future and the eternal, so earthly competition and reduction point toward hell. Lewis is intent on drawing relations between actions and attitudes in ordinary life that point toward heaven and those that point to hell. Indeed, when human life is taken as a zero-sum game, when it moves toward homogenization, when it is fundamentally conflicted, and, when it is controlled bureaucratically, it not only begins to resemble hell but is actually continuous with it.

Lewis offers a statement of hell's philosophy in *The Screwtape Letters*. It is a philosophy of external relations, competition, and conflict. It is a summary of the philosophy by which many people live today, which is implied by their attitudes and actions. Let us hear Screwtape as, in a clear policy statement, he articulates the underlying belief of modern society and the official dogma of hell:

> The whole philosophy of Hell rests on recognition of the axiom that one thing is not another thing, and, specially, that one self is not another self. My good is my good and your good is yours. What one gains another loses. Even an inanimate object is what it is by excluding all other objects from the space it occupies; if it expands, it does so by thrusting other objects aside or by absorbing them. A self does the same. With beasts the absorption takes the form of eating; for us, it means the sucking of will and freedom out of a weaker self into a stronger. "To be" *means* "to be in competition."[15]

The doctrine of external relations, which Lewis presents as the basic dogma of both hell and modern culture, is inseparable from its political and social consequences. It means that every other entity is an external obstacle and a potential threat to me, defined, as I am, by self-interest. Particular people increase at the expense of others. The fittest and most powerful survive.

I do not think, however, that Lewis calls for an end to all competition. While competition is often continuous with the philosophy of hell, it need not be. Competition can be seen as a form of imitation and as the way in which progress occurs. When a child, for example, sees an adult do something, the child may want to do it, too. The realization of "I can do that, too" can easily lead to "I can do that differently" and even, "I can do that better." I do not think that Lewis distrusts this cultural process by which imitation moves toward advancement. Indeed, at many points he speaks against a homogenized culture, one that fails to allow for the recognition of excellence and the ability of some people to do certain things better than others. What he rejects is the notion that human beings come into their own primarily by means of opposing one another, by dynamics of difference and opposition. He would not translate, as Herbert Spencer does, the putatively antagonistic relation that animals have with one another into a description of human relations. As he says, "It is our business to live by our own law not by hers [Nature's]: to follow in private or in public life, the law of love and temperance even when they seem to be suicidal, and not the law of competition and grab, even when they seem to be necessary to survival."[16] Indeed, he would argue, I think, that our perception that animals are unavoidably antagonist to one another is at least in large part a projection of attitudes that we have accepted as defining the relations of people to one another. For Lewis, animals have real or potential internal relations both to one another and to human beings. The doctrine of external relations and inevitable antagonism shapes our understanding of competition. Even more, our understanding of competition is based on our characteristic self-preoccupation. As Lewis says, "Now what you want to get clear is that Pride is essentially competitive—is competitive by its very nature—while the other vices are competitive only, so to speak, by accident. Pride gets no pleasure out of having something, only out of having more of it than the next man. . . . It is the comparison that makes you proud: the pleasure of being above the rest."[17] Competition becomes a very different kind of thing when it is based not on opposition and self-interest but on the primacy of human relations and a desire for the well-being of other people and for Creation as a whole.

IV

To return to our question: Does celebration as presented by Lewis serve to conceal injustices, inequalities, and conflicts? This question is made more insistent by the fact that Lewis seems to have a less than sharp eye for political, economic, and social inequities. Not only can he be gender elitist and, perhaps even more disturbing in the context of a children's book, *The Last Battle*, racist, he also appears politically elitist in his affirmation of hierarchy and of royalty, especially in the Narnia Chronicles.

In response to this very important question, I think we must acknowledge that Lewis shares the racist, sexist, and homophobic aspects of mid-twentieth-century white, male culture. And it will not do to argue in his defense that his culpability is less than that of many of his well-known literary contemporaries. It should be said that Lewis did not take adequately into account how social, political, and economic factors affect the relations of people to one another and to the nonhuman context of their lives. The "wicked witch" represents much of the structure by which our daily lives are organized and under which many people suffer. One of our advantages over Lewis is that we are in a position more critically to assess the connections between theological or ontological statements about human relations and the effects of social, economic, and political arrangements.

However necessary it is to amend Lewis on these points, we must not dissolve ontological and theologically described relations into social or economic ones. Neither should we obscure the belief that humans are in states of primary relations with one another and with their world. The difficult task is to retain a more complicated and finely calibrated analysis of social evil while retaining the sense of internal relations and of the communal character of Creation. It is easier to subject Christian faith to political interests than to subject political interests to Christian faith. It is far easier to subject Christian faith to self-interests than it is to subject self-interests to the reality that Christian faith affirms, the relational character of human life. Political beliefs and critiques must be made forceful in Christian thought and practice without positing difference and conflict as more basic to human life than internal relations and celebration.

It should also be said that Lewis was not entirely unaware that forms of evil not only create the homogenizing, controlling, and arrogant powers of bureaucratic structures but also create political, social, and economic injustices. For example, at the end of *Prince Caspian* captives are released and the sick are healed. In *Mere Christianity* Lewis calls for Christians constantly to transform their relation to money by giving it away and giving until giving makes a difference to the giver. He also declares himself to be a democrat, although it is not because he has faith in the choices that people make but rather because he does not trust one or a few to rule over the many.[18] On the economic side, he suggests that if we were to come upon a truly Christian society we would probably find it more socialist than we expected.[19]

Lewis also wants to see Christians with the appropriate training and vocation placed in positions where political and economic factors are paramount so that they can employ their faith in that work. Lewis does not go very far himself in articulating what it would take to liberate the captives or redistribute wealth. But if celebration is basic, then limited conflict is warranted when its goal is to remove the conditions that militate against celebration, including, by implication, social, political, and economic repression and injustice. The doctrine of primary relations that celebration brings to light forces us to be conscious of the relations that we have with other people and with the non-human creatures with which we share the earth, relations that have strong political and economic dimensions The trick is to retain a critical eye and a combative readiness without falling into conformity with hell's philosophy.

The stances and strategies of conflict are always alien to the Christian. The goal of conflict is not to overcome the enemy but to overcome the conditions that make the other an enemy. No celebration is complete until all the conditions that militate against celebration are removed and until all who can possibly be included in the celebration find their places in it, including, it is hoped, the former enemy.

V

When Dante, in *The Divine Comedy*, enters the heaven of fixed stars, the eighth circle of the Ptolemaic cosmos, he enters under his own sign, Gemini. This signifies that he enters as no one else or as anything less than his own very self. But in the completion of his journey he joins a multitude of those who have preceded him.[20] The sense of fulfillment is at one time both highly singular and fully communal. The culmination of Christian faith, hope, and love can be seen as nothing less than that.

We must keep in mind that for Lewis all moments of celebration, all moments when self-actualization and communal completion coincide, are gifts. All celebrations have an eschatological direction and point beyond themselves to the final feast.

As we have seen, the language of grace has lost much of its force in our culture because gift giving has become part of our economic practice. However, there is a kind of gift giving that stands out as different from the giving of gifts as part of a system of required payments and of being repaid. It is the gift I receive and do not know that I so deeply and fully want until I receive it. A gift is truly a gift when in receiving it I become aware for the first time of what all along I have lacked and for which I have always hoped.

For Lewis, celebration is a gift of that kind. When a person enters into and is included by a celebration, that person receives the capacity to recognize how primary, internal, and substantial are our relations with other persons and with the world. The sense of inclusion is the reception of grace. It is a recognition that one is now what one wanted and needed to be all along, a valued and even indispensable part of a much larger and richer whole.

The fullest form of grace is the moment when a person is incorporated into an occasion as though he or she were the one who all the time was wanted to make the celebration complete. It is as though the lack referred to above as "John and Janet" is filled because John and Janet heard the call and felt, as never before, needed. It is the call and incorporation that the children in *Prince Caspian* or *The Last Battle* feel when they find themselves summoned to Narnia. It is the corporate that creates that possibility, and it is the particularity of the person called for that articulates what in the corporate is lacking. As Lewis says, "Your soul has a curious shape because it is a hollow made to fit a particular swelling in the infinite contours of the divine substance, or a key to unlock one of the doors in the house with many mansions. For it is not humanity in the abstract that is to be saved, but you—you the individual reader, John Stubbs or Janet Smith."[21] To recognize that within completion there is a lack that only you can fill is to be awakened for the first time to your potential particularity. The sound of one's name and the welcoming fulfillment in the community create the moment when particular and communal are inseparable. It is the heart of celebration.

Celebration is homecoming; it is being taken in by a will to fill the house. The fullness is not quantitative; it is a fullness of irreplaceable particulars. It is like the individual voices in a piece of polyphonic music, each indispensable to the whole.

Celebration, then, is incorporation that grants particularity. It is the basic direction of all things. It is that for which the whole creation groans. It is that for which we most deeply long and that we grow weary waiting for.

From without this may resemble narcissism, this longing to hear one's name and to be incorporated within a fullness as an indispensable and irreplaceable particular. But it is narcissism's opposite. It is not a matter of bringing a world to the self or mistaking the self for the world; rather, it is a desire to be summoned by and incorporated in a world that precedes, outstrips, and is more significant than the self. It is a world without which a self could never be conferred and a world that is so gracious and commodious as to receive each particular as though without it the sense of the whole could not have been achieved.

It is crucial to the moral and spiritual improvement of our own culture that we clarify and enhance a shared sense of the relationships that we do and can have. It is only in appreciation of constant, primary, and internal relations that genuine celebration can occur. And it is only people who know what celebration is because they have experienced it who can begin to understand what religious hope, the language of grace, and the Christian vision imply.

CONCLUSION

The question that we have been postponing until now must finally be faced. What would it be like to attempt a project similar to Lewis's here on American soil? One cannot simply transport the house that Lewis constructed to these shores and move into it. We can visit his and get a feel for what a comparable construction would be like, but it is not possible to avoid building again. Positioned as we are in a different time and culture, we cannot simply appropriate Lewis.

Indeed, Lewis would not want us to. He had a firm sense of history and the particularity of cultures, and he would recognize that what may have done the job in his time and place would not be adequate or appropriate to ours. More than that, he had a strong sense of the impermanence of any construction, including theological ones: "My idea of God is not a divine idea. It has to be shattered time after time. He shatters it Himself. He is the great iconoclast."[1] Lewis wrote that during a particularly dark period of his life, but it is a comment consistent with his position on the relation of conscious constructions to changing times and conditions. I do not think Lewis would want us to shirk the difficult work of giving our own account of the world, one that our attitudes and actions presuppose and our moral vision and spiritual longings point to. Constructing a Christian account of things cannot mean simply using the accounts of others, however helpful other accounts may be. I think he would especially be amused by Protestant Christians who, while recoiling from the Catholic idea of benefiting from the good works of saints, are ready to include themselves within his theological good work and to treat Lewis as a kind of Protestant saint.

The question of what it would take to begin a project similar to Lewis's here and now is too complex to answer fully in a few pages. I shall only sketch a plan for such a beginning, a project that would give us a more positive relation to our culture, especially our literary culture, than we seem now to have.

To begin with, the cultural criticism that Lewis aimed at modernity continues largely to be relevant to our own situation. While it is far from uniform, modernity has retained most of the characteristics that Lewis deplored and attacked. Postmodernist reactions to modernity have changed academic and literary culture so that they are more aligned with Lewis's interests and style, but substantial continuity remains between our present cultural situation and modernity.[2] Lewis's cultural critique and his alternative way of giving an account of the world continue to apply.

There are, however, two main differences between Lewis's relation to modern culture and our own. The first is that there remained in English culture recognizably religious resources yet within reach that could be retrieved, resources that the acids of modernity had not corroded. This is less true of our situation today. American culture has been far more identified with the flowering (if that's the right word) of modernity than English culture, and we are a half century further along in that process than was Lewis. Consequently, the response to modernity here must take more the shape of reconstruction than of retrieval.

The second difference is that Lewis could look to a far more homogeneous culture and a more shared religious identity than can we. English society was diverse in his day but not nearly so diverse as it is today. And even present-day English society is not as diverse as our own. If a generally Christian account could work in Lewis's time and location, it cannot be general enough to work for us. While Lewis operated somewhat aside from the restrictions of an institutionally specific form of Christianity, we have to step back even further than he did to engage a work analogous to his own. We shall have to draw on much more diffuse cultural potentials to support a religiously useful account of the world and of our relations to and within it.

The fact that the moral and spiritual aspects of our literary tradition are less retrievable and less Christian than were his throws doubt on the project. However, while one cannot be sanguine about the results, it is not an effort that we should abandon. The effort itself has value irrespective of results. But I would also venture to say that there is enough evidence to anticipate that significant results, while not guaranteed, are likely. Those of us who are involved in the study of religion along with other Americans who are concerned about the moral and spiritual well-being of our culture have a responsibility not to hold only a critical, negative attitude to contemporary culture but to propose projects for its cure. Even more, we should not retreat from the challenge into the security and relative simplicity of our own separated faith communities. As responsible people we should work assiduously toward the clarification of shared beliefs or of beliefs that we as Americans can or should share. I think, in fact, that were Lewis on the scene today, he would robustly join—perhaps even lead—such an effort.

While the sources of sharable beliefs are not readily accessible and the cultural situation is deteriorating, it would be a mistake to conclude that there are no resources available or no audience ready to receive them. It is not the case that the effects of modern culture on American life leave us without any cultural resources at all upon which to draw in order to articulate shareable beliefs. Difficult as it may be, we can and must speak in public about the moral and spiritual needs and potentials of American culture. However incomplete the results, the work must be undertaken and sustained.

The work also must be undertaken even for the sake of religious people who lack connections with the wider culture. It is not possible to have healthy religion within the context of an unhealthy culture. Cultural deficiencies and distortions seep into the churches. In fact, it can be argued that the sense of distance from and disdain for American culture that religious people express is itself an effect of the culture. For a principal characteristic of that culture is to form identity by opposition and disdain and to think of oneself as not affected by or related to others. American culture is above all a culture of taking exception or of being an exception. The prevailing means of identity formation in American society reflects what is most problematic about modern culture, namely, the dogma of external relations by which it lives. It follows that Christian despisers who withdraw from the culture because of its weak moral and spiritual condition mimic the culture in securing identity by separation, rejection, and opposition.

Moreover, to despise modern culture is to demonize it. To do so is adolescent. As Julia Kristeva points out, it is a Romeo and Juliet model of bonding, the attempt to create community by projecting and magnifying a common threat.[3] The attempt to build unity between Christians by casting the rest of culture in the role of an enemy suffers from this Romeo and Juliet negative-identity syndrome.

While there is much to reject, oppose, and correct in the culture, there also are traits that need to be surfaced and reinforced. What is called for is neither wholesale rejection of the culture nor uncritical endorsement of it. Needed instead is a sagacious discrimination of those aspects of American culture that can be related to traditional beliefs, beliefs that may yet provide some support for more adequate accounts of the world and of our relations within and to it.

In an important paper, Robert N. Bellah asks if there are beliefs that Americans share.[4] He points out that Americans share a culture created by such factors as their common form of government, their common language, and their common orientation to the market. Americans also share the means by which this culture is conveyed, the educational system and the mass media. Bellah then goes on to add another common element of American culture, its individualism. The principal argument of his essay is that American individualism is grounded in religious belief, namely, belief in the sacredness of personal freedom and conscience. The conclusion he draws is that Americans are multicultural not out of indifference or a bland tolerance but out of a more positive conviction concerning the sanctity of a person's and a group's right to form and to follow their own beliefs.

I think that Bellah is right on this point. But I also think that he neglects a larger cultural context in which the belief in the sanctity of individual freedom and conscience should be seen. If we bring that larger context into view, I believe that we will have more to draw on as we try to identify moral and spiritual strains in American culture.

I propose that Americans actually share more than Bellah's essay allows. I believe that there is a surprisingly rich and complex moral and spiritual content to American culture that can be retrieved and shared. This content is not a watered-down version of some more full-fledged Christian theology and morality. Nor is this content to be understood as the sort of general religiousness characteristic of all human cultures, something that American culture has simply by virtue of being a culture.[5] The moral and spiritual content of American culture has an identifiable source, character, and history. This content is in the present time heavily taxed and diluted. Nonetheless, right now it still is there, still available to be retrieved, reconstructed, and redeployed, although it may not be there for long!

The common life of the Republic was shaped by and developed within a sapiential religious system, a set of beliefs, norms, and practices whose primary source and warrant was the Wisdom books of the Bible. Ingredients of that sapiential religious system, albeit attenuated and scattered, persist in our culture today. The primary sites of these beliefs are literary.[6]

A sapiential religious system carries beliefs that can be shared and can operate without ecclesiastical sponsorship. One reason is that in the Wisdom literature the person is central. Wisdom texts focus on individuals: Job, Qoheleth, the young men being trained in the classrooms from which much of the material in the book of Proverbs may have been drawn, or the heroes of such Wisdom tales as the story of Joseph in Genesis. However, the individual in these texts is located, as we shall see, in a set of relationships. Individuality in Wisdom is relational.

Wisdom texts served the public interests of the Republic by being neither institutional nor parochial. They address humanity in general and in inclusive terms. The appeal is not to a special people, not to a people who stand in contrast or opposition to their neighbors. Wisdom in ancient Israel was an international phenomenon. Solomon, the biblical patron of Wisdom, conversed about wisdom with heads of other states.

Wisdom literature provided usable texts for the emerging Republic not only because they focused on the individual and because they were not institutionally specific but also because they stressed the importance of experience and everyday life. Wisdom offers a guide and response to living in the ordinary world. Wisdom provides accounts of the world and of the place of people in it. It addresses all areas of ordinary life, and it represents Wisdom as, among other things, the accumulation of insights and truth drawn from experience. These general characteristics of Wisdom go a long way to explain why biblical Wisdom literature could provide the basis for a common American culture and allow many beliefs and values crucial for American culture to be recoverable yet today.

In addition to these general characteristics, wisdom texts advance three more specific beliefs or affirmations concerning the relation of persons to their world. All three were major factors in the development of American culture, and all three beliefs continue to have an effect today.

The first is that human beings, if they are not to go awry, must maintain a relation with the natural context of their lives. There are many appeals in Wisdom literature to the authority of the natural context of human life. Those who are instructed by Proverbs are enjoined to observe animals and plants, for example. The natural context of life is not merely used as a source of metaphors to clarify moral and spiritual issues. Rather, human beings are asked to align themselves with the natural. Human life is increasingly falsified when it drifts away from its attachments to and alignment with its natural context. So, in the Book of Job, Yahweh rebukes Job for his failure to relate his own situation to the cosmic context of his life. Yahweh doesn't ask Job to consider such events as the Exodus from Egypt or the conquest of Canaan, but to consider the beasts in the mountains and under the sea, the great trees, and the storehouses of snow.

This belief that human life must constantly renew its relationship or alignment with nature continues in the Western, Christian tradition, becoming increasingly important toward the end of the sixteenth century. While it comes into American life earlier, we can pick it up during the founding of the Republic in Tom Paine and in the Jeffersonian agrarians. We can trace it from there through such literary writers as Cooper, Melville, Twain, Cather, and Hemingway down to the present day in such contemporaries as John Gardner, Annie Dillard, Norman Mailer, and E. Annie Proulx.

I realize that the category of the "natural" is, today, problematic. Many people live entirely in humanly made and controlled environments. All natural places are owned by someone or by some nation. There is also no place where one can see nature without the effects of human constructions inscribed on it—even the sky offers not only clouds and stars but also planes and satellites. Nevertheless, "natural" continues as an important cultural contrary not, as in the past, to "supernatural" but to "humanly constructed and controlled." There is no clear or fixed boundary dividing the natural from the humanly constructed, but we have a strong sense that some things are more natural than others. The natural has prestige as base and resource, and the natural has value that is morally as well as physically beneficial. While these qualities of the natural are cheapened and eroded by the marketplace—"the natural way to fight constipation" or "the natural look created by this hair coloring"— normative use of "natural" in advertising suggests its continuing significance and authority. The natural has force as a value in our culture.

A retrieval and reconstruction of this belief would not posit the natural as something independent from and unrelated to human culture but would affirm the cultural standing of the "natural" and of our relation to it. It would mean trying to locate as fully as possible where the natural comes to expression. It would involve a quickening of our desire, deep as it is in American cultural history, for the natural. We are enlarged and we live in a larger world, a world that draws us away from self-centeredness, when we turn from the work of our own hands and bring the natural into awareness.

I think that Americans from differing backgrounds and religious orientations or lack of them could agree on this belief. They could agree that a relation with the natural context of human life in terms both of appreciation and responsibility is a valuable and beneficial part of American culture. The various reasons for affirming this belief need not be resolved or even addressed. For example, there are many reasons why people have become environmentally aware, reasons that run along differing religious identities, cultural values, and personal convictions. Many kinds of people for many reasons share beliefs about responsibility toward the natural context of our lives. One of the reasons that this development is beneficial for the culture is that it provides a public, sharable counter-thrust to narcissism. People recognize that they are related to a larger world and that this relationship needs to be taken into account. Unfortunately, the ecology movement tends to fall into oppositional configurations that compromise its role as a belief that Americans could share. What needs to be emphasized, and our literary culture can help here, is that internal relations with the natural context of our lives have a moral and spiritual significance that is crucial to our shared identities as Americans.

The second sapiential affirmation concerns human diversity. The Wisdom literature takes a positive stance in relation to the fact that people differ from one another. Joseph in Egypt neither lives as though in a place that only will defile him nor denies or compromises his own cultural origins and religious identity. In the Proverbs we find warnings to keep the complexities of human interactions in mind. The fool is a person who fails to appreciate differences between people, differences of age and gender, for example. The Wisdom literature carries within it many signs of contributions from other cultures, such as Egypt and Mesopotamia. Wisdom neither rejects people of other cultures nor ignores or collapses the differences between people and cultures. There are all the marks of internal relations, of dynamics of difference and similarity, between people. Diversity is not first of all a problem; it is a resource.

There is a tradition in American cultural history of celebrating diversity, seeing human life as expanded and enriched by it. I have in mind texts by Roger Williams, William Penn, Benjamin Franklin, Thomas Jefferson, and W. E. B. Du Bois and the fiction of Hawthorne, Henry James, Willa Cather, Faulkner, Jack Kerouac, Ralph Ellison, and Bernard Malamud. Our writers and other artists are ahead of the rest of society in this regard, and we should listen to and follow them. Diversity should be recognized in American culture not as a problem or as something only to tolerate. It should be recognized as carrying enormous, positive moral and spiritual potential. And it should be recognized as part of what it means to be American.

A Lewis-type reconstruction of cultural diversity would stress internal relations between people not only in spite of but also because of their differences. This means that I am both continuous and discontinuous, like and unlike someone who is different from me by virtue of gender, race, culture, sexual orientation, or religion. My relations with that person constitute an exploration into the complex of difference and similarity; I do not know beforehand how much of each there will be. That exploration will lead me to understand how important other people with other cultures are, how they grant access both to a larger human world and to the particularity of persons and groups. From diversity we learn that cultures carry moral and spiritual content that creates and reinforces right relations between people and their world. A Lewis-like reconstruction of this belief would recognize both the differences and the continuities between human cultures. It would remind us that despite their differences religious people and others concerned about the moral and spiritual well-being of Americans have more in common with one another than they have with those who live only by the prevailing values of the market culture or view other people as unrelated and even as threats to themselves.

American life is now marked by greater and more sharply defined cultural diversity than ever before. Diversity has become undeniable and unavoidable. Rather than fear or flee it, Americans, especially religious people and others concerned about the moral and spiritual health of our society, should attend to it. They can affirm that people are always already in relation to one another, and these relations can be positive rather than negative, affirming rather than rejecting. Christians must become aware that they, perhaps more than others, have good reasons to view other people positively. People of differing cultural and religious backgrounds may have differing reasons than Christians for affirming internal relations with people with whom they differ, but these differing reasons need not be resolved for the force of the belief to be released.

Religious communities need to formulate positive accounts of the relations of their adherents to differing people. Diversity in American society seems less affirmed by religious than by nonreligious people. Indeed, religion seems more the basis for separation and conflict between people than for an affirmation of their positive relations to one another. Given this situation, it seems to me that religious people and especially Christians should formulate clear and forceful arguments as to why the differences that mark American life are a resource and not simply a problem or threat. The challenge is to develop positive, internal relations with people of differing faiths and cultures that do not require an attenuation of one's own religious identity and location.

The third belief of a sapiential religious system is that people should imagine a better, more morally and spiritually resonant common life for the future. Wisdom texts, especially Proverbs, project the future as a realm in which human life may more fully participate in Wisdom itself. Wisdom underwrites an imagination of the whole and of a goal. Its forward thrust is inclusive, corrective, and edifying.

This vision is an integral part of our literary tradition. Many of our writers, as Irving Howe put it, "establish a realm of values at a distance from the setting of actual life, thereby becoming priests of the possible in a world of shrinking possibilities."[7] Indeed, American identity is upheld by a line of visionaries who run almost without interruption from John Winthrop, who gave us his shipboard sermon on a "City upon a Hill," to Martin Luther King Jr., who gave us his view of the future from Mount Nebo in Washington, D.C. Although the stress of Emerson is on self-reliance, his moral and spiritual interests are not limited to the individual. Life is also, for Emerson, a pilgrimage toward a celestial city.[8] And like him Thoreau and Whitman do not neglect the vistas of a more inclusive and peaceful common life. Their legacy continues to be borne by such varied writers in recent times as Flannery O'Connor, J. D. Salinger, Kurt Vonnegut Jr., and Thomas Pynchon.

The problems of our society, its violence, its vulgar materialism, its habits of exclusion and competition, and its injustices, seem to overwhelm the moral imagination and its capacity to propose more equitable and spiritually enhancing possibilities. But this belief and this activity in American life should be reaffirmed and celebrated. A Lewis-like effort in this direction would try to undo the hold on us as Americans of addictive dreams of power and pleasure that sap and sour not only our moral vision but our capacity to entertain one. We are not, in our moral capacity, threatened so much by the size and complexities of the problems as by the diversion of our capacity for imagining the moral into self-gratifying national, group, and individual projections. It is part of our culture as Americans not to tire of imagining a better society, a society with the kinds of internal relations that Lewis projects, an American Malachandra. Could we have a society in which people, without ignoring immediate and concrete problems, would also have constantly in view what it might mean to create a more just and civil common life? I realize that the complexities and problems of American social and economic conditions daunt the imagination and that visionaries and reformers can easily be intimidated by the typical bureaucratic appeal to efficiency and cost. The last few decades have seen a growing fatigue of the moral imagination in our society, especially in young people. But we should recognize that there is still receptivity to the call to envision and create, on however small a scale, a more just and civil society. Belief in the possibility of becoming morally better not just as individuals but as a people, of providing a better life for others as well as for ourselves, has not been wholly suppressed by competitive ideologies and the lure of personal aggrandizement.

Again, Americans of differing religious orientations and nonreligious people concerned with social justice will come at this project with different motivations. But those differences need not be resolved or even addressed. The shared desire for a more just, joyful, and peaceful common life is what is important. And the most urgent task, it seems to me, is for those who reject what is destructive and divisive in our culture to articulate what kind of alternative common life might be possible. Such people, including those who argue a religious and even Christian basis for their objections to American culture, too often imply or even insist that the negative aspects of American culture are irremediable. The question that must be put to them is not only what kind of common life their criticism aims for but also how that alternative culture might be encouraged to emerge. The urgent need is to mobilize the energy that is now given to protesting and taking exception and to direct it toward formulating alternative accounts of how things should be. For the great damage attending the loss of moral imagination is the death of the desire for a more fully human life. The anger and frustration that mark so much of American life do not stem only from injustice and oppression. They also reflect the failure of the culture to encourage and enable people to articulate for themselves what in our common life needs to be changed and to imagine the kind of world that would be less harmful to all of us.

Many American readers of Lewis will not want to engage in such acts of cultural reconstruction. They will want to keep their religion to themselves as a warrant for their own self-concerns. They will deny that the kind of cultural work that Lewis engaged needs to be done here anew. They will not accept that without such work Christianity also cannot escape cynicism and self-preoccupation. But proponents of the reconstitution of culture in American life cannot be shouted off the stage as long as the remnants of a hope in the future persist in public life.

American religion is so often bizarre, haphazard, or jejune because religious people in this country have been cavalier with regard to the common culture. The terms for reconstruction lie yet at hand, although scattered and attenuated, largely in American literary culture. Our Lewis-like task is the long and slow process of gathering these fragments, reconstructing, and redeploying them. The goal is to foster a culture that emphasizes a shared sense of right relations between people and their environment, between people and their neighbors, and between people and future prospects for a common life. When that culture has begun to restore our humanity, Christians can then turn to the larger task of giving a more specifically Christian account of the world and recommending it to their nonreligious neighbors as coherent and revealing.

This project carries the risk of falling into errors. Sapiential religious systems were once themselves exclusive, and their adherents tried to discredit other religious systems, especially more institutionally specific ones. The beliefs I have rehearsed need to be understood as limited and not as displacing other, more fully religious belief systems. They are beliefs that people can share, and they can be approached from different directions and affirmed for differing reasons. Sapiential cultural beliefs ought to be the bath water that supports the rubber duckies of religious institutions and communities. My great concern is not that people without religious identity will resist affirming these beliefs or even making them, say, structuring components of educational curricula for public schools. What concerns me is that Americans with distinctive religious identities will see the affirmation of shared beliefs as the reappearance of that monster, liberal or cultural Protestantism with all its prejudices and entrenched institutional power. The goal cannot and should not be the restoration of a religious culture, even a vaguely Protestant one. Religion and culture, while open to, requiring, and completing one another, should also be kept apart. One advantage that our own time and place give us over Lewis is that we will not be tempted, as perhaps he was, by nostalgia for a Christian culture.

Cultural norms and beliefs do not constitute a religion, even though they may have their sources in an identifiable religious system. I am not calling for a civil religion. I am not arguing that a shared set of cultural beliefs is all we need to meet our moral and spiritual needs. On the contrary, I think that if these beliefs and the relations they warrant were to inform our common lives, they would point beyond themselves to higher and fuller relations. And these further directions can only be articulated by the more fully developed religious beliefs and practices that traditional religions provide.

I do not want to speak too freely for Lewis. But if my sketch for the retrieval and reconstruction of a more viable culture and my call for beginning a Lewis-like project on our shores and in our time have been to any degree compelling, it may be possible at least to say that Lewis, were he with us, would throw his weight behind this project. Indeed, I think that he would do more. He would engage it in such forceful and ingenious ways that those of us who work at it haphazardly and with little effect against all that opposes it would find ourselves carried along by his wake.

NOTES

Introduction

1. Charles H. Lippy, *Being Religious, American Style: A History of Popular Religiosity in the United States* (Westport, Conn.: Greenwood Press, 1994), pp. 4, 7, 9. There are, of course, many Americans whose belief systems conform to those of the religious institutions with which they are affiliated. And, at the other end of the spectrum, there may be an equal number of Americans who do not find it necessary or possible to hold a worldview at all, particularly one fashioned to any degree according to moral and religious beliefs. But I agree with students of popular religion in America that there is a large percentage, perhaps a majority, of Americans who experience a significant degree of cognitive dissonance with the tenets of the religious tradition or institution with which they are identified but do not think of themselves for that reason as any less religious. Such people resemble those with no formal affiliation who, for contrary reasons and moving from contrary positions, are also engaged in the task of giving accounts of their world and place in it, accounts that to some degree include or support explicit moral and religious beliefs.

2. See R. Laurence Moore, *Selling God: American Religion in the Marketplace of Culture* (New York: Oxford University Press, 1994).

3. Nicholas Wolterstorff, *Reason Within the Bounds of Religion* (Grand Rapids: William B. Eerdmans Publishing Co., [2d ed.], 1984), p. 75.

4. Since the category of "nature" or the "natural" arises in Lewis often and since I use it, too, it would be good to point out that neither he nor I use the term as though it refers to something that is not conditioned by language and culture. "Nature" and "natural" are always culturally conditioned categories. For an excellent study of the differing ways in which the category of the "natural" has been used in the history of Western culture, see Peter Coates, *Nature: Western Attitudes since Ancient Times* (Berkeley: University of California Press, 1998). We shall take up the question of "nature" as a category in American culture in the Conclusion of this book.

5. See my *Take, Read: Scripture, Textuality and Cultural Practice* (University Park: Pennsylvania State University Press, 1996).

1: Retrieval

1. "I should like to be able to believe that I am here in a very small way contributing ... to the encouragement of a better school of prose story in England: Of story that can mediate imaginative life to the masses while not being contemptible to the few." C. S. Lewis, "On Stories," in Walter Hooper, ed., *Of This and Other Worlds* (London: Collins, 1982), p. 42.

2. C. S. Lewis, *Preface to Paradise Lost* (Oxford: Oxford University Press, 1967 [1942]), p. 53. Stanley Fish is well known for his collapse of the distinction between rhetoric and literature and between knowledge and power. See his *Doing What Comes Naturally: Change, Rhetoric, and the Practice of Theory in Literary and Legal Studies* (Durham, N.C.: Duke University Press, 1989).

3. I have not included a brief but significant chapter in my narrative of the American reception of Lewis's work, namely, the role Lewis played in the formation of the Yale school of theology during the post–World War II period. A crucial text is Paul L. Holmer's *C. S. Lewis: The Shape of His Faith and Thought* (New York: Harper and Row, 1976). Holmer, who was thoroughly acquainted with Lewis, attributes to him some of the crucial intellectual moves and assumptions of his own and, by extension, of his colleagues' work. It would be worth measuring the direct and indirect influence of Lewis on the work not only, then, of Holmer but also of such otherwise differing scholars as Paul Ramsey, Hans Frei, and W. H. Poteat.

4. For a discussion of the complexity of postmodernist developments in literary studies and the moral deficiencies they contain, see my *"Take, Read:" Scripture, Textuality and Cultural Practice* (University Park: Pennsylvania State University Press, 1996), especially chapter 3, "Postmodernism: Not Reading Anything at All As Though It Were Scripture."

5. See C. S. Lewis, *Surprised by Joy: The Shape of My Early Life* (New York: Harcourt Brace & Co., 1956), pp. 174–81.

6. Terry Eagleton, *Literary Theory: An Introduction* (Oxford: Basil Blackwell, 1983), pp. 31, 32.

7. Ibid., p. 27.

8. See also Fred Inglis, *Cultural Studies* (Oxford and Cambridge: Blackwell, 1993), especially "English for the English," pp. 27–58.

9. For an excellent study of the status of Idealism, especially Hegelianism, in Oxford in Lewis's time, see Franklin Arthur Pyles, "The Influence of the British Neo-Hegelians on the Christian Apology of C. S. Lewis" (Evanston, Ill.: Northwestern University, Ph.D. diss., 1978). See also James Patrick, "C. S. Lewis and Idealism," in Andrew Walker and James Patrick, eds., *Rumors of Heaven: Essays in Celebration of C. S. Lewis* (Guilford, Surrey, Eng.: Inter Publishing Service Ltd., 1998), pp. 156–73.

10. See, for example, "The New Men," which is the concluding chapter of his *Mere Christianity* (New York: Macmillan, 1960 [1943]), pp. 169–75.

11. He records the role in his intellectual/spiritual development that Owen Barfield played in ridding Lewis of his "chronological snobbery," that is, "the uncritical acceptance of the intellectual climate common to our own age and the assump-

tion that whatever has gone out of date is on that account discredited." *Surprised by Joy*, p. 207.

12. "Though we ought always to imitate the procedure of Christ and His Saints this pattern has to be adapted to the changing conditions of history." C. S. Lewis, *Present Concerns*, ed. Walter Hooper (San Diego, New York, London: Harcourt Brace Jovanovich, 1986), p. 61.

13. Lewis, *Surprised by Joy*, p. 208.

14. Human temporality is vexed by the perennial problem that temporality is not only marked by both continuity and change but also that it is not possible beforehand to say in what the change and continuity will consist or how much of each there will be. I take this problem in human temporality to reside, *mutatis mutandis*, as well in the relation of human cultures to one another. The interpreter, whether working with other historical periods or with the cultures of other peoples, must be prepared to learn in each case in what the differences and continuities will reside and how much of the one and how much of the other there will be.

15. For example, Lewis begins his *The Problem of Pain* in this autobiographical way: "Not many years ago when I was an atheist. . . ." He then goes on to use his own previous anti-Christian views as typical of the cultural objection to Christianity that it is the intention of the book to address. Lewis, *The Problem of Pain* (New York: Macmillan, 1962), p. 13.

16. C. S. Lewis, *The Pilgrim's Regress* (London: Geoffrey Bles, 1945 [1933]), p. 5.

17. *Surprised by Joy*, p. 168.

18. Lewis refers to self-preoccupation primarily in the traditional language of self-regard and pride. I shall often be using the term "narcissism" as what I take him to have in mind by the form that self-preoccupation takes in modern culture. The term suggests that what preoccupies is not simply the self but an image of the self. I think that Lewis would agree with this characterization of modern self-concern.

19. C. S. Lewis, *Reflections on the Psalms* (London: Geoffrey Bles, 1958), p. 40.

20. C. S. Lewis, "Religion without Dogma?" in his *God in the Dock: Essays on Theology and Ethics*, ed. by Walter Hooper (Grand Rapids: William B. Eerdmans, 1970), p. 131.

21. Richard W. Ladborough, "In Cambridge," in James T. Como, ed., *C. S. Lewis at the Breakfast Table and Other Reminiscences* (New York: Macmillan, 1979), p. 103.

22. See C. S. Lewis, *That Hideous Strength* (New York: Macmillan, 1946), pp. 61–68.

23. C. S. Lewis, *Reflections on the Psalms*, p. 112.

24. Alan Bede Griffiths, O.S.B., "The Adventure of Faith," in Como, ed., *C. S. Lewis at the Breakfast Table and Other Reminiscences*, p. 15.

25. See "Literary Impact of the Authorised Version," in C. S. Lewis, *They Asked for a Paper: Papers and Addresses* (London: Geoffrey Bles, 1962), pp. 26–50.

26. Lewis's principal opponent is post-Christian, secular culture. He does not offer a Christian account of the world in opposition to other religious accounts. For Lewis religious people of various kinds have more in common with one another than any of them has with modern, post-Christian secularism or skepticism: "The gap between those who worship different gods is not so wide as that between those who

worship and those who do not." C. S. Lewis, *De Descriptione Temporum* (London: Cambridge University Press, 1955), p. 7.

27. A question arises as to whether or not Lewis tries to argue people into Christian belief, and it often arises in relation to John Beversluis's book, *C. S. Lewis and the Search for Rational Religion*, a book in which Beversluis argues that Lewis's attempts fail. See, for example, the discussion of this matter in "Reflections on C. S. Lewis, Apologetics, and the Moral Tradition: Basil Mitchell in Conversation with Andrew Walker," in Walker and Patrick, eds., *Rumors of Heaven: Essays in Celebration of C. S. Lewis*. My position on this question is that Lewis tries to argue that a Christian account of the world is more adequate and coherent than competing, secular accounts. This is something less than trying to use rational arguments to lead inevitably to Christian belief. One could, for example, conclude that neither account, religious nor nonreligious, is compelling.

28. Lewis, *The Problem of Pain*, pp. 23–24.

29. Christology generally and the doctrine of Atonement particularly hold clear positions in Lewis's theology that are both crucial and unusual. We shall take up these matters more directly in the essay on celebration.

30. Peter Bayley, who, as a student, knew Lewis and who himself became a literary scholar, says of him, "his greatest [strength] lay in extraordinary powers of clarification and illumination. His weakness lay in this very strength: he could not resist oversimplification and beautifully neat conclusions." Peter Bayley, "From Master to Colleague," in Como, ed., *C. S. Lewis at the Breakfast Table and Other Reminiscences*, p. 81.

31. C. S. Lewis, *The Voyage of the "Dawn Treader"* (New York: Harper Collins Publishers, 1980 [1952]), pp. 115–16.

32. Matthew Arnold, "Literature and Dogma: An Essay Towards a Better Apprehension of the Bible," in *Dissent and Dogma*, R. J. Super, ed. (Ann Arbor: University of Michigan Press, 1968), p. 182.

33. Lewis, *The Problem of Pain*, especially pp. 26–54.

34. See his *Miracles: A Preliminary Study* (New York: Macmillan, 1960).

35. Lewis, *Mere Christianity*, pp. 165–66.

36. See, for example, *The Screwtape Letters* (New York: Macmillan, 1961), p. 73.

2: Reenchantment

1. ". . . I sometimes wonder whether we shall not have to re-convert men to real Paganism as a preliminary to converting them to Christianity." C. S. Lewis, *Present Concerns*, ed. Walter Hooper (San Diego New York London: Harcourt Brace Jovanovich, Publishers, 1986), p. 66.

2. What are being described here are cultural tendencies and dominant attitudes. Lewis, it is important to remember, does not dismiss the culture entirely because of these characteristics. Nor does he claim that all people have been so affected by the negative characteristics of modern culture that they are incapable of, for example, genuinely courageous or charitable acts unless they have replaced religious or

Christian attitudes for those inculcated by the dominant culture. Indeed, as we shall see in the chapter on Character, Lewis prized highly the continuing virtues in the culture despite the influence within the culture of attitudes he deplored. I would say the same of our own culture today. Religious and secular cultural criticism that is only negative obscures and damages those aspects of the culture worth affirming. Indeed, the task of the cultural critic is to discriminate the positive and negative in the culture from one another.

3. Language of this kind recalls the address of Friedrich Schleiermacher to the cultural despisers of Christianity, an address in which Schleiermacher radically altered, even reversed, the terms by which Christianity should be viewed and understood. This address of 1799 is often cited as an important turning point in the history of Christian theology, one in which Christian theology became hostage to the drifts of cultural currents. One must, however, be careful here. As we shall see later, Christian theology is not a fully developed and fixed project, for Lewis, one that, like a completed structure, needs only a vacant lot to locate itself. As I pointed out in the previous chapter, cultures change, and these changes require not only recastings but new understandings of religious belief and practice. Furthermore, Lewis would not, as do many who cite Schleiermacher's moves as misguided, treat the problem as one necessarily caused by giving a positive reading to human culture. Lewis does not respond to the cultural despisers of religion by becoming a religious despiser of human culture, although he has serious problems with some dominant characteristics of modern culture.

4. C. S. Lewis, *Present Concerns*, p. 85.

5. See Anthony J. Cascardi, *The Subject of Modernity* (Cambridge University Press, 1992), especially the chapter "The disenchantment of the world," pp. 16–71.

6. William Golding, *A Moving Target* (New York: Farrar, Straus, Giroux, 1982), p. 99, and *The Hot Gates* (New York: Harcourt, Brace and World, Inc., 1966), pp. 100 and 87.

7. C. S. Lewis, *Rehabilitations and Other Essays* (London: Oxford University Press, 1939), p. 17.

8. Holmer stands out among interpreters of Lewis's work both in his recognition of Lewis's identification of this assumption as basic to modern culture and in his recognition of the refutation of this assumption as central to Lewis's project. Paul L. Holmer, *C. S. Lewis: The Shape of His Faith and Thought* (New York: Harper and Row, 1976), p. 56.

9. C. S. Lewis, *The Abolition of Man* (New York: The Macmillan Company, 1947), p. 13.

10. Ibid, p. 21.

11. For a fuller description of these developments and their formative roles in the production of modern culture, see my *"Take, Read": Scripture, Textuality and Cultural Practice* (University Park: Pennsylvania State University Press, 1996), pp. 41–45.

12. Screwtape, for example, urges Wormwood to use humility as a way of leading the "patient" to discount the value of the talents he possesses. "By this method thousands of humans have been brought to think that humility means . . . clever men trying to believe they are fools." *The Screwtape Letters*, p. 64.

13. See C. S. Lewis, *Mere Christianity* (New York: Macmillan Publishing Company, 1960 [1952]), p. 57.

14. Let me quote a passage in which Lewis is explicit about the limits or counterbalances that should be placed on the typical strategies of scientific inquiry. What he calls a "regenerate" scientific method would have these characteristics: "When it explained it would not explain away. When it spoke of the parts it would remember the whole. While studying the *It* it would not lose what Martin Buber calls the *Thou*-situation." C. S. Lewis, *The Abolition of Man*, p. 49.

15. While I strongly agree with Paul Holmer that Lewis does not operate from the general modern separation of fact and value from one another, I tend to see Lewis's project as more complex than Holmer takes it to be. I think that Lewis upholds the usefulness and legitimacy of both reduction and separating fact from value as marks of modern methods of rationality and analysis that need not be rejected. But those methods are particular strategies that should be housed within a culture that arises from primary relations and that offsets analysis by reduction with an analysis or interpretation that expands and edifies. See Holmer, p. 56.

16. Examples of these theological moves, in the order in which I list them, would be those basic to the work of Rudolf Bultmann, Reinhold Niebuhr, and Karl Barth.

17. See Kenneth Surin, "*Contemptus Mundi* and the Disenchanted World: Bonhoeffer's 'Discipline of the Secret' and Adorno's 'Strategy of Hibernation'" in *Journal of the American Academy of Religion*, Vol LIII, No. 3 (September, 1985), pp. 383–411.

18. C. S. Lewis, *The Abolition of Man*, p. 44.

19. For Lewis's discussion of pride as the root of sin and his reliance on St. Augustine concerning this matter, see his *The Problem of Pain*, p. 75.

20. C. S. Lewis, *Surprised by Joy* (New York: Harcourt Brace and Company, 1956), p. 107.

21. C. S. Lewis, *The Abolition of Man*, p. 35.

22. Ibid., p. 38.

23. It could be argued that "shared values" constitute no less than does a situation free of them conditions in which an adult can impose will on children. Lewis would respond to this rejoinder, as we shall see in the chapters on Culture and Character, by arguing that what is taught is both the way by which students are incorporated within the values of the culture and the way by which those values are both affirmed and questioned. Lewis is not opposing collective values to individual values. Rather, he is contrasting a situation in which it is acknowledged that both teacher and students already operate within a structure of values. The values already there should be acknowledged, examined, and, when possible, affirmed or, when necessary, challenged.

24. In an excellent essay on Lewis and H. G. Wells, Thomas C. Peters comments, "Perhaps the most unsettling of Lewis's arguments against Wells is that scientism leads in the end to evil." Thomas C. Peters, "The War of the Worldviews: H. G. Wells and Scientism Versus C. S. Lewis and Christianity," in David Mills, ed., *The Pilgrim's Guide: C. S. Lewis and the Art of Witness* (Grand Rapids, Michigan: William B. Eerdmans Publishing Company, 1998), p. 217. While I agree with this conclusion, I hope that I have

made clear how and why this occurs. It does because what Peters calls "scientism" is really the ideology of the arrogant, modern self freed from restraint by the removal of primary relations of actual or potential value with the larger world, both human and non-human.

25. It is doubtful, however, that Ransom would have provided Devine the kind of plaque of appreciation that he puts up at the site of Weston's death, had Devine been his final adversary rather than Weston.

26. C. S. Lewis, *Out of the Silent Planet* (New York: The Macmillan Publishing Company, 1965), p. 30.

27. See *Surprised by Joy*, pp. 132–148.

28. For Lewis, as for St. Augustine, evil is the perversion of good and requires good for its existence. Evil does not have a content or being of its own but is parasitic. "What we call bad things are good things perverted. This perversion arises when a conscious creature becomes more interested in itself than in God, and wishes to exist 'on its own.' This is the sin of Pride." C. S. Lewis, *Preface to Paradise Lost* (New York: Oxford University Press, 1967 [1942]), p. 66. It should be pointed out, however, that this quotation could easily create a misinterpretation of Lewis because of its context in his discussion of "Paradise Lost" and Satan. Lewis affirms the whole intermediary world between an individual person and God as providing a large context in relation to which an alternative to pride and self-centeredness is offered.

29. Paul L. Holmer, *C. S. Lewis: The Shape of His Faith and Thought*, p. 25.

30. Lewis does not address this issue directly. I think that he would agree that at times it may be beneficial to human beings to address them and their interests in ways consistent with modern forms of analysis. For example, disputes may be settled or long-term solutions of social problems can be projected in ways that, by being detached or abstract, may be more effective than if proposed with a sense of relation between the investigator or theorist and the interests of particular people. The key consideration, then, is the condition that such stances are defensible because they are beneficial in particular cases.

31. Quoted from her autobiographical sketch, "The Longest Way Round," by Walter Hooper, *C. S. Lewis: A Companion and Guide* (London: Harper Collins Publishers, 1996), p. 58.

32. When Lewis describes science within the context of a human culture, he describes scientists who, among other things, "would not be free with the words *only* or *merely*." *The Abolition of Man*, p. 49.

33. C. S. Lewis, *That Hideous Strength*, p. 255.

34. *Surprised by Joy* (New York: Harcourt Brace and Company, 1956), p. 169.

35. See Max Weber, *Economy and Society*, Vol 3, pp. 950–1736.

36. C. S. Lewis, *Present Concerns* p. 83.

37. *The Abolition of Man*, p. 45.

38. C. S. Lewis, *The Four Loves* (New York: Harcourt Brace and Company, 1960), p. 170.

39. Ibid., pp. 118–19.

40. See C. P. Snow, *Two Cultures and the Scientific Revolution* (Cambridge University Press, 1959).

41. For a valuable study of the assumption that to be modern means basically not to possess or be affected by culture see Bruno Latour, *We Have Never Been Modern*, trans. Catherine Porter (Cambridge, Massachusetts: Harvard University Press, 1993).

42. I think that one of the reasons why Lewis does not agree with the cultural assessments of most of his literary contemporaries such as those I already have mentioned—T. S. Eliot, Graham Greene, and William Golding, for example—is that he does not share the belief that the world wars stripped away the illusion of culture and revealed the human condition or human nature to be what it really is. There is, for him, no view of reality apart from culture. There are particular times, such as in acts of analysis or comparison, when it is desirable as much as possible to view something as though the view were free from culture. But the object and the view in such cases are, for him, artificial and abstract.

43. Paul L. Holmer, *C. S. Lewis*, p. 86.

44. C. S. Lewis, *The Abolition of Man*, p. 44.

45. "The individuality of the Absolute points up the doctrine of the concrete universal. . . . The individual exhibits the particular instance of a universal." ". . . he [Lewis] completely rejected the teaching that the Absolute is not a particular. . . ." Franklin Arthur Pyles, "The Influence of the British Neo-Hegelians on the Christian Apology of C. S. Lewis," (Evanston: Northwestern University Ph.D. Dissertation, 1978), pp. 41 and 42.

46. We shall address this matter in Lewis of the mutuality of particulars and the whole in the chapter on Celebration.

47. "Great stories take us outside of the prison of our own selves and our presuppositions about reality." Colin Duriez, "The Romantic Writer: Lewis's Theology of Fantasy" in David Mills, ed., *The Pilgrim's Guide*, p. 103.

48. C. S. Lewis, "On Three Ways of Writing for Children" in *Of This and Other Worlds*, Walter Hooper, ed., (London: Collins, 1982), pp. 64–65.

49. Arthur Pyles, "The Influence of the British Neo-Hegelians on the Christian Apology of C. S. Lewis," p. 55.

3: Houses

1. C. S. Lewis, *Surprised by Joy: The Shape of My Early Life*, p. 10.

2. Gaston Bachelard, *The Poetics of Space*, trans. Marie Jolas, foreword by Etienne Gilson (New York: The Orion Press, 1964), pp. 61–63.

3. Ibid., pp. 17–18.

4. Ibid., pp. 81–88.

5. Ibid., pp. 91–104.

6. I have already indicated that Lewis, primarily by the range of his cultural interests and critiques, the variety of genre, and his rhetorical style, seems more at home in a postmodernist than in a modernist academic setting. This is also the case with his willingness to understand a person's or group's relation to their world primarily in textual terms. I would add, in relation to the textual theory implied in his work, that, unlike those theories derived from Jacques Derrida, Lewis retains some sense of the par-

ticularity of texts in addition to their interrelatedness. This does not mean that Lewis is assuming some kind of autonomy for texts or some point in or behind them of origination. It is consistent with so much of his work that Lewis would, in the present debates about texuality, take a position that would avoid the options of "canon" and "writing," that is, either the autonomy of texts or their lack of particularity. All of the splits that plague debates on these and related issues Lewis would try to avoid because they reveal assumptions about human life as basically defined by contraries and oppositions. I tend to agree with him on these points. See my *Story, Text and Scripture* (University Park: Pennsylvania State University Press, 1988), pp. 119–24.

7. Lewis sees a major change occurring in Western culture during the opening decades of the nineteenth century due largely to the increasing dependence of human culture on machines. This dependence turned attention to the latest and newest, since improvements in machinery displaced the value of what they superseded. See his *De Descriptione Temporum* (London: Cambridge University Press, 1955), p. 11.

8. Not only does Lewis believe that premodern texts should be part of the house of contemporary English culture, he also advocates a medieval way of relating to the past, that is, with a strong sense of appreciation for and continuity with it. While he neither undermines a historical sense nor promotes anachronism or nostalgia, he does see periodization in particular and a sense of distance from or discontinuity with the past as typically modern and highly questionable habits of mind. See, e.g., his *Discarded Image: An Introduction to Medieval and Renaissance Literature* (Cambridge: Cambridge University Press, 1964), pp. 183–84.

9. Fredric Jameson, "Postmodernism and the Cultural Logic of Late Capitalism." *New Left Review* 146 (1984): 64.

10. Lewis comments on the stimulating potential for the imagination that such microcosms offer in *Surprised by Joy*, p. 7.

11. See his essay, "On Stories," in Walter Hooper, ed., *Of This and Other Worlds* (London: Collins, 1982), p. 27.

12. C. S. Lewis, *Out of the Silent Planet* (New York: Macmillan, 1965), p. 32.

13. C. S. Lewis, *Perelandra*, pp. 63, 65.

14. William James, *The Varieties of Religious Experience: A Study in Human Nature* (New York: Collin Books, 1961), p. 57.

15. Rudolf Otto, *The Idea of the Holy*, trans. John W. Harvey (New York: Oxford University Press, 1958).

16. C. S. Lewis, *Mere Christianity* (New York: Macmillan, 1960), p. xi.

17. C. S. Lewis, "Dogma and the Universe," in *God in the Dock: Essays on Theology and Ethics* (Grand Rapids: Eerdmans, 1970), p. 45.

18. C. S. Lewis, *A Grief Observed* (New York: Seabury Press, 1961), p. 33.

19. See, for example, the essays in David Mills, ed., *The Pilgrim's Guide*. While all of them are valuable studies of Lewis's work and complicate one's understanding of it fruitfully, some of them do have an edge to them, a desire to conscript Lewis in some ongoing theological or cultural war. While Lewis was a warrior, he saw the battle lines not defined by theological points but by a more inclusive understanding of the world. Differences are recognizable in terms of the sense of the world and of one's place in it. For Lewis, a religious, and especially a Christian, sense of being in

the world is a more capacious, complex, and open sense than is that of alternative, secular accounts.

20. There are many points at which Lewis makes clear that his project is not one that poses Christianity in opposition to other religions but one that poses Christianity as an alternative account of things to the principal forms of Western secularism, namely, materialism and narcissism. His view of other religions in their relation to Christianity tends to be a rather traditional Catholic view, namely, that other religions anticipate Christianity and find their fulfillment in it. This is nowhere more firmly or clearly stated in his work than in the character of Emeth in *The Last Battle*. Emeth, whose name means "truth," lived outside the domain of Aslan but is included in that domain at the end by virtue of his desire to live truthfully.

21. C. S. Lewis, *The Problem of Pain* (New York: Macmillan, 1962), p. 25.

22. Although many instances of this move could be cited, one of the more influential is George A. Lindbeck, *The Nature of Doctrine: Religion and Theology in a Postliberal Age* (Philadelphia: Westminster Press, 1984). See my response to this book in *Bound to Differ: The Dynamics of Theological Discourses* (University Park: Pennsylvania State University Press, 1992), pp. 37–40.

23. See Pierre Bourdieu, *Distinction: A Social Critique of the Judgement of Taste*, trans. Richard Nice (Cambridge, Mass.: Harvard University Press, 1984).

24. The difficulty of affirming social space is an aspect not only of Lewis's work but also, it appears, of his life. The "Inklings," a group of friends and colleagues who shared ideas and work in progress, formed a social space that stood, at least in some ways, as an alternative to the general college climate at Oxford. Lewis seemed to be, of all the participants in the group, its most devoted member. "Jack held meetings of the Inklings in his rooms for fifteen years, until one horrible Thursday in October 1949 when nobody turned up." George Sayer, *Jack: C. S. Lewis and His Times* (New York: Harper and Row, 1988), p. 152.

25. C. S. Lewis, *The Magician's Nephew* (New York: Harper Collins, 1955), p. 8.

26. Ibid., p. 146.

27. C. S. Lewis, *Arthurian Torso: Containing the Posthumous Fragment of the Figure of Arthur by Charles Williams* (London: Oxford University Press, 1948), p. 105.

28. See Max Weber, *Economy and Society*, vol. 3, pp. 950–1136.

29. C. S. Lewis, *Present Concerns*, p. 63.

30. See John Sears, *Sacred Places: American Tourist Attractions in the Nineteenth Century* (New York: Oxford University Press, 1989).

4: Culture

1. Kathryn Tanner, *Theories of Culture: A New Agenda for Theology* (Minneapolis: Fortress Press, 1997), p. 157.

2. C. S. Lewis, *Present Concerns,* ed. Walter Hooper (San Diego: Harcourt Brace Jovanovich, 1986), p. 61.

3. A classic study of this question and of the ways Christians have differed in their response to it is H. Richard Niebuhr's *Christ and Culture* (New York: Harper, 1951).

4. C. S. Lewis, *The Discarded Image: An Introduction to Medieval and Renaissance Literature* (Cambridge: Cambridge University Press, 1964), pp. 43–47.

5. Paul Holmer, *C. S. Lewis: The Shape of His Faith and Thought* (New York: Harper & Row, 1976), p. 94.

6. C. S. Lewis, "On Stories," in *Of This and Other Worlds*, ed. Walter Hooper (London: Collins, 1982), p. 39.

7. The reader could easily expect to find a reference at this point to Clifford Geertz and his definitions of culture and of religion, especially his "Religion as a Cultural System" in *The Interpretation of Cultures: Selected Essays* (New York: Basic Books, 1973). While Geertz is valuable for his inclusion of religion within culture, a move important to anthropological attitudes toward religion, he does not, it seems to me, grant a way of securing the difference and possibly critical relation between religion and culture that Lewis retains. While there are hazards in retaining distinctions between reality, culture, and religion, there are greater hazards in occluding those distinctions. Again, Lewis wants to see the three as separable but not as separate.

8. Lionel Adey, *C. S. Lewis: Writer, Dreamer, and Mentor* (Grand Rapids: William B. Eerdmans, 1998), p. 90.

9. C. S. Lewis, "Lilies That Fester," in *They Asked for a Paper: Papers and Addresses* (London: Geoffrey Bles, 1962), p. 110.

10. This situation finds its full expression in Screwtape's frustrated attempts to understand the "Enemy's" motives. They are motives that simply cannot be understood and that must be distorted in and by the "culture" or total lack of culture in Hell. The "culture" of Hell is one built entirely on self-interest.

11. C. S. Lewis, "First and Second Things," in *God in the Dock*, p. 281.

12. E. M. W. Tillyard and C. S. Lewis, *The Personal Heresy: A Controversy* (London: Oxford University Press, 1939), p. 30.

13. C. S. Lewis, *The Abolition of Man* (New York: Macmillan, 1947), p. 13.

14. "The dogmatic belief in objective value is necessary to the very idea of a rule which is not tyranny or an obedience which is not slavery." C. S. Lewis, *The Abolition of Man*, p. 46.

15. See C. S. Lewis, *The Abolition of Man*, p. 9, and *The Problem of Pain* (New York: Macmillan, 1943), p. 17.

16. "It is by these steps that I have come to regard as the greatest of all divisions in the history of the West that which divides the present from, say, the age of Jane Austen and Scott." "For in the world of machines the new most often really is the better and the primitive really is the clumsy." C. S. Lewis, *De Descriptione Temporum* (London: Cambridge University Press, 1955), pp. 11, 12.

17. "Yet Lewis's quarrel is not with the scientific method. It is with the bogus priests of technology and progress who would apply science to all of life in such a way that the spirit dwindles or is channeled into an evangelistic, well-placed secularism." Corbin Scott Cornell, *Bright Shadow of Reality: C. S. Lewis and the Feeling Intellect* (Grand Rapids: William B. Eerdmans, 1974), pp. 116–17.

18. *The Abolition of Man*, p. 37.

19. Ibid., p. 35.

20. Ibid., p. 57.

21. Ibid., p. 69.

22. Lewis does not carry over his collapse of the distinction between rhetoric and poetry into a collapse of the distinction between culture and forms of social, political, and economic power. This is because he wants to see culture as the regulatory and directing context of power, analogous to the "chest" that orders and regulates human energies and impulses.

23. Lewis, *Present Concerns,* p. 7.

24. See John Guillory, *Cultural Capital: The Problem of Literary Canon Formation* (Chicago: University of Chicago Press, 1993), and Pierre Bourdieu, *Distinction: The Social Critique of the Judgement of Taste*, trans. Richard Nice (Cambridge, Mass.: Harvard University Press, 1984).

25. See Lewis's preface to "Screwtape Proposes a Toast" in *The Screwtape Letters*, p. 151.

26. Tillyard and Lewis, *The Personal Heresy*, p. 30.

27. We shall address the relation in Lewis of the doctrines of Creation and of Redemption to one another in the chapter on Celebration. However, to prevent misunderstanding, it should be noted that, as we shall see in the next chapter, Lewis posits discontinuity between the self that must be rejected or abandoned and the self that is received or put on.

28. Barbara Herrnstein Smith, *Contingencies of Value: Alternative Perspectives for Critical Theory* (Cambridge, Mass.: Harvard University Press, 1988).

29. Among the many studies of this kind, one of my favorites is Timothy Mitchell, *Colonizing Egypt* (Berkeley: University of California Press, 1991).

30. Steven Connor, *Theory and Cultural Value* (Oxford: Basil Blackwell, 1992).

31. Stanley Fish, *Doing What Comes Naturally: Change, Rhetoric, and the Practice of Theory in Literary and Legal Studies* (Durham, N.C.: Duke University Press, 1989), p. 156.

32. C. S. Lewis, *The Discarded Image*, p. 6.

33. C. S. Lewis, *An Experiment in Criticism* (Cambridge, Mass.: Harvard University Press, 1961), p. 138.

5: Character

1. C. S. Lewis, "The Weight of Glory," in *They Asked for a Paper* (London: Geoffrey Bles, 1962), p. 210.

2. C. S. Lewis, *The Screwtape Letters* (New York: Macmillan, 1961), p. 56.

3. C. S. Lewis, *Mere Christianity* (New York: Macmillan, 1960), p. 55.

4. Ibid., p. 57.

5. Ibid., p. 64.

6. Ibid., pp. 64–65.

7. "I am a democrat because I believe in the Fall of Man. I think most people are democrats for the opposite reason." C. S. Lewis, *Present Concerns*, ed. Walter Hooper (New York: Harcourt, Brace, Jovanovich, 1986), p. 17.

8. C. S. Lewis, *The Abolition of Man* (New York: Macmillan, 1947), pp. 39–43.

9. Ibid., p. 42.

10. For a well-known and influential description of the ways in which knowledge in modern culture is bound to powers that condition the internal lives of people, see Michel Foucault's *Discipline and Punish: The Birth of the Prison*, trans. Alan Sheridan (New York: Vintage, 1979).

11. C. S. Lewis, *The Abolition of Man*, p. 34.

12. C. S. Lewis, *The Great Divorce* (New York: Macmillan, 1946), p. vi.

13. The most influential text of philosophical ethics that is in basic agreement with Lewis on these matters is Alasdair MacIntyre, *After Virtue: A Study of Moral Theory* (Notre Dame: University of Notre Dame Press, 1984).

14. C. S. Lewis, *The Abolition of Man*, p. 57.

15. See Joseph Fletcher, *Situational Ethics: The New Morality* (Philadelphia: Westminster Press, 1966).

16. For Lewis's comments on the difficulties of creating fictional characters that are good rather than wicked, see his *Preface to Paradise Lost* (Oxford: Oxford University Press, 1967 [1942]), p. 102.

17. For a discussion of some of these issues, see his *Preface to Paradise Lost*.

18. See "On Three Ways of Writing for Children," in C. S. Lewis, *Of This and Other Worlds,* ed. Walter Hooper (London: Collins, 1982), pp. 64–65. Lewis distinguishes between two kinds of imagination by calling one of them "baptized" and the other "unbaptized." It should be stressed that Lewis is not, in this distinction, drawing a line between Christians and non-Christians. It is not as though Christians have baptized and non-Christians have non-baptized imaginations. He has a more general distinction in mind.

19. C. S. Lewis, *The Lion, the Witch and the Wardrobe* (New York: Harper Collins, 1978), p. 51.

20. C. S. Lewis, *Mere Christianity*, p. 87.

6: Pleasure

1. C. S. Lewis, *Present Concerns,* ed. Walter Hooper (New York: Harcourt, Brace, Jovanovich, 1986), p. 55.

2. C. S. Lewis, *The Screwtape Letters* (New York: Macmillan, 1961), p. 58.

3. Ibid., p. 47.

4. C. S. Lewis, *The Four Loves* (New York: Harcourt Brace, 1988 [1960]), p. 11.

5. It should be noted that Lewis places pleasure as the counterpart to the sublime in contrast to Kant in the third Critique, who constructs the beautiful as the contrary of the sublime.

6. See, e.g., Corbin Scott Carnell, *Bright Shadow of Reality: C. S. Lewis and the Feeling Intellect* (Grand Rapids, Michigan: William B. Eerdmans, 1974), pp. 116–17.

7. Bruce L. Edwards, ". . . The Abstractions Proper to Them: C. S. Lewis and the Institutional Theory of Literature" in Bruce L. Edwards, *The Taste of the Pineapple: Essays on C. S. Lewis as Reader, Critic, and Imaginative Writer* (Bowling Green, Ohio: Bowling Green State University Popular Press, 1988), pp. 41, 55.

8. C. S. Lewis, *An Experiment in Criticism* (Cambridge: Cambridge University Press, 1961), p. 138.

9. On the matter of "canon" in literary studies, see Robert von Hallberg, ed., *Canons* (Chicago: University of Chicago Press, 1984). On the matter of the construction of the text by the reader, see Stanley Fish, *Is There a Text in This Class? The Authority of Interpretive Communities* (Cambridge: Harvard University Press, 1980), and Jane Tompkins, ed., *Reader-Response Criticism: From Formalism to Post-Structuralism* (Baltimore, Md.: Johns Hopkins University Press, 1980).

10. It should also be noted that Lewis does not neglect the principal point in Stanley Fish's amended theory of reader response, in a word Fish's identification of the literary profession as the site where reading is stabilized. However, Lewis is not ready to give up the dependence of that profession and of changes in it on texts. For this aspect of Fish's work and for a larger critique of it, see my *"Take, Read": Scripture, Textuality and Cultural Practice* (University Park: Penn State University Press, 1996), pp. 80–85.

11. *An Experiment in Criticism*, p. 138.

12. Ibid., p. 19.

13. Ibid., p. 83.

14. Roger Lundin, *The Culture of Interpretation: Christian Faith and the Postmodern World* (Grand Rapids: William B. Eerdmans Publishing Company, 1993), p. 221.

15. *An Experiment in Criticism*, p. 138.

16. It may be of interest to some readers to note that Lewis's theory of reading resembles closely the theory of reading that is the heart of John Calvin's doctrine of Scripture, which is a doctrine of the reading of Scripture. I have tried to argue that this theory of reading epitomizes a tradition of theory and practice in regard to reading and finds new expression today in the work of Maurice Blanchot and Julia Kristeva. See my *"Take, Read,"* chaps. 1, 4.

17. C. S. Lewis, *Surprised by Joy: The Shape of My Early Life* (New York: Harcourt Brace, 1984 [1956], p. 169.

18. Ibid., p. 107–8.

19. C. S. Lewis, *Perelandra* (New York: Macmillan, 1944), pp. 87–88.

20. C. S. Lewis, *They Asked for a Paper: Papers and Addresses* (London: Geoffrey Bles, 1962), pp. 166–82.

21. *Perelandra*, p. 32.

22. Ibid., pp. 42–43.

23. C. S. Lewis, *Surprised by Joy*, p. 218.

24. Ibid., p. 168.

25. "Nicomachean Ethics," in *The Complete Works of Aristotle,* ed. Jonathan Barnes, vol. 2 (Princeton, N.J.: Princeton University Press, 1984), Book II/7, p. 1749.

26. Ibid., Book X/1, p. 1853.

27. Amelie Oksenberg Rorty, "Akrasia and Pleasure: Nicomachean Ethics Book 7," in Amelie Oksenberg Rorty, ed., *Essays on Aristotle's Ethics* (Berkeley: University of California Press, 1980), p. 282.

28. "Nicomachean Ethics," Book VII/9, p. 1820.

29. C. S. Lewis, *Out of the Silent Planet* (New York: Macmillan, 1965 [1938]), p. 73.

30. For a discussion and bibliography on this matter, see Steven Connor, *Theory and Cultural Value* (Oxford: Blackwell, 1992), pp. 34–54.

31. C. S. Lewis, *Perelandra*, p. 48.

32. Ibid., p. 130.

33. C. S. Lewis, *That Hideous Strength*, p. 185.

34. See John Milbank, "Can a Gift Be Given? Prolegomena to a Future Trinitarian Metaphysic," in L. Gregory Jones and Stephen E. Fowl, eds., *Rethinking Metaphysics* (Blackwell, 1995). pp. 119–32.

7: Celebration

1. C. S. Lewis, *Prince Caspian* (New York: Macmillan, 1951), pp. 170–171.

2. Ibid., p. 177.

3. Readers with theological interests or who know Lewis well will recognize that behind his theory of persons whose particularity is revealed in their relationships stands Lewis's doctrine of the Trinity. Indeed, his doctrine of the Trinity stresses that God, rather than being single, isolated, and static, is complex, relational, and dynamic. I do not want to underestimate the importance of the doctrine of the Trinity in his work, but I think that his theory of human particularity in relationship is based primarily on his doctrine of Creation.

4. C. S. Lewis, *Miracles: A Preliminary Study* (New York: Macmillan, 1947), pp. 198–99.

5. C. S. Lewis, "Membership," in *The Weight of Glory and Other Addresses* (New York: Macmillan, 1949), p. 34.

6. C. S. Lewis, *Mere Christianity* (New York: Macmillan, 1960 [1943]), p. 141.

7. Ibid., p. 42.

8. C. S. Lewis, *Letters to Malcolm: Chiefly on Prayer* (New York: Harcourt, Brace & World, 1964), p. 85.

9. See, for example, John Milbank, *Theology and Social Theory* (Oxford: Blackwell, 1990), for an extended and detailed study of the variations and force in Western thought of assumptions that human life is marked primarily by conflict.

10. Jean-François Lyotard, *The Postmodern Condition: A Report on Knowledge*, trans. Geoff Bennington and Brian Massumi (Minneapolis: University of Minnesota Press, 1984), p. 88.

11. See Michel Foucault, *Power/Knowledge: Selected Interviews and Other Writings 1972–1977*, trans. Colin Gordon et al. (New York: Pantheon Books, 1980).

12. C. S. Lewis, *Surprised by Joy* (New York: Harcourt Brace and Company, 1956), p. 32.

13. However, it should be added that Lewis did not translate England's role in the war against Germany fully into the terms of good versus evil, since he did not

have a readiness to consider all that England represented as standing for righteousness and truth.

14. C. S. Lewis, *The Lion, the Witch and the Wardrobe* (New York: Harper Trophy Edition, 1994 [1950], p. 128.

15. C. S. Lewis, *The Screwtape Letters* (New York: Macmillan, 1944), p. 92.

16. C. S. Lewis, *Present Concerns*, ed. Walter Hooper (New York: Harcourt Brace Jovanovich, 1986), p. 79.

17. C. S. Lewis, *Mere Christianity*, p. 95.

18. "A great deal of democratic enthusiasm descends from the ideas of people like Rousseau, who believed in democracy because they thought mankind so wise and good that every one deserved a share in the government. . . . The real reason for democracy is just the reverse. Mankind is so fallen that no man can be trusted with unchecked power over his fellows." C. S. Lewis, *Present Concerns*, p. 17.

19. "If there were such a society in existence [i.e., a Christian society] and you or I visited it, I think we should come away with a curious impression. We should feel that its economic life was very socialistic and, in that sense, 'advanced,' but that its family life and its code of manners were rather old-fashioned—perhaps even ceremonious and aristocratic." C. S. Lewis, *Mere Christianity*, p. 66.

20. "But when Dante saw the great apostles they affected him like *mountains*. There's lots to be said against devotion to saints; but at least they keep on reminding us that we are very small people compared with them." C. S. Lewis, *Letters to Malcolm*, p. 13.

21. C. S. Lewis, *The Problem of Pain* (New York: Macmillan, 1943), p. 135.

Conclusion

1. C. S. Lewis, *A Grief Observed* (New York: The Seabury Press, 1961), p. 52.

2. See Frederic Jameson, *Postmodernism: Or, the Cultural Logic of Late Capitalism* (Durham, N.C.: Duke University Press, 1991).

3. Julia Kristeva, *Tales of Love*, trans. Leon S. Roudiez (New York: Columbia University Press, 1987), pp. 279, 294.

4. See Robert N. Bellah, "Is There a Common American Culture?" *Journal of the American Academy of Religion* 66, no. 3 (Fall 1998): 613–26.

5. Accounts of religious strains in American culture take either of these approaches. An example of the first, namely, that such strains are vestiges of a former, more ecclesiastically located form of religion, is the work of Sacvan Berkovitch, especially his *The American Jeremiad*. Examples of the second approach, that is, accounting for such strains in terms of general theories of the role of religious beliefs and practices in human cultures, are the work of Catherine Albanese, especially her *Faith of the Fathers*, and that of Giles B. Gunn, especially his *The Interpretation of Otherness: Literature, Religion and the American Imagination*.

6. See my *Moral Fiber: Character and Belief in Recent American Fiction* (Philadelphia: Fortress Press, 1972), esp. the conclusion; *Bound to Differ: The Dynamics of Theo-*

logical Discourses (University Park: Pennsylvania State University Press, 1992), esp. chaps. 3, 6; and "Beliefs Americans Share," in *Journal of General Education* 39, no. 2 (1987): 85–97.

7. Irving Howe, *Decline of the New* (New York: Harcourt, Brace and World, 1970), p. 110.

8. Michael Cowan, *City of the West: Emerson, America and Urban Metaphor* (New Haven, Conn.: Yale University Press, 1967), pp. 89–112.

INDEX